Western Queers in China

Western Queers in China

Flight to the Land of Oz

D. E. Mungello

ROWMAN & LITTLEFIELD PUBLISHERS, INC.
Lanham • Boulder • New York • Toronto • Plymouth, UK

Published by Rowman & Littlefield Publishers, Inc.
A wholly owned subsidary of The Rowman & Littlefield Publishing Group, Inc.
4501 Forbes Boulevard, Suite 200, Lanham, Maryland 20706
www.rowman.com

10 Thornbury Road, Plymouth PL6 7PP, United Kingdom

Cover image: Xia Gui (active 1180–1224). Detail "Geese Forming Calligraphy Against the Distant Mountains (Yao shan shu yan)" of Twelve Views of Landscape, Southern Song Dynasty (1127–1279). Handscroll, ink on silk, 11 × 90¾ inches (28.0 × 230.5 cm). The Nelson-Atkins Museum of Art, Kansas City, Missouri. Purchase: William Rockhill Nelson Trust, 32-159/2. Photo credit: John Lamberton.

British Library Cataloguing in Publication Information Available

Library of Congress Cataloging-in-Publication Data
Mungello, D. E. (David Emil), 1943–
   Western queers in China : flight to the land of Oz / D.E. Mungello.
     p. cm.
   Includes bibliographical references and index.
   ISBN 978-1-4422-1556-6 (cloth : alk. paper) — ISBN 978-1-4422-1558-0 (electronic)
   1. Gay immigrants—China—History—20th century. 2. Homosexuals—China—History—20th century. 3. Homosexuality—China—History—20th century. 4. China—Emigration and immigration—Social aspects—History—20th century. I. Title.
   HQ76.3.C6M86 2012
   306.76'608909051—dc23

2011051200

♾™ The paper used in this publication meets the minimum requirements of American National Standard for Information Sciences—Permanence of Paper for Printed Library Materials, ANSI/NISO Z39.48-1992.

Printed in the United States of America

Contents

Illustrations

Preface

This book is based on two main types of sources. One source involves published works that are listed in the footnotes and bibliography. The second source consists of information supplied by professional acquaintances and personal friends of seven of the twenty-three men who form the subjects of this study. These men are all deceased, but because of the deeply personal nature of the subject matter, I have not (with a few exceptions) made detailed citations of the information from acquaintances and friends. Instead, I acknowledge their contributions below by linking them with the respective subjects of my queries. Their contributions were made mainly through paper and electronic mail, but also by telephone.

For information on Harold Acton, I am indebted to Prof. Paul N. Bailey, Prof. Cyril Birch, and Signora Ellyn Toscana. For information on Alan Priest, I am indebted to Dr. Maxwell Hearn. For information on Laurence Sickman, I am indebted to Dr. Thomas Lawton, Prof. Roderick Whitfield, and Mr. Marc F. Wilson. Mr. Wilson, director emeritus of the Nelson-Atkins Museum of Art, was particularly helpful in offering detailed information both by telephone and mail. For information on Arthur Waley, I am indebted to Prof. T. H. Barrett, Dr. E. Bruce Brooks, and Prof. Joanna Waley-Cohen. I am indebted to Prof. Susan Naquin for providing me with a high-resolution scan of map 2, which appeared in her book *Peking Temples and City Life, 1400–1900*. I am indebted to Prof. Erwin J. Haeberle for providing a copy of the photograph of Magnus Hirschfeld visiting Beijing in 1931.

For information on Glen Baxter, I am indebted to Dr. Elling Eide, Prof. Harold L. Kahn, and Prof. Patrick Hanan. For information on Howard Wechsler, I am indebted to Prof. Patricia Buckley Ebrey, Dr. Elling Eide, and Prof. Harold L. Kahn. For information on Marston Anderson, I am indebted to Prof. Cyril Birch, Prof. Suzanne Cahill, Prof. Kang-I Sun Chang, Prof. Donald Harper, Prof. Theodore Huters, Prof. Wendy Larson, Prof. Leo Ou-fan Lee, Dr. Jocelyn (Nash) Marinescu, and Prof. Jon Von Kowallis.

I was also assisted with information on the remaining sixteen men of this study. For information on J. J. M. De Groot, I am indebted to Dr. Ad Dudink and Prof. Wilt Idema. For information on Joseph Schedel and Vincenz Hundhausen, I am greatly indebted to Dr. Hartmut Walravens who also was instrumental in helping me to secure inaccessible materials, including photographs. For information on Victor Segalen, I am indebted to Prof. Timothy Billings. For information on Witter Bynner, I am indebted to Mr. William Benemann. For information on David Kidd, I am indebted to Prof. Grant Goodman. For information on Rewi Alley, I am indebted to Prof. Anne-Marie Brady and Ms. Phebe Gray. I am indebted to Prof. Michele Fatica for his assistance in securing permission to publish the portrait of Matteo Ripa.

In addition, I am indebted to numerous people who responded to my other queries for information and requests for assistance. These include Dr. Jens Damm, Mr. Brian A. Dursum, Mr. Don Kenny, Dr. Theodore N. Foss, Prof. Eugenio Menegon, Prof. Greg Pflugfelder, Prof. Leonard Pronko, Prof. Timon Screech, Prof. Jonathan Spence, Prof. Giovanni Vitiello, Prof. Sophie Volpp, and Mr. Edmund White. For assistance in securing rare materials, I am indebted to Dr. R. G. Tiedemann. For assistance in several instances of translation, I am indebted to Dr. Catherine Jami, Prof. Vincent Yang, and, above all, Prof. Jonathan Chaves who provided scholarly clarification on a number of Chinese terms. Finally, I am deeply grateful to my editor at Rowman & Littlefield, Susan McEachern, for her patience in seeing the manuscript through to its final form.

This book is dedicated to my grandson, Austin Dale Pflum.

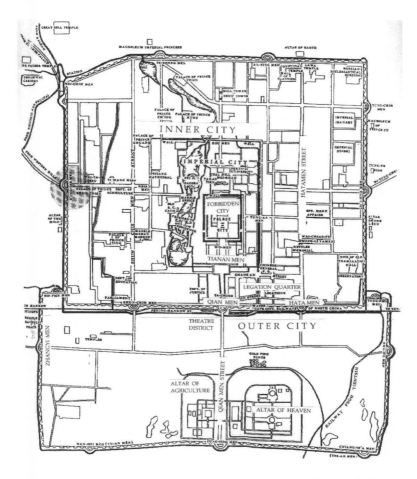

Map 1. Beijing, ca. 1922. Traditionally Chinese capitals were built on a north–south axis which reflected and reinforced cosmological forces. In Beijing, Qianmen Street lay at the core of this axis linking the imperial palace at the center of the city with the Temples of Heaven and Agriculture to the south. Qianmen (Front Gate) was the most central and important of all the city gates. It straddled the main north–south thoroughfare of Qianmen Street and divided the Inner City from the Outer City to the south. Joseph Schedel lived and worked near Hatamen Street in the Legation Quarter, a foreign enclave located directly to the northeast of Qianmen. The theater district was located just four blocks south of Qianmen and immediately west of Qianmen Street. Vincenz Hundhausen's lakeside house was located directly to the west of the Outer City wall and just outside the southwestern gate marked Zhangyimen. Adapted from "Cook's Skeleton Map of Peking," 1922.

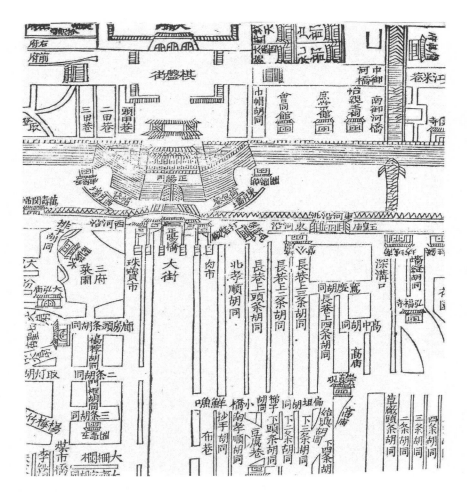

Map 2. The area around Qianmen (Front Gate), labeled here with its official title of Zhengyangmen (South-Facing Gate), early nineteenth century. Until the fall of the imperial dynasty in 1911, the middle of the three gates was normally closed, except when the emperor processed through them. The area immediately to the south was the main center for lodges, shops, restaurants, and entertainment. The theater district was located on Dazhalan Street (an east–west street that intersected with Qianmen Street), which is the last street shown at the bottom left of this map. Until 1900 the gates of Qianmen were closed at dusk, but briefly reopened after midnight so that officials who had been indulging in the pleasures of the entertainment section (theaters, food, and boys) could return to the court for the imperial audience at dawn. *Shoushan quan tu* (complete map of the capital), early nineteenth century.

Introduction

This is a story of how twenty-three different men with same-sex desire fled to China and influenced history. The story is told through the themes that shaped their lives and experiences: flight from homophobia in their home countries, the exotic attraction of Chinese boy-actors, friendships with Chinese men, intellectual connections with the Chinese, and the reorientation of Western aesthetics toward China.

In its great encounter with China, the West needed cultural guides who could lead the way. Some of the first cultural guides to China were Jesuit missionaries who realized that they could not convert the souls of the Chinese unless they understood their culture. They were followed by translators, diplomats, pharmacists, teachers, scholars, aesthetes, expatriates, adventurers, and physicians, all of whom contributed to developing a deepened connection with China. Within each of these groups were men who felt same-sex desire.

Unlike the growing tendency among gay men today to be open about their sexuality, prior to the mid-1990s most men who felt same-sex attraction lived in closeted fear of disclosure. For those men, sexuality had to remain a private matter, and this led them to express their sexual feelings in more subliminal ways. In this repressive atmosphere, China emerged as a land of exotic escape. This escape was limited to a fairly select group. It included men adventurous enough to travel to China and live there for a time, but it also included men with the ability to immerse themselves in the Chinese language and culture while never setting foot in China.

China was a siren's call to the gay sensibility. Whether in the aesthetics of its calligraphy, the wonder of its scenic landscapes, the exotic quality of its philosophy and theater, or the lithe and dark-haired beauty of its men, China exerted a powerful attraction on many who felt same-sex desire. This attraction continued even during the last half of the twentieth century when homosexuality in China practically disappeared under the repression of a homophobic, totalitarian regime. It is an attraction that I myself felt, although for many years I thought it was merely a personal idiosyncrasy that did not apply to others. I began to study Chinese in 1963 because of the beauty and exotic quality of its characters. At the time, I saw no sign of homosexuality in Chinese culture. Ironically, I later learned that the well-known gay writer Edmund White (born only three years before me in 1940) majored in Chinese at the University of Michigan for similar aesthetic reasons and was likewise unaware of any homosexuality in contemporary China. While White declined an offer of a graduate fellowship in Chinese from Harvard and became a pioneering writer of gay literature in New York, I went to Berkeley to pursue a doctorate in Chinese history.[1]

Writing a book like this presents unique challenges to a historian. The trails left by these deceased men are difficult to follow. Some trails have grown cold with time. Others are hidden by secrecy and intentional obfuscation. Most of these men discovered their sexual attraction to other males at an early age, and they learned the need to hide it (from their family, friends, and almost everyone else). In order to protect themselves, secrecy became a way of life, and the habits of secrecy became ingrained and second nature.

Because the subjects of this study were closeted in various degrees, the written documents associated with them often require a key or secret code to unlock their meaning. This key consists of certain signs, learned through the experiences of men who feel same-sex attraction in a hostile society, whose meaning is recognizable to them, though usually not to others. This involves a sensitivity (half jokingly called "gaydar") heightened by the constant anxiety of their secret sexual desires being discovered and exposed. The fear of the betrayal of their secret is so great that there is enormous reluctance to share it with anyone who is unlike them. In today's more tolerant climate, the degree of fear that most men in this study experienced strikes us as extreme and even paranoid. This is why the topic requires us to reconstruct the tensions of the past to make the behavior of these men understandable.

A second key to unlocking the secrets of men (at least recently deceased ones) with same-sex attraction involves surviving friends, colleagues, and family members. However, their usefulness depended on their willingness to talk. In attempting to contact these potential sources, I found that many of them did not want to talk. Painful memories and embarrassment are still very powerful. However others were willing to share information and insights with me. The overwhelming need for secrecy among these men was so strong that many people still regard disclosures about a friend's same-sex attraction as a form of disloyalty and betrayal. While admitting a friend's or colleague's attraction to his own sex, they often feel the need to defend that person as if the recognition of this attraction unfairly casts an aspersion or reveals a fatal flaw. I note this not to criticize these reluctant sources, but to recognize the powerful protective feelings that surround the realm of closeted men. Coming out (publicly declaring one's same-sex attraction) has become for many gay men and lesbians today a rite of passage in their development. However, prior to 1969 and the gay liberation movement, it rarely occurred.

I will briefly address the terminology question, which can be troublesome and even controversial. Each of the terms used to refer to male same-sex attraction is loaded with meaning which has fluctuated in connotation over time. The word *homosexual* was invented by the Germans in 1869. In current usage, it has clinical connotations. It tends to be used more by critics of same-sex attraction, while those sympathetic to male same-sex attraction tend to prefer the term *gay*. The term *gay* has been in wide usage only since the late 1960s and was restricted in use by the *New York Times* until 1986.[2] I have generally followed the definitions of the influential theorist Eve Kosofsky Sedgwick in using *homosexuality* and *gay* with similar meaning, but with some reference to their different times, that is, applying *homosexuality* more to the century 1869–1969 and *gay* to the period afterward.[3]

The list of expletives for men who feel same-sex attraction is long and ugly. It includes *aunties, cocksuckers, fudge pounders, faggots, fruits, nellies, queens, sissies,* and *swishes.* Some remember the shift in nasty pejoratives. In the United States in the 1950s, *nigger* was commonly used among men as a demeaning term, but by the 1960s it was being replaced by *faggot.*[4] The term *fairy,* with its mocking connotations, was commonly used for homosexuals from the late nineteenth century until the mid-twentieth century. The term *pansy,* with its connotations of weakness, was often applied to homosexuals in the twentieth century. The transformation in usage of the word *queer* is particularly symbolic. From the 1940s to the 1960s, it was extremely pejorative, but more recently it has been favored by same-sex advocates championing a nonconformist quality and by queer theorists. Consequently *queer* is used today with an ironically positive tone. The acronym *GLBT* (or *LGBT*) has political connotations and tends to be used by forceful advocates. The acronym is still in flux, since it began as *GLB* (gay, lesbian, and bisexual) and then added *T* (transgenders), then *Q* (queers), then *I* (intersex), and is still in the process of expanding. One new form is *LGBTTIQQ2S.*[5] In short, the meanings of all these terms are still evolving.

The two dominant and opposing positions in explaining human sexual orientation have been "biological essentialism" and "social construction-ism." While essentialists claim that the prime influence shaping sexual orientation is inherent and biological, constructionists argue that the main influence is social and cultural. Essentialists believe that a gay identity in some form has existed throughout history, while constructionists argue that the sex drive is undefined and that the gay identity has been created by developments of the last century. However, most essentialists and construc-tionists agree that one's sexual identity is discovered rather than chosen.[6]

This is a highly controversial debate. The late queer theorist Eve Ko-sofsky Sedgwick tried to reorient the constructionist-essentialist debate by recasting it as a "minoritizing versus universalizing" issue.[7] Actually, Sedgwick preferred to avoid the constructionist-essentialist debate on the grounds that "a conceptual deadlock between the two opposing views had by now been built into the very structure of every theoretical tool we have for undertaking it." Her views have been very influential among academics, but many nonacademic writers and historians vehemently reject the constructionist leanings of queer theorists.[8]

For many men with same-sex desire, China was a Land of Oz—a coun-try whose remoteness and radical differences filled their imaginations. Initially it was accessible to only a few, and this inaccessibility helped to foster its mystique. The differences in the body type of its people as well as its language, food, clothing, music, and culture were all part of its ap-peal. These differences had a particular attraction for many men. As the homophobia in Europe and North America intensified in the late nine-teenth and early twentieth centuries, the attractiveness of China increased as a realm of escape from this oppressiveness. Until the mid-twentieth century, the Chinese were relatively tolerant of homosexuality. A filial son was obliged to marry and procreate, but sexual diversions with fe-male impersonators and other men were commonly accepted.

All too often, the history of Sino-Western contacts is told in terms of rul-ers and wars and striking differences, which Rudyard Kipling immortal-ized in the lines "East is East and West is West, and never the twain shall meet."[9] The big picture however obscures rich patterns of small personal dimensions that need to be excavated like buried treasures. The allure of China for men with same-sex desire involved much more than the physi-cal attraction of Chinese men with their seemingly prolonged youth, lithe bodies, and—in an age rife with the lingering images of imperialism—houseboy subordination. For these Western men, the attraction of China was also cultural. Its calligraphy, art, architecture, philosophy, theater, and literature exerted a powerful appeal.

Soon after the 1939 musical film adaptation of Frank Baum's 1900 novel *The Wizard of Oz* was released, homosexuals appropriated the main character Dorothy as one of their own. The youthful actress of that film, July Garland (1922–1969), became a homoerotic icon, and her vocal "Some Day Over the Rainbow" became their theme song. Her death in 1969 sparked the iconic Stonewall Inn riots in New York that marked the beginning of gay liberation. Like many gay men of that time, the character Dorothy dreamed of escaping the drab black-and-white landscape of Kansas (a metaphor for their oppression) into a Technicolor Land of Oz (where fantasies were realized). For the men of our study, China was the metaphorical Land of Oz. A few went to China as adventurous sex tourists and ended up living there for years. Others were more serious from the outset. Some never went there at all but were equally entranced by a historical or literary China that lived in their imaginations. Some were professional scholars. Others were amateur aesthetes who were enraptured by the architecture and atmosphere of Beijing. Still others were altruists who served as missionaries or teachers. Some were practically oriented and sought to make their fortune in China.

China's initial modernization beginning around 1900 involved a wholesale borrowing of Western culture, which included homophobia. By historical irony, China's tolerant traditions of same-sex relations between men were temporarily suppressed as culturally backward by these forces of modernization. The reformers and revolutionaries of twentieth-century China promoted puritanical attitudes toward sex for the people at large, if not for themselves, which led to the harsh persecution of homosexuals. Consequently, 1949 was a great watershed for gay men in China in which tolerance gave way to a long homophobic nightmare. Homosexuals were imprisoned, and repeat offenders were sometimes executed. During his imprisonment in 1958–1964 at the Clear Stream Labor Camp at Chadian, Bao Ruowang witnessed a gay fellow prisoner being executed with a pistol shot through his head at close range.[10] While the severest persecution of gay men occurred on the Communist mainland, homosexuals in Nationalist Taiwan were also persecuted. Gay men who had been gathering in New Park (Xin Gongyuan) in downtown Taipei since the end of Japanese rule in 1945 were subject to police raids and arrests in 1970.[11] The famous novel *Niezi* (Whore's Son) (1983) by Bai Xianyong (Pai Hsienyung) portrayed the plight of these gay men in Taipei, ostracized by their families and society. The novel was translated into a widely read English edition under the title *Crystal Boys*.[12] Not until the 1990s did the traditional tolerance for same-sex relations in China begin to reemerge. On the mainland, the Chinese government revoked the legal ban on same-sex acts in November 1992, though social ostracism remained.

It would be a mistake to view the men treated in this book as part of a cohesive group. They were extremely diverse, and their same-sex feelings sometimes never rose above the subliminal in manifesting themselves.

This study is interested in these men as much for their sexual identities as for their sexual activities. Some of them had sexual relations with Chinese; others did not. In most cases, their same-sex attractions were hidden by men who were far more reticent about such things than contemporary gay men. It is inconceivable that these men would have written a book like Philip Gambone's novel *Beijing* (2003), which is an American man's fictionalized and sensitive account of a love affair with a Chinese man, based on his experiences teaching in Beijing in 1996. And yet the similarities in sensibility between these pre-1995 men and their post-1995 counterparts are instantly recognizable.

Compiling a list of closeted men with same-sex attraction who were fascinated by China presents a challenging degree of complexity. Our sexual identities are too complicated to be defined with mathematical precision, in spite of Alfred Kinsey's seven-point (0–6) scale that attempted to calibrate the heterosexual-homosexual balance of males in terms of experience and psychic reactions.[13] While some men exhibit clear and exclusive sexual preferences for men, others do not. Moreover, this book is as much about getting into these men's minds as getting into their bedrooms. For their own protection, closeted men tended to avoid writing about their sexuality. They tended to think of themselves as having a secret or double life and wearing a mask that they would remove on occasion. They did not refer to themselves as being "closeted" until the 1960s when the closet metaphor was first used by homosexuals.[14]

Some of these men expressed their same-sex attraction in private correspondence, but others were too secretive to leave any written record. Discreet talk and rumors were the safest forms of communication. And so, in order to pick up the trails of these men with same-sex feeling who were attracted to China, I tried to engage with these circulating rumors. In trying to substantiate these rumors, I examined their biographies and writings. Memoirs written by friends and associates were sometimes very useful. In the cases of the more recently deceased, I was able to contact surviving friends and colleagues. Sometimes I succeeded in making a clear identification, but at other times the ambiguity could not be resolved.

In the absence of clear confirmation, I looked for patterns that have tended to recur in the lives of closeted men, such as a certain kind of sensibility, certain attitudes toward women, isolation or flight from one's family, and special male friendships. The result was a list of twenty-three men with widely varying ranges of confirmation of their same-sex attraction. Sometimes I failed to find any corroboration to a rumor, as in the case of the prolific German Sinologist Erwin Ritter von Zach (1872–1942), and so I omitted him from consideration. Similarly fruitless were my efforts to corroborate the rumors of homosexuality surrounding the misanthropic explorer and botanist Joseph Francis Charles Rock (1884–1962), whose adventures with the Nakhi people in the remote areas of southwest China were chronicled for thousands of readers in the *National Geographic* magazine in the 1920s and 1930s. His articles were said to have inspired James Hilton's novel *Lost Horizon* (1933), which created the myth of Shangri-La.

With the China theater historian A. C. Scott (1909–1985), the rumors were compelling, but the trail of surviving friends and associates had grown too cold to substantiate them. However, I do include several men (Matteo Ripa, J. J. M. De Groot, and George N. Kates) for whom the rumors and lifestyle combine to yield a gray area, a sexual limbo, in identifying them as men who felt same-sex desire. While the proof for including these men among my subjects may not be conclusive, it is necessary to recognize that when treating human sexuality, complexity is the reality with which we are dealing.

1

Flight to the Land of Oz

BLACKMAIL, ARREST, AND JAIL

On May 2, 1909, as he walked through the Zoologischer Garten in Berlin, Josef Schedel was too distracted to appreciate the beautiful, warm spring day in Berlin. He was focused on the train departing at 7:15 that evening. It would carry him to China and far away from Peter K. in Hannover who was attempting to blackmail him. (See figure 1.1.) When Peter's letter had arrived in February, Josef had panicked. He knew about others who had been arrested for violating Article 175 of the German Criminal Code, which prohibited sexual contact between men.[1] Six weeks later he signed a contract with Betines & Co. to work as a pharmacist in China. He was not happy about leaving "his dear boys" in Munich, but he knew from working with the Wissenschaftlich-humanitäre Komittee (Scientific-Humanitarian Committee) that the dangers were real. The WhK was dedicated to the decriminalization of sexual relations between men and had been founded in 1897 by the homosexual researcher and advocate Magnus Hirschfeld, among others. Two days before, Schedel had visited the Charlottenburg office of the WhK, and although Hirschfeld was away, he had spoken with Dr. Tischler.

After dinner with a friend, Schedel boarded the train at the Friedrichstrasse Station and departed on a route that would take him eastward almost ten thousand miles on the Trans-Siberian Railway to China. Finally, on May 27 he arrived via Mukden in Tianjin and the next day traveled on to Beijing. Time would show that Schedel's flight from Germany was based on more than paranoia. On June 17, 1910, one year after arriving in Beijing, he received an ominous visit from Dr. Erich Hauer, who was serving as a translator for the German embassy.² Hauer in his capacity as an official representative of the state court of Munich was investigating additional incriminating letters from individuals identified by Schedel only as "N. and F. H." The matter involved Article 175.

Why did Schedel choose China as his land of flight? Germans of his time were aware of the Chinese boy-actors. Ferdinand Karsch-Haack (1853–1936) was a homosexual who had written about them in his book about same-sex behavior in non-European cultures. The first volume appeared in 1906 under the title *Das gleichgeschlechtliche Leben der Kulturvölker—Ostasiaten: Chinesen, Japaner, Koreer* (The Same-Sex Life of Civilized Peoples—East Asians: Chinese, Japanese, Koreans). Karsch-Haack was an entomologist and ethnologist who had a particular interest in

Figure 1.1. Joseph Schedel (1856–1943), portrait as a young man. Schedel was born in Bamberg, Germany, as an illegitimate child and spent 1909 to 1921 in China working as a pharmacist in Beijing and Tianjin. Courtesy of Dr. Hartmut Walravens.

China.[3] He was curator of the Zoological Museum of Berlin University, but an armchair ethnologist who never engaged in field research. Although Karsch-Haack was trained as a biologically based entomologist, he argued that homosexuality was socially constructed. He argued that the "Sian-Kon" (*xianggong*), escort-prostitutes or singsong boys, of China were proof of his social constructionist theory because their training in homosexual behavior made them indistinguishable from other homosexuals. His theory was praised by Magnus Hirschfeld, but other contemporaries criticized it harshly. Karsch-Haack also defended Chinese culture against Western "scientific" approaches, which condemned Chinese acceptance of homosexuality as immoral, and he criticized Western civilization for its ascetic Christian outlook which fostered intolerance toward homosexuality.

In the debate between biological essentialists and social constructionists over the cause of same-sex attraction, Karsch-Haack's formulation of social constructionism was a pioneering effort, but it was handicapped by his incomplete knowledge of China and its popular influence was limited by his turgid academic style of writing, with long, convoluted sentences. However, he did demonstrate personal integrity in being one of the first authors involved in the homosexual movement in Germany to use his own name rather than a pseudonym.

Schedel was not alone in fleeing to China. On May 25, 1895, in London, Oscar Wilde had been found guilty of violating section 11 (the Labouchière Amendment) of the Criminal Law Amendment Act of 1885, which criminalized any act of "gross indecency" between men, whether in public or in private.[4] The magistrate refused to allow bail and sentenced him to two years of hard labor. Wilde's sensational trial revealed what had previously been hidden from the British public—the existence of extensive clandestine same-sex activity among upper-class men in Great Britain. Wilde's conviction shattered the confidence of this elite group in their feeling of invulnerability to exposure and punishment. Wilde's friend and biographer Frank Harris may have exaggerated the hysteria following Wilde's arrest when he claimed that the trains and cross-Channel ferries were crammed with wealthy sodomites fleeing England to France and Italy, but the flight of gay men was real enough.[5]

Edmund Backhouse (1873–1944) had good reason to join in the flight because he was closely connected with this elite group of men and was vulnerable to guilt by association. Backhouse had helped to raise money for Wilde's legal defense, although he later said it was a base slander to call him a homosexual. He admitted to admiring Oscar Wilde's wit, but he claimed to know nothing of his "perverted tastes."[6] This was but one of many fabrications that littered Backhouse's life.

At Merton College, Oxford, Backhouse had demonstrated a remarkable facility for languages, which he applied to the private study of Asian languages. Socially he was eccentric and had a tendency to disappear from social gatherings that he was hosting. His career at Oxford was erratic—academic success mixed with a nervous breakdown—and he never took a degree. His Oxford friends consisted of a small group of homosexuals who glorified the ancient Greeks and promoted "Uranianism," a common late nineteenth-century euphemism for homosexuality.[7] In December 1894 this group produced one issue of a magazine called _The Chameleon_, which contained the poem "In Praise of Shame" by Lord Alfred Douglas, the word _shame_ being slang in the 1890s for same-sex love.[8] That issue of _The Chameleon_ attracted notoriety at Oscar Wilde's trial and raised questions over Wilde's degree of involvement in its production. In another poem, "Two Loves," Douglas made the famous allusion to homosexuality as "the love that dare not speak its name," a poetic allusion apparently derived from the Latin legal term _"peccatum illud horrible inter Christianos non nominandum"_ (that horrible sin unmentionable among Christians).[9]

One of Backhouse's fatal habits first emerged at Oxford. In three years as an undergraduate, he incurred extravagant debts (possibly £23,000, a large amount of money for that time) which he could not pay. His reaction to this crisis became the first of a lifetime pattern—he fled, pleading a serious illness. Because he left England, he was officially declared bankrupt in 1895. His father paid off his debts but reduced his inheritance to a modest allowance. Backhouse was expelled from his social club (the National Liberal Club) on the grounds that he had violated a rule prohibiting its members from incurring public disgrace, conviction, or bankruptcy.[10]

Between 1895 and 1898 when he arrived in China, Backhouse's whereabouts are unknown.[11] Trevor-Roper's biography of Backhouse explains his life as driven mainly by the search to fund an affluent lifestyle and the fraudulent means he used to do so. In this perspective, Backhouse's homosexuality is viewed as a sideshow—more fantasy than reality, and secondary rather than essential in explaining his life. However, the timing of Backhouse's disappearance indicates otherwise.

Backhouse had good reason to flee. Bankruptcy brought disgrace, but a conviction for homosexual acts would have brought him imprisonment, as it did for Wilde. While Wilde demonstrated a certain (perhaps foolhardy) bravery in defending himself, Backhouse was not brave. China beckoned as a land of refuge and escape. There his linguistic talents, combined with his social contacts in a colonialist setting, provided the means for a comfortable survival.

For most closeted homosexuals, secrecy and deception about their sexuality were necessary means of survival, but for Sir Edmund Trelawny Backhouse, secrecy and deception were part of his personality and character that extended into all areas of his life. Among the homosexuals attracted to China, Backhouse stands out as a black sheep who exploited his upper-class connections and Sinological knowledge in the manner of a sophisticated thief.

Trevor-Roper published *The Hermit of Peking* in 1976 when homosexuality was for most authors still an embarrassing and difficult topic to explore. In the intervening thirty-five years, there has been a flood of studies that have raised the awareness of same-sex love. This includes information on Backhouse's homosexual relations in Britain, which was not available to Trevor-Roper, and enables us to make a fuller interpretation of Backhouse's sex life. Viewing Backhouse as an active rather than latent homosexual would not make him less fraudulent in character, but it might help explain why he spent most of the last forty-seven years of his life in China.[12]

FLIGHT TO ITALY AND CHINA

For many years, northern European men who were inclined toward same-sex love had been fleeing to southern Italy, where boys and young men were available for sex at low cost in the form of money, clothing, or housing. Naples and the nearby island of Capri were particularly favored sites. Naples was first settled by migrating Greeks (the Italian name "Napoli" is derived from the Greek word *Neapolis* [New City]), and some of the classical Greek affinity for same-sex love seems to have been transmitted to the Greek colony at Naples. The Blue Grotto on Capri where the Roman emperor Tiberius had played sex games with boys was rediscovered in 1826, transforming Capri into one of the most popular European sites for homosexuals.[13] From the time of the German art historian Johann Joachim Winckelman, who lived in Rome from 1756 to 1768, the Mediterranean became an obsession of the mind for homoerotically inclined thinkers from northern Europe. They blended classical Greek, Roman, and Renaissance images with modern Italy to create an idealized image of male beauty and a homosexual place of escape from the repressive homophobic attitudes of northern cultures. Naples became famous for the beauty and availability of its boys and young men (ephebes). Numerous visitors from northern Europe have left written accounts of the homoerotic culture they encountered there.

During the years 1824–1835, the German Count August von Platen was living in Italy, entranced by its homoeroticism. Von Platen was part of the expatriate group of scholars at Rome but focused most of his attention on Naples, not only on its fifteenth-century history, but also on its young males.[14] He found Neapolitan men not only particularly attractive, but also very available, and he described love between men in Naples as commonplace. Other gay men followed. Oscar Wilde found refuge in Naples after his release from prison in 1897 while his companion Lord Alfred Douglas prowled the streets for boys, an attraction he later claimed to forswear with his conversion to Catholicism.[15] The poet W. H. Auden and his lover Chester Kallman lived on the island of Ischia in the Bay of Naples in the 1950s.[16] The tradition of same-sex love in Naples continues today.[17]

The sensibility of this homoerotic aesthetic is portrayed in the photographs of the German nobleman and homosexual Wilhelm von Gloeden (1856–1931). In 1879, Gloeden moved to Sicily in search of a warmer climate to treat his tuberculosis and established a home in the seaport of Taormina.[18] After his family became impoverished and his income was cut off, he took up photography as a source of income, selling postcards of photographs he took in Sicily. These featured peasant scenes, but his specialty was nude or thinly clad young men in poses that portrayed classical Graeco-Roman antiquity. His home in Taormina became famous, and his visitors included prominent figures like Anatole France, Richard Strauss, Edward VII of England, the king of Siam, Wilhelm II, and Oscar Wilde, as well as the Morgans, Rothschilds, and Vanderbilts. In one well-known photograph, Gloeden posed some of his boy models on a belvedere overlooking the Bay of Naples and Mt. Vesuvius.[19]

The tendency of men with same-sex desire to flee the oppressive laws of northern Europe intensified with several scandals that occurred at the turn of the twentieth century. Seven years after the conviction and imprisonment of Oscar Wilde, a second homosexual scandal occurred in 1902 and involved the wealthy German arms manufacturer and nobleman Friedrich Krupp.[20] Krupp was married with two children and was one of the most prominent men in Germany. He spent a great deal of money in Capri, building a house, renovating the island's main hotel, and inviting many guests. His liaisons with the boys and young men of Capri, although quite typical and even welcomed by most Capresi, attracted the attention of left-wing newspapers in Italy and Germany which opposed Krupp's politics. The Italian government banned Krupp from returning to Italy, and shortly thereafter he was found dead, though whether the strain of the scandal contributed to a fatal heart attack or caused his suicide is unclear. Another scandal echoing that of Wilde occurred in France where the wealthy Jacques d'Adelswärd-Fersen (1880–1923) was disgraced in 1903 by the charge of indecent behavior with minors and was imprisoned for six months. He took refuge on Capri where he cultivated a young Italian lover named Nino Cesarini. D'Adelswärd-Fersen acquired posthumous fame when Roger Peyrefitte published a fictionalized account of his life entitled *L'Exilé de Capri*.[21]

The parallels between homosexuals fleeing to southern Italy and homosexuals fleeing to China involved more than just escaping from arrest
and imprisonment. In both southern Italy and China, social attitudes
toward same-sex love were more permissive than in northern Europe.
When the Suez Canal was opened in 1869 and travel eastward to Asia
became easier, the destinations for escape were expanded. In 1886 the
British explorer and writer Sir Richard Francis Burton concluded his ten-
volume translation of *Arabian Nights* with a "Terminal Essay" in which
he proposed the theory of the "Sotadic Zone."[22] In this theory, Burton
claimed that "pederasty" was caused by geography and climate, not race,
and that it was more prevalent in the tropical and semitropical regions of
the world. This zone involved the Mediterranean (northern latitude 43°
to 30°) and included Italy, Greece, the Iberian Peninsula, southern France,
and the northern coastal regions of Africa from Morocco to Egypt. The
Sotadic Zone ran eastward to include Asia Minor, the Levant, the Middle
East, Afghanistan, and northern India, continuing onward to include
Turkistan, China, and Japan. In addition, it included the South Sea Islands
and Central America. Burton's theory enjoyed a great vogue in the late
nineteenth century and was widely believed.

Since the sixteenth century, China had been an object of fascination for
Europeans, but it now became an attractive destination for same-sex love.
It was widely known that the atmosphere for casual sex with other males
was far more welcoming in East Asia than in Europe. Moreover, the material affluence of Westerners enabled them to live well in China where
the economy was in decline. This colonialist atmosphere shaped sexual
relationships by giving gay men an economic and social superiority over
Chinese "boys."

Prohibitions against sodomy in China had been introduced into law
in the Ming dynasty (1368–1644) but were not rigorously enforced. The
Ming Zhengde emperor (r. 1506–1521) was known to enjoy male favorites. In the seventeenth century, a wave of literature fascinated with
homosexuality led to a backlash by the conservative Manchu government.[23] Consequently in 1679 these prohibitions against sodomy (*jijian*)
were incorporated into the legal code (*Daqing luli*) of the Qing dynasty
(1644–1911).[24] Even then, the provisions appear to have been more lightly
applied than in Europe, where in a small country like the Netherlands in
the brief period 1730–1732, there were 276 convictions for sodomy and at
least 75 hangings.[25] Unless rape or homicide was involved, the Chinese
punishment for sodomy was light. A sentence of a hundred blows with a
heavy bamboo often amounted in practice to forty strokes with a lighter
stick. One might have to wear a cangue (square wooden collar) day and
night for a prescribed period. A man convicted of sodomy might suffer a
loss to his reputation as a "decent man" (*liangren*), and he might be called

the derogatory names of "little rabbit" (*tuzi*) or "turtle" (*wangba*). He would also be vulnerable to blackmail.

Nevertheless male same-sex love was relatively common in the Qing dynasty. Boys and young men were seduced by their Confucian teachers while neophytes were seduced by Buddhist monks.[26] Sexual activity between males occurred at barber stalls and bathhouses, which frequently were fronts for male prostitution.[27] This activity reached to the very top of the Chinese social structure, with several Manchu emperors cultivating male favorites, including the Qianlong emperor (r. 1736–1796), the Xianfeng emperor (r. 1851–1861), and the Tongzhi emperor (r. 1862–1874).[28] In fact, three of the last four Qing emperors appear to have been notably lacking in procreative virility.

In both southern Italy and China, same-sex relationships between foreigners and native people rarely amounted to relationships between equals. The foreigners involved were usually older, wealthier, and sexually dominant. Their native partners were normally younger, poorer, and penetrated sexually. The Italian language reinforces this distinction. Dating from ancient Greek and Roman cultures, there was a strong distinction between active and passive (insertive versus penetrated) sexual partners, with the latter regarded as subordinate or slavelike in behavior.[29] In Italian culture, a man maintained his social status only if he proved his virility and played the active role in intercourse. Prior to the invention of the modern terms *omosessuale* (homosexual) and the colloquial *frocio* (faggot), the traditional Italian language had no specific term to refer to the sexual penetrator in anal intercourse (top), but only terms to refer to the one who was penetrated (bottom), such as *arruso* and *ricchione*.[30] Younger men who had played the bottom role tended to be excused their youthful digressions and could maintain their status in society if with adulthood they made the transition from the passive to the active role in intercourse.

The situation in China bore remarkable similarity to Italy. Homosexuality was widespread and generally tolerated. The laws against same-sex activity were invoked only in cases of egregiously indiscreet behavior or when a crime was involved. In eighteenth- and nineteenth-century China, sexual penetration of the anus signified domination, and penetrated males suffered a loss of respect, unless they were young and poor.[31] As in Italy, youthful bottoms (receptive partners) in China tended to be excused on the assumption that they were in a stage of development that would lead eventually to them becoming tops (penetrating partners). Also as in southern Italy, the Chinese tolerance of homosexuality easily enabled foreign men to find sexual partners among lower-class Chinese males, particularly among actors and destitute boys.

FLIGHT OF THE IMAGINATION

The word *flight* involves two different but complementary meanings. One involves escape, and the other refers to flying through the air. The flight to China of men with same-sex attraction involved both meanings in the broadest metaphorical sense. The Frenchmen Victor Segalen (1878–1919) and George Solié de Morant (1879–1955) fled to China for different reasons than Josef Schedel and Edmund Backhouse. There is no evidence that Segalen or Morant ever engaged in the physical acts of same-sex love, and yet both of them wrote a highly homoerotic novel. Their flight to China was not to escape arrest for illegal homosexual acts, but rather a flight from the restraints of a homophobic European culture into the artistic freedom of a homoerotic culture. Both men used their experience in China to construct a literary work that was fictional enough to avoid identifying themselves as same-sex love adherents and yet close enough to reality to create a pair of believable homoerotic fantasies.

Harold Witter Bynner (1881–1968) was the first-known American poet to seek inspiration in China. For a few years around 1920 he was one of the most prominent names in American poetry in an age when poetry was more widely read than today.[32] He was prolific and wrote for literary magazines as well as major periodicals, producing over thirty volumes of verse and prose.[33] Raised by a middle-class family, he met many of New England's literary leaders at Harvard and after graduating in 1902 had planned to stay on and teach there, but another opportunity arose.[34] His mother had married a wealthy and generous man who offered to fund a tour of Europe for him followed by a year in New York, working in the business world. Bynner went and was intrigued but not inspired by Europe, and this set him off from contemporaries like T. S. Eliot and Ezra Pound. Bynner was sexually attracted to other men, and the homophobic atmosphere that pervaded not only Harvard, but American and European cultural life, alienated him.

Uninterested in the imagism of Amy Lowell and Ezra Pound, Bynner and his best friend from Harvard, Arthur Davidson Ficke (1883–1945), tried to create a new movement called spectrism. In 1916 they published a literary hoax called *Spectra* in which Bynner and Ficke wrote poems using the pseudonyms Emanuel Morgan and Anne Knish of Pittsburgh.[35] Spectrism turned out to be an ephemeral phenomenon in literary history, and Bynner's lyric style grew increasingly out of favor in the 1920s. He was acutely conscious of this, particularly since he was personally acquainted with more successful poets like Ezra Pound and Robert Frost. When Frost later visited Bynner's home at Santa Fe in 1935, Bynner's resentment surfaced, and he poured a glass of beer on Frost's head.[36]

Bynner seems to have had a mental block in his development, which he broke through by moving westward, first to Berkeley and then to China, before finally settling in New Mexico. His move was not only part of a venerable American tradition of searching for new frontiers, but also part of a homosexual pattern of leaving family restraints to pursue his sexuality in the freedom of new surroundings. His pacifism, same-sex desire, and attraction to China defined him and set him off from the dominant literary movements of early twentieth-century American culture. He was an un-usually open homosexual who was in the vanguard of twentieth-century authors in shifting American aesthetic models from Europe to Asia.

Bynner's contact with China was stimulated by World War I. He op-posed the war and refused to fight in it. He was in a fluid state, looking for answers, when Ficke proposed that they make a trip to East Asia.[37] Fleeing from the frustration of a dead end in his own life, the trip to China was to be a turning point for him. Like his contemporaries George Solié de Morant and Victor Segalen, Bynner's attraction to China was more homoerotic than homosexual, in the sense that it was more cultural than explicitly sexual. He was looking for meaning rather than boys.

Harold Mario Mitchell Acton (Aikedun) fled to China in 1932 to escape a changed cultural environment in Europe in which his homoeroticism was out of style. Only a decade before, Europe had been quite different in tone and had produced a movement of aesthetes generated at elite institu-tions like Eton and Oxford. This was a movement led by young, upper-class males who came of age in the disillusionment that followed the end of World War I (1914–1918). They very consciously rejected the values of their fathers (discipline, responsibility, patriotism, simplicity, sports, horses, dogs, and heterosexuality) and cultivated egotism, eccentricity, extravagance, aesthetics, ballet, internationalism, and homoeroticism. The movement included some of the most famous literary and cultural figures of that time, including Howard Acton, Cecil Beaton, Brian Howard, Ste-phen Spender, and Evelyn Waugh.

Acton and his classmate Brian Howard (1905–1958) began their re-markable ascent to leadership of this generation of dandy-aesthetes at a precocious age while at Eton (1918–1922). Eton was a fashionable boarding school that reflected social and dynastic power.[38] At that time, a student's status at Eton was based more on his eloquence and wit than on his parents' wealth or his intellect or even his ability in sports. Acton and Howard developed a cult of ephebic beauty and rode the cult to prominence. After Eton, they moved on to Oxford where the movement came into full bloom. Evelyn Waugh later immortalized them as Oxford aesthetes in his famous novel *Brideshead Revisited* (1945) in the character of Anthony Blanche, who was a composite of Acton and Howard.[39] Their prospects looked bright. Acton's Oxford tutor felt it was obvious that he would be "the literary leader of his generation."[40] That never happened, in part because his talents did not match his promise and in part because the 1930s brought a radical change in social climate and culture. The dandy-aesthetes became cultural refugees in the sober social realism that took hold in the thirties, and this is one of the reasons why Acton went to China.

In 1929, with his poetry and other works meeting a dismal reception, he returned deeply discouraged to his parents' home near Florence. Acton's memoirs reflect his style of the dandy-aesthete in seeking to be witty and amusing. He described actions and people with lots of name-dropping and an air of superficiality. He was not a profound thinker, and one will look in vain for any meditations that led to his decision to go to China. Acton's friends encouraged him to "get out of Europe and go to the Far East," and finally he made his decision to go and stay for a while.[41] He seems to have gone as a form of escape from his disappointments in Europe. He wrote, "So long as I remained in Europe my writings were bound to be affected by Italy. It was therefore necessary for me to change my conditions, of place if not of time." A more candid assessment by a gay friend who knew Acton well is that he went to China because of his fascination with its antiquity, his craving for its opium, and his sexual attraction to its young men.[42]

Acton left for China in January 1932 and—apart from one brief return to Florence—remained there until 1939. He departed Le Havre on the *Ile de France*, a ship built for the rich. Winter and the Depression fostered a gloomy atmosphere on the crossing, and Acton described the ship as half empty and devoid of gaiety. He compared it to a vast hotel with hundreds of waiters standing idle beside empty tables. He disembarked at New York and traveled across the United States. He never seems to have felt comfortable in America, in spite of his maternal family in Chicago. He traveled to Honolulu where he visited relatives, and then on to Japan. Acton disliked the Japanese and opposed their aggressive military policies toward the Chinese.[43] Finally he reached northern China with growing excitement. He had long had an interest in this land and had been waiting for years to see it. He compared his feelings on entering Beijing to what the historian Edward Gibbon (1737–1794) felt when he first entered his fabled Rome.[44] One of the first things he did was visit the imperial palace. Of all the palaces he had seen, only the Vatican could compare to the Forbidden City in the magnificence of its open courtyards and pavilions.

Acton lacked passion—both for his art and for his sexual partners—but one should not rely too much on his wealth in explaining his lack of passion. Witter Bynner was also a poet who inherited wealth, but unlike Acton, Bynner came out and revealed his same-sex love in literary form in the poem "The Eden Tree" (1931).[45] Bynner shows the importance of

China to this process by describing a Chinese funeral procession that opens the poem and anticipates his death.[46] Wealth provided Acton with a substitute for passion and although his same-sex preferences were well known, he refused to reveal them publicly. For Bynner, poetry was his passion, and coming out involved a matter of artistic integrity.

Numerous foreign homosexual aesthetes found refuge in Beijing. If Acton symbolized the upper-class aesthete, the middle classes were represented by the German Vincenz Hundhausen (1878–1955). Hundhausen was an attorney who went to China in 1923, ostensibly on a professional matter, but with the underlying intention of escaping the unfavorable *"politische Entwicklung"* (political development) in Germany.[47]

It is unclear whether Hundhausen was referring to the rise of the National Socialists or to the increasing harassment of homosexuals, both of which he vehemently opposed. After 1923, arrests and convictions under Article 175 doubled in the Weimar Republic even before Hitler came to power and then increased almost twentyfold in the 1930s under National Socialism.

While handling the legal business of the estate, Hundhausen began studying Chinese literature and philosophy and became enthused over serving as a literary intermediary in an East–West cultural exchange. He remained until he was expelled in 1954. He and Acton were acquainted, though Acton mocked the bourgeois *Gemütlichkeit* of Hundhausen's German adaptations of Chinese poetry and drama.

Rewi Alley (1897–1987) was well known in the 1960s and 1970s as a foreigner who had chosen to live in China out of sympathy for the Communists. In actuality, Alley fled to China in 1927 to escape from the homophobic culture of New Zealand. At the time he was an imperialist in outlook who settled in Shanghai because of its colonialist environment and sexually free atmosphere which enabled him to have sex with Chinese youths. Over time, he developed a genuine concern for the well-being of Chinese youths. After the Communist victory in 1949, he was successful in adopting a closeted lifestyle such that even longtime acquaintances remained unaware of his homosexuality.

The flight of the British author W. Somerset Maugham (1874–1965) to China was part of a series of travels he made to East Asia in search of boys and materials for his novels. Maugham was a deeply closeted man whose successful dramas and best-selling literary works gave him the financial means to travel in grand style with his longtime companion Gerald Haxton (1892–1944), who served as his procurer. Traveling to East Asia in search of sex partners suited his style of hiding his homosexuality, whose concealment became more and more obsessive as he aged.

David Kidd (1926–1996) fled to China in 1946 to escape the post–World War II American triumphalism and hypermasculine culture of Detroit where his father worked in the auto industry. He arrived in Beijing at the age of nineteen. His youth, sexually ambiguous personality, and the civil war between the Nationalists and Communists drew him into remarkably intimate contact with the Chinese. A wealthy Chinese (Manchu?) woman arranged for them to marry, even though his homosexuality probably prevented them from ever consummating the marriage.

The flight of aesthetes and scholars to China was as much imaginative as physical. Sometimes the flight involved an attempt to recapture the past. The Communist revolution was so destructive of the traditional culture of Beijing that in the 1950s and 1960s an appetite developed in the West for books about old Beijing before its fall. It was an appetite driven by nostalgia and intensified by the horrifying destruction of so many grand monuments and traditions of the past. The best books in this genre were written by people who had loved traditional Chinese culture to the point of romanticizing it. Some of them were homosexual aesthetes. These authors described Beijing as they experienced it in the 1930s and 1940s.

The first of the more notable books in this category to appear was written by George N. Kates (1895–1990). Kates was born in Cincinnati, Ohio, to parents who had both emigrated from Europe—his father from Poland and his mother from Germany.[48] Possibly the family was Jewish. His father was a successful industrialist who provided him with the financial means to travel widely and develop proficiency in several European languages. Kates served as a translator in the American Army during World War I and graduated from Harvard in 1922. He spent the 1920s commuting between Hollywood where he was a cultural consultant for Paramount Pictures and Queen's College, Oxford, where he completed his doctorate in 1930. He became interested in Chinese literature, began studying Chinese, and moved to Beijing in 1932. Like the other foreign aesthetes, he avoided the commercial and diplomatic community of the Legation Quarter. He described them as people who

> moved in another sphere. In these asphalted streets the multitudinous sights and sounds of the old capital did not exist. Trees were planted along their well-swept borders as in some model European city; and local peddlers were excluded by special police guarding the entrance barriers. . . . It was not alluring.[49]

Kates wrote that antiforeign feeling in Beijing, which had been so strong three decades earlier, was "almost completely nonexistent" in the 1930s.[50]

The aesthetes were usually distinguished from China scholars by a difference of focus. Scholars came to Beijing to study the language, with the aim of achieving professional proficiency and completing a research project. They were dependent for financial support on institutional stipends of finite duration. Consequently, their stays in Beijing had a clear objective and were usually of shorter duration than the aesthetes, who came to live there indefinitely. Kates thought that he was putting down roots to stay in Beijing, but the threat of hostilities between Japan and the United States forced him to leave after seven years. He would have much preferred to stay longer.

During his seven-year stay, Kates' proficiency in Chinese enabled him to negotiate with a former palace eunuch to secure a residence inside the Forbidden City. Like Harold Acton, he had the financial means to collect art and antique pieces of furniture, rugs, and porcelain. His sister Beatrice M. Kates shared his interest in antique Chinese furniture and joined together with two other women to photograph outstanding pieces of traditional furniture found in the homes of friends. Kates wrote the text to accompany the photographs they collected, and the result was published in London in 1948 under the title *Chinese Household Furniture*. Kates' sexuality is unknown, but his life resembled the life of many men with same-sex attraction who lived in an age when being closeted was essential to one's professional and social acceptance. After returning to the United States, he served in the Office of Strategic Services in the Chinese wartime capital of Zhongqing in 1943–1944. Later he contributed, as a language research specialist, to the draft of the Chinese text of the United Nations Charter. Finally, he became curator of Oriental Art at the Brooklyn Museum.

Sometimes physical and political obstacles prevented the men we are discussing from setting foot in China, but at other times their absence was just a matter of choice. In any case, the literary and historical documents as well as the museum artifacts and works of art made it possible for them to flee to a China that existed out of time and space. The physical and imaginative remoteness of China had particular appeal to closeted and latent homosexuals whose secrets caused them to be already in flight from family and friends. The supreme challenge to any neat categorizing in this matter is Arthur Waley (1888–1966). Waley was an intense individualist whose alienation from convention was shaped by his Jewish ancestry, his withdrawn nature, his association with famous eccentrics of the Bloomsbury Group, and his friendships with women that appear to have been devoid of any sexual interest. He never set foot in China, and yet he was one of the greatest translators of Chinese literary works in the twentieth century.

The gay Tang dynasty historian Howard Wechsler (1942–1986) was hindered from visiting China by the strictures of Cold War diplomacy. Nevertheless, he did flee, metaphorically speaking, to the field of Chinese history. In the process, he escaped the obscurity of his middle-class origins in the Bronx in an upward trajectory that duplicated the manner and even the physical locale of the legendary character Jay Gatsby in F.

Scott Fitzgerald's novel *The Great Gatsby*. At Yale, Wechsler cultivated the China historian Arthur Wright, whose eminence, wealth, and expensive house on Long Island Sound impressed him. With Wright's support and his own hard work, Wechsler used his scholarship of Tang history to go far, all the way to the *est* seminars of Werner Erhard on the West Coast as well as to the gay bathhouses of San Francisco. Along the way, he contracted the AIDS virus, and his rising star in the Chinese field abruptly crashed.

The flight to China of the gay scholar Marston Edwin Anderson (1951–1992) was of a different sort. Shaped by his midwestern Scandinavian Lutheran background, Anderson was a far more repressed personality than Wechsler. He fought his same-sex desires with an intensity that led him to conceive a child. Instead of marrying the child's mother, he fled to Berkeley where he studied Chinese, and then to China where he did language study and dissertation research. One of the most promising young scholars of his generation, his career was cut short by AIDS. He remained deeply closeted until his death.

2

The Exotic Appeal
of Chinese Boy-Actors

THE RISE AND FALL OF THE BOY-ACTOR AESTHETIC

In 1925 George Soulié de Morant published one of the most striking expressions of Chinese homoeroticism that had appeared in Europe.[1] *Bijou-de-Ceinture, ou le jeune homme qui porte robe, se poudre et se farde, roman* (The Belted Gem, or the Young Man Who Wears Dresses, Powder, and Makeup: A Novel) portrayed the story of a real-life Chinese actor who was trained to perform female Peking Opera roles. Soulié de Morant described him as "a precious stone, a treasure, a true *baobei* [gem]."[2] The English translator named the boy-actor "Pei Yu" (*beiyu*), which means "gem" or "bijou."[3] Although many of the characters and events in *Bijou-de-Ceinture* are historical, Soulié de Morant tells the story in a deeply personal way and transforms it into a work of art. As a result, it is difficult to discern the exact dividing line between reality and art.

Actors belonged to one of the lowest-ranking professions in China. In legal and social status, they ranked as slaves.[4] They were recruited as boys from the bottom of the social scale, and their entry into the acting profession condemned them to remain in the lowest legal status. They were one of four classes—prostitutes, actors, lictors, and constables—who traditionally were disqualified from participating in the examinations. In 1770 the prohibition on actors participating in the official examinations was extended to their sons and grandsons, thereby excluding three generations from the paramount path to success in China.[5]

The careers of these actor-prostitutes began with their selection as delicate-looking boys who had pale skin and effeminate mannerisms. Their parents contracted them to a theater troupe at a young age, and the acting troupe leader signed a formal agreement with the boy's father in return for payment of a fee. For the boy, this represented indentured servitude which would end only after a specified number of years. The training of the boys was sometimes very harsh, and most of the income they generated was appropriated by their trainers. Nevertheless, some actors had so much talent and such striking good looks that they ascended to occupy a niche in society in which they were cultivated by wealthy and powerful men.

Prior to the Taiping Rebellion, most of these boys in the Beijing theaters were recruited from the lower Yangtze River region, but after the 1860s, Beijing-area boys predominated. They were trained to play female roles (*dan*) and to work as escort-prostitutes (*xianggong*). The preparation was quite strenuous and involved diet, exercise, and training in feminized appearance and manner. The highly valued white skin was cultivated through ointments and avoidance of the sun. Theater audiences particularly appreciated a boy-actor who could skillfully imitate a female, although the emphasis was more on appearance than acting technique.

The main theater district in Beijing was located directly south of the Qianmen (Front Gate), officially known as Zhengyangmen (South-Facing Gate) (maps 1 and 2 in the front matter and figures 2.1–2.3).[6] This was the most important of the nine Beijing gates built in the Ming dynasty and the only one to survive largely intact into the present.[7] It straddled the main north–south thoroughfare in Beijing and divided the Inner City (*Neicheng*) to the north from the Outer City (*Waicheng*) to the south. The Forbidden City and Tiananmen Square lay at the northern end of Qianmen Main Street (*Qianmen Dajie*), while the Altar of Heaven and the Altar of Agriculture lay at its southern extremity. Chinese emperors processed between the Forbidden City and these altars to make ritual sacrifices at specified times during the year, such as at the summer and winter solstices.

Figure 2.1. Qianmen Street, looking south from the Inner City toward Qianmen (Front Gate) of Beijing, by J. D. Zumbrun, ca. 1900. Library of Congress Prints and Photographs Division, Washington, DC.

Figure 2.2. Outside Qianmen (Front Gate) of Beijing, looking north from the Outer City, ca. 1931. Library of Congress Prints and Photographs Division, Washington, DC.

After the Manchu conquest of 1644, Chinese residents of the Inner City were forced to relocate their homes to the Outer City.[8] Wealthy Chinese families were expelled from their spacious compounds to the congested streets beyond the southern wall. The areas close to the wall of the Inner City became densely occupied with concentrations of shops and markets near the gates. There was a major relocation of restaurants and expensive shops to these locations. The area outside of the Qianmen became an entertainment center with theaters, male and female prostitutes, and restaurants. The Kangxi emperor, out of his concern for their debilitating influence on the elite Manchu bannermen, had banned theaters from the Inner City in 1671, forcing them to relocate to this Dazhalan district of the Outer City.

Figure 2.3. Outside Qianmen (Front Gate) of Beijing, Outer City (south) side, donkey carts awaiting passengers, 1902, by C. H. Graves. Library of Congress Prints and Photographs Division, Washington, DC.

At the fourth intersection south of Qianmen Gate, one turned west onto a narrow, busy street called Dazhalan, after the large gate posts at each end of the street that divided the wards and which were closed at night to protect against thieves and civil disturbances (map 2).[9] A typical restaurant on the Dazhalan was the Houdefu (Unbounded Generosity and Happiness), which served Beijing-style food.[10] The dishes included boiled bear claws served with various condiments and sliced fish served with soy. Traveling west on Dazhalan Street, one soon reached the Tianqiao (Heavenly Bridge) section where most theaters (usually about ten in number) were located. The foul smell of the meat markets failed to diminish the popularity of the numerous wine houses and theaters in the area.[11] One of the most famous theaters was named, with dramatic flair, the Dapeng (Roc), after the great fabulous bird that appears in the opening chapter of the famous Daoist work *Zhuangzi*.[12] Seven of these theaters were still functioning—albeit as faded, aging queens—in the early 1930s.[13]

Although commoners and bannermen flocked to the theaters, their popularity was due in large part to the relationships between upper-class men and boy-entertainers who combined the roles of actors and prostitutes. The patronage of them by upper-class men flourished from the late Ming dynasty (ca. 1550) until the fall of the Qing dynasty in 1911.[14] Men of status and wealth made contact with these boy-entertainers in the theaters as well as restaurants and private residences (*siyu*) which doubled as pleasure houses. Contact might be made by reserving table seats in the theater balcony stalls, which cost seven times the amount of a regular seat.[15] The boy-actors would watch for the arrival of these gentlemen and visit them in the balcony. Once they had been matched, they would often depart for a restaurant before the stage dramas had concluded.

There was a close relationship between the theaters and the restaurants that were located nearby.[16] Nineteenth-century postperformance gatherings were venues for being seen by other people, with lively discussion between tipsy theatergoers and pretty actors scurrying about. Banquets were arranged in advance. The host signed a contract with the restaurant manager, who in turn signed a contract with a theater troupe to provide actors, and then formal invitations were sent out to the guests. Boy-actors were well paid for pouring drinks at a banquet, although most of the money went to the acting troupe master-trainer. It was expected at the more prestigious restaurants that one actor would be ordered for each guest. Each boy-actor was expected to formally greet each guest at the table, to pour his wine, to sit beside the assigned guest, to sing arias, and to display physical affection. As the liquor flowed, the guest might pull the boy-actor onto his lap, and they might play a common game, such as "the skin cup" (*jing pibei*).[17] In this game, the actor might straddle the guest's lap, tilt back the guest's head and press his lips to the guest's mouth, letting the wine flow from his mouth into the mouth of the guest.

While it was possible to have sex with one of the boy-actors in special rooms in the restaurant, more discriminating men preferred to meet in the private residence of the boy-actor's master-trainer. In many cases, this amounted to the master-trainer functioning more as a brothel master than a drama coach. These boy-actors were a source of significant income for their master-trainers, who exploited them as prostitutes during the peak of their adolescent attractiveness (thirteen to eighteen years of age).[18] By the age of eighteen, their pubescent beauty and desirability began to fade, and they were cruelly cast aside.

While Josef Schedel's Western friends in Beijing were his peers, his Chinese friends were of distinctly lower social standing and included *dan* (female impersonators) who worked in the theater district near the Qianmen Gate. Schedel mentions spending time with these "singsong boys" in the theater district of Beijing in October of 1910.[19] The Qianmen was located a short distance from the southwest corner of the Legation Quarter and was close to Schedel's residence and workplace. In January of 1911, Schedel spent an evening with a singsong boy who stole his silver cigarette case. He dismissed the evening as a "nice but expensive pleasure."

Over time, Schedel seems to have developed some appreciation for the Chinese theater. In 1910, soon after arriving in Beijing, he left the theater after only one hour because he found the sounds of the music and singing to be cacophonous. However, by 1918 he attended a pleasure establishment with a Chinese business acquaintance in which he saw three Chinese dramas—a tragedy, a comedy, and a military play—not arriving home until nearly midnight. His comments on the splendid costumes, the lute playing, the juggler, and acrobatics indicate that he had learned to enjoy Chinese theater.[20] One suspects that he enjoyed the boy-actors in particular.

The romantic role of boy-actors was an accepted part of the aesthetic of Ming and Qing literary culture. The masterpiece of Chinese fiction, Cao Xueqin's *Story of the Stone* (Shitouji) (1791), also known as *The Dream of the Red Chamber* (Honglou meng), is built around a love triangle between one man and two women.[21] However, the novel also features a same-sex attachment between the main character Jia Baoyu, an upper-class youth, and a female impersonator (*dan*) with the stage name of Qiguan (Bijou, Gem) and the offstage name of Jiang Yuhan.[22] Later, in the nineteenth century, a novel glorifying male same-sex attraction and male "flowers" (*hua*) (i.e., prostitutes) was produced by Chen Sen (ca. 1796–1870). This *Precious Mirror for Judging Flowers* (Pinhua baojian) (1849) blended fictional characters modeled on the *Story of the Stone* with prominent and identifiable real-life figures who patronized the boy-actors of Beijing.[23]

Boy-actors became very popular in the Ming and Qing, and this was only partly due to the absence of women from the stage. Their exclusion dates from the decree of the homosexually inclined Xuande emperor in 1429 banning scholar-officials from patronizing female prostitutes. A more significant reason for prominent men increasing their patronage of these "singsong boys" (*xiaochang*) seems to have been the development of a homoerotic sensibility. Scholar-officials with wives and concubines at home turned to boys and young men not merely as substitutes for women, but as something desirable in their own right.[24] From the late eighteenth century until the early twentieth century, these young males served as highly coveted prostitute-entertainers.[25] In addition to being trained in the dramatic arts of singing, acting, and applying makeup, they were taught the art of escorting and performing sexual services. Part of their training was said to involve sitting on wooden pegs, which would stretch their anuses to ease sexual intercourse with their patrons.[26]

Chinese sensibility began to shift around 1910 under the impact of the West and modernization. As the Chinese began to imitate Western sexual values, the aesthetic features of the *dan* and the related role of prostitute-entertainer began to lose their attraction for the reform-minded younger generation. The influential cultural reformer Hu Shi (Hu Shih) returned from studying in the United States in 1917 and condemned traditional Chinese homoeroticism.[27] By 1912 the *dan* themselves were attempting to divorce their acting role from that of prostitution. With the end of the examination system in 1905, scholar-officials were no longer being produced, and the traditional literati sensibility appears to have faded under the onslaught of all that was new and modern. As for the appeal of the boy-actors, what had previously been seen as aesthetic and erotic was increasingly viewed as ugly and repulsive. The area of the male brothels south of the Qianmen became a squalid section that self-respecting men avoided.[28]

This change in sensibility is reflected in the 1937 short story "Tu" (Rabbit) by the leading twentieth-century writer Lao She (Shu Qingchun) (1899–1966).[29] The story is set in Beijing of the thirties and features a youth called Young Chen who wished to become a famous Peking Opera star by playing *dan* (female impersonator) roles. The narrator presents Chen as a pathetic figure who succumbs to the glitter of a tawdry world, comparable in our own day to a poor boy becoming a porn star. Although Chen is sincere, his naïveté is exploited by a sinister handler and bankrolled by a corrupt government minister who seduces Chen's sister and then casts both sister and brother aside. The author expresses pity for Chen and condemns a society that allows for such exploitation.

Lao She was very homophobic. He had been deeply influenced by the modernizing forces of the May Fourth Movement which condemned the *dan* roles as culturally backward. In addition, he had been a lecturer in Chinese at the University of London from 1924 to 1930 and had read widely in English, particularly the works of Charles Dickens, which he admired and tried to adapt to China.[30] He also had absorbed British homophobia. Consequently, it is not surprising that his treatment of homosexuality in "Rabbit" reflects a Chinese version of the Victorian British view of homosexuality as "the love that dare not speak its name." There are no explicit references to homosexual acts in "Rabbit." Homosexuality is treated as so repulsive that references are made only implicitly through the use of the powerfully pejorative metaphor "rabbit."

Lao She's homophobia was typical of leading Chinese writers of the early twentieth century. Lu Xun (1881–1936), the leading writer in the movement to modernize Chinese culture, criticized the *dan* actors as part of China's old and weak feminine image. He was preoccupied with creating a new and masculine national character.[31] Li Yaotang (1904–2005), who wrote under the pseudonym of Ba Jin, was also very homophobic. His most famous work was the autobiographical novel *Family* (Jia) (1933), which tells the story of generational conflict in his wealthy family in Sichuan province in the early 1920s. On the occasion of the sixty-sixth birthday celebration of the family patriarch, an acting company performs in the family compound, and the female impersonators are rewarded with money. Ba Jin described what followed:

> But even this did not satisfy the honourable guests. When an opera was over, the actors who had been rewarded had to drink with them at their tables, still wearing their make-up and costumes. The honourable gentlemen fondled the performers and filled them with wine; they behaved with such crass vulgarity that the younger guests were shocked and the servants whispered among themselves.[32]

Ba Jin's novel reflects how the previously stylish and admirable homoerotic cultivation of *dan* actors had become old fashioned and disgusting for the reform generation of the early twentieth century.

EUROPEAN MEN AND CHINESE BOY-ACTORS

George Soulié de Morant was born in Paris in 1879, and his father was an army engineer who was lost at sea when young George was seven. His father's death prevented him from studying medicine, but a family friend in France enabled him to learn Chinese at a young age and to secure employment in Shanghai in 1900.[33] After working as secretary-interpreter for the Chinese Railway Association, he was engaged by the French Ministry of Foreign Affairs as French Consul in Shanghai and later sent to posts in Hankou and Yunnan-fu (Kunming). During a cholera epidemic, he was impressed by the effectiveness of treatment with acupuncture, to which he devoted a lifelong study.

He returned to France in 1911 where he married, began a family, and became a prolific writer on a wide range of topics in Chinese culture. He promoted the development of acupuncture in the French medical profession in spite of a great deal of skepticism and hostility. He also wrote translations of Chinese literature and articles on Chinese art, history, music, and theater in a popular vein. He was sent back to China by the French government for a final trip in 1917 that lasted for one year and was filled with secrecy. He died in 1955.

After returning from his last visit to China, Soulié de Morant wrote a book about his friendship with a Chinese *dan* (female impersonator) whom he called Bijou-de-Ceinture (Belted Gem) and claimed that the boy-actor was a real person. His use of the name Bijou seems to have been a conscious echo of the name of the boy-actor Bijou (Qiguan) in the well-known *Story of the Stone*. The events in *Bijou-de-Ceinture* cover a twenty-year period which roughly paralleled Soulié de Morant's stays in China of 1900–1911 and 1917–1918. One difference between the historical chronology and the novel lies in the book's setting of the first meeting of the author with the boy Beiyu around 1895, which was five years before Soulié de Morant actually arrived in China. According to the novel, they met on a canal barge heading northward toward Beijing on the Grand Canal. The ten-year-old boy's beauty had a striking effect on the author.

Soulié de Morant explains the Chinese exotic in a way that would have been quite shocking to a European audience of that time. (The pedophilic connotations are capable of creating discomfort in an audience today.) He explains the attraction of Chinese men to boys in universal terms: "Old men in all countries have a passionate love of youth. As their potency decreases, one could almost say that their desire increases to test their strength against greater and greater challenges."[34] This statement is used to explain why Beiyu's teacher sodomized him. His father treats the event as one of minor abuse without the horror that accompanies pedophilic scandals in contemporary Western societies. Later, desperate poverty forced Beiyu's father to sell him to the director of a theater company for five ounces of silver. Beiyu's striking beauty stirred a dangerous obsession in a Prince Li, a close relative of the emperor. Much of the book centers around the attempts of this powerful but disreputable figure to seduce Beiyu. While Prince Li was portrayed as incarnating the corruption of the Manchu throne, two Chinese officials were presented in a favorable light as Beiyu's protectors.

The English translator claimed that Prince Li was "probably" Shiduo, great-grandson of Zhaolian (1780–1833), from whom he inherited the title Prince Li (Li xinwang).[35] Shiduo served as a grand councilor from 1884 to 1901. However, since Shiduo lived until 1914, he could not be the Prince Li of *Bijou-de-Ceinture* because that author claims that his Prince Li "died in precisely the circumstances" described in the Boxer Rebellion in Beijing in 1900.[36] By contrast, Beiyu's protectors in the novel are clearly identified by Soulié de Morant as the real-life figures Yuan Chang (1846–1900) and Xu Jingcheng (Hsü Ching-ch'eng) (1845–1900). Yuan was a prominent scholar (*jinshi* degree, 1876) and official in the Foreign Office (Zongli Yamen) who conducted treaty negotiations with the French.[37] Yuan was a close friend of Xu Jingcheng, a scholar (*jinshi* degree, 1868) and diplomat who had served as foreign minister to Germany.[38] Because Yuan and Xu were critical of the Boxers, they were condemned as proforeign and were executed at the height of the xenophobic Boxer frenzy in 1900.

But what makes *Bijou-de-Ceinture* so striking as a homoerotic work is that the author did not use the conventional moral context of early twentieth-century Europeans in defining forces of good and evil in binary terms of heterosexuality and homosexuality. Instead, he defined good and evil in terms of the tenderness versus the abusiveness of the different characters' love for Beiyu. While Prince Li sought to possess Beiyu through force (and ultimately failed), the bisexual Minister Yuan protected him. Rather than criticizing men loving men, Yuan made an eloquent defense of bisexuality. Over a shared pipe of opium, he compared the love of women to "peaches overripened by the sun" and love of men to an apple whose "dry freshness stimulates the palate even while satisfying it."[39]

Whether the boy-actor in his novel *Bijou-de-Ceinture* was a real person or fabricated for literary purposes, Solié de Morant's detailed knowledge indicates a fascination with boy-actors that would have been based on some degree of personal contact with them during his stay in Beijing. He was clearly aware of the shock effect of the Chinese boy-actors on European readers.[40] His sympathetic portrayal of them reveals his own feelings. What is not clear is his exact relationship to Beiyu. In the novel, he portrayed himself as a friend and observer of events, but his emotional attachment to Beiyu indicated that he was more than a friend. Several reasons might have prevented him from revealing the whole story. After he returned to France in 1911, Soulié de Morant married and had a family. The translator Gerald Fabian mentions meeting his son Nevile, who was also his father's literary executor.[41] This would seem to confirm Soulié de Morant's bisexuality.

Another reason for not revealing the details of a romantic and sexual relationship with Beiyu would have been fear of a hostile reaction from the French reading public in 1925 when *Bijou-de-Ceinture* was published. So long as the author remained a narrator, the story could be received as a form of exotica, but the cultural environment was not receptive to homosexuality and very few books about same-sex experiences had been published in France in the 1920s. When André Gide published his defense of pederasty in *Corydon* in 1924, he personally distanced himself from the narrator of the book. When Jean Cocteau anonymously published his semiautobiographical novel *Le Livre Blanc* (The White Book) in 1928, it was attacked as obscene, and Cocteau continued to deny its authorship throughout his life.[42] If Soulié de Morant had presented himself as a lover of Beiyu, his novel would probably have been rejected out of hand on moral grounds as degenerate. Given his wish to maintain professional respectability for his other works on China, his portrayal probably went as far as he possibly could go in 1925 without damaging his reputation.

Harold Acton's interest in the classical drama of China had a homo-erotic component. He was particularly fascinated with the tradition of *dan* actors who played female characters. He believed that the role of heroine was best played by males who created an illusion of ultrafemininity, which he called "a genuine triumph of art over nature."[43] Foreigners had to develop an appreciation for it because the shrill music that accompa-nied the falsetto singing of the actors offended the uncultivated ears of non-Chinese. Desmond Parsons had been one of Acton's few friends who did not shrink from attending.

In his regular visits to performances of Peking Opera (*jingju* or *jingxi*), Acton saw great female impersonators, such as Cheng Yanqiu (Ch'eng Yen-ch'iu) (1904–1958) and Mei Lanfang (1894–1961).[44] Although women had been appearing on stage since before the 1930s, the standards were still set by female impersonators. Mei was the greatest actor of that time.[45] He came from a family of actors, traditionally a disreputable class in China, and his grandfather was the well-known Mei Qiaoling (1841–1881) who directed a Peking Opera group and played *dan* roles. Mei Lanfang began training at the age of seven and made his debut in Beijing in 1904 at the age of ten. During his long career he was unrivaled as a female im-personator, and he gave the *dan* roles an importance that they had never before enjoyed. He appeared in productions in Shanghai and Hong Kong in 1919 and in Tokyo in 1924. His fame became so great that he attracted prominent viewers, including the Indian poet Rabindranath Tagore and the Crown Prince of Sweden.

In 1929–1930, Mei and his theater troupe traveled to the United States to play in Washington, D.C.; New York; Chicago; San Francisco; Los Ange-les; and Honolulu (figure 2.4). In 1935 he traveled to Europe but was un-able to perform because of the unsettled political situation there. Lu Xun, obsessed with creating a new virile cultural model for China, ridiculed Mei's overseas tours as a female impersonator, claiming that they were a sign of Mei's declining popularity in China rather than his growing fame abroad.[46] In the fall of 1936, Mei performed in Beijing for the last time before the outbreak of the Sino-Japanese War. In July of 1937 when the Japanese attacked, he moved to Hong Kong. After the Japanese occupied Hong Kong in December 1941, he refused their requests to perform. He even grew a mustache to symbolize his resistance to playing female roles under the Japanese occupation.

Although the high tide of homoerotic adulation of *dan* actors was past, they continued to be cultivated by certain Western aesthetes in the 1930s. In his satirical novel *Peonies and Ponies*, Acton playfully portrays a relationship between an Englishman named Philip Flower and a young Peking Opera actor named Yang Pao-ch'in ("Yang Baoqin" in pinyin ro-manization). Flower was an English expatriate who had lived in Beijing

Figure 2.4. Mei Lanfang (1894–1961), famous *dan* actor (female impersonator) of Peking Opera, photographed during a visit to New York in 1930. ©Billy Rose Theatre Division, New York Public Library for the Performing Arts.

for fifteen years. He extravagantly claimed that he was half-Chinese because although his body was foreign, his soul was Chinese.[47] He was only moderately affluent, but because of the relative poverty of the Chinese, he was able to live in a grand style in Beijing with a house and servants. He is described as a "pansy," and this fits the dandy-aesthete model that Acton knew so well.[48] Acton mocks his superficiality but portrays his interest in the boy (actually, ephebe) as genuine.

Flower first saw the boy in a Peking Opera performance in which he was playing a *dan* role. He was entranced by the boy's mixture of virility and femininity in impersonating a young bride.[49] After the performance, he went backstage and introduced himself, inviting the boy to visit him at his home. Consonant with Acton's satire, the boy is presented as a poor actor who is dying to get out of China and go to the West. Since the boy is basically an orphan who was sold to an acting master by his grandmother, he views Flower as a way out of his poverty. Flower adopts him, buys clothes for him, and hires a private tutor to educate him since the boy never went to school. Although Flower is Victorian in his prudery, an undertone of sexuality runs throughout the account. Yang is said to be "as pretty as a girl."[50] But Flower's sexuality is very repressed, and he never seems able to cross the line from adoptive father to daddy lover.

SAME-SEX MALE LOVE IN CHINA

On the whole, the Chinese were more tolerant of homosexuality than were Europeans, but there were numerous critics of same-sex practices. Homosexuality was indeed condemned by the Chinese if it interfered with the demands of filial piety and with its primary obligation to procreate and continue the family line.[51] There were regional variations in Chinese attitudes toward homosexuality, reinforced by regional differences of dialect and culture. Fujian province was one of the more accommodating areas of same-sex attraction. Also the literati culture of the Ming dynasty (1368–1644) which was centered in the Lower Yangze River region (Jiangnan) of east-central China was fascinated by homoeroticism. In this milieu, boy love became fashionable, and its practitioners, rather than being closeted, made a public display of cultivating boys as a mark of their elite social status.[52] These sophisticated sexual tastes were not widely shared by the common people in the countryside.

After the Manchu conquest and the establishment of the Qing dynasty (1644–1911), these cultural tendencies continued. The seventeenth century featured a flourishing homoerotic literature among Confucian scholars, novelists, and playwrights. Works such as *Cap and Hair Pins* (Bian er chai) developed the theme of love being fulfilled by a homosexual relationship.[53] There is some question about whether this proliferating homoerotic literature reflected actual sexual practices or an intellectualized phenomenon. While most scholars think it reflected a greater practice of same-sex love, another interpretation regards it as more of a literary and intellectual fascination with passion (*qing*) and with what was strange (*qi*), that is, same-sex relationships as a form of strange passion.[54]

In the capital region of Beijing in northern China, attitudes were more complicated. The explosion of homoerotic literature in the seventeenth century provoked a negative reaction from some conservative Manchus. The Kangxi emperor (r. 1661–1722) was particularly homophobic.[55] It is unlikely to have been coincidental that prohibitions against sodomy (*jijian*) were incorporated for the first time into the illicit sex section of the Qing legal code in 1679, two years after the Kangxi emperor assumed personal control of the government from the regents.[56]

Chinese names for same-sex relations are just as variant as Western terminology. In the West, the terms *sodomia* (sodomy) and *Sodomitae* (Sodomites) have been used since the Middle Ages and stemmed from the famous biblical account of sexual abuse in the ancient city of Sodom in Genesis 19. The term *Homosexualität* (homosexuality) first appeared in an 1869 German pamphlet by Karl Maria Kertbeny (1824–1882).[57] Kertbeny and several other Germans had developed the new idea that same-sex attraction was an inherent part of an individual's personality. His pamphlet took the form of an open letter to the German minister of justice. It was an attempt to influence the drafting of a new German penal code concerning whether sex between members of the same gender should be a crime. Other nineteenth-century Western terms for same-sex relations were "inversion" or "invert" and "pederasty" or "pederast," which had negative connotations, and "Uranianism" or "Uranian," which had positive connotations.

In Chinese antiquity, men who had sex with emperors were called "favorites" (*bi*), although the term was also applied to women.[58] Famous homoerotic metaphors from classical texts include "half-eaten peach" (*fentao*) from the sweet peach that the male favorite Mizi Xia shared with his lover Duke Ling of Wei (534–493 BC).[59] Other classical homoerotic metaphors are the name Longyang (*longyang*) from the royal favorite Lord of Longyang (third century BC) and "cut sleeve" (*duanxiu*) from the Emperor Ai (6 BC–AD 1), who cut off his sleeve rather than disturb the head of his favorite Dong Xian who was sleeping on it. During the later Ming and Qing (1644–1911) dynasties, the most common terms for homosexuality were *nanse* (male beauty) and *nanfeng* (male custom). The term *nanfeng* (southern custom) was also commonly used, from the belief that homoeroticism had originated in the southern provinces of Zhejiang and Fujian. There were also names with derogatory connotations, such as "little rabbit" (*tuzi* or *tu'er*) and "turtle" (*wangba*).

New terms have been added in modern times, each of which carries slightly different meanings. In the 1920s the terms *tongxingai* (same-sex love) and *tongxinglian* (same-sex attraction) were absorbed into China by way of Japan. These terms were basically Chinese translations of the Western term "homosexuality," and they conveyed the negative Western connotations which had not traditionally been part of Chinese culture. In the 1990s, Hong Kong and Taiwan were leaders in a movement to develop new Chinese terms for same-sex love.[60] In Hong Kong, British colonialism had imposed a European homophobia in the colony's legal system, although prosecution of same-sex male activity seldom occurred. Homosexual activity in Hong Kong was decriminalized in 1991 as part of an anticolonialist movement that revived more tolerant traditional Chinese attitudes. As part of an attempt to define same-sex love in more indigenous cultural terms, the Chinese term *tongzhi* (comrade), with sexual, not political (i.e., Communist) connotations, was given a new meaning. The *tongzhi* movement focused on developing a same-sex identity for all of China, including overseas Chinese in Taiwan, Singapore, and the West.

While the *tongzhi* movement spread to Taiwan and gave rise to a literary movement called *tongzhi wenxue (Tongzhi* literature), others in Taiwan took a different path. Taiwan was more deeply influenced by Western postmodernism than Hong Kong, and a group at Taiwan National University (Taida) developed a more radical school called *Kuer* literature (*kuer wenxue*).[61] The term k*uer* is a new Chinese term (neologism), essentially a transliteration of the Western term "queer" that is formed by combining the characters *ku* (cruel, cold, very, extremely) and *er* (child, youngster, son). The meaning of *kuer* is derived less from Chinese tradition, which *kuer* proponents rejected as patriarchal and feudal, than from Western movements, such as American gay liberation.

In some ways, the *kuer* movement is reminiscent of the New Culture Chinese reformers of the early twentieth century with their moralistic condemnation of the past and championing of the new. The movement has attempted to blend global (rather than traditional Chinese) values with the local context of Taiwan. It identified with a "modern" and "progressive" lifestyle and with the upwardly mobile new middle class of Taiwan whose models lie in the West and in Japan rather than in China.[62] As with queer studies scholars in the West, it represents a highly theoretical approach that emphasizes extreme social constructionism over essentialism and a preference for viewing sexuality in terms of socially constructed "gender" (*xingbie*) rather than biologically based "sex" (*xing*).

A carefully constructed cloud of obfuscation has been thrown over the subject of clerical same-sex relationships in early Sino-Western history. Among Catholic missionaries, who began entering China in 1579, two factors have combined to limit information about priests with same-sex desire. The Catholic Church was obsessed with preventing same-sex liaisons among celibate priests. Jesuit novices were introduced to practices like the "no touching" rule at the beginning of their novitiate.[63] Superiors took great pains to guard against clerical homosexuality and, when it (inevitably) occurred, suppressed the public dissemination of information about it. In 1601 a new secret code for use by Jesuit provincials in com-municating with the Jesuit father general in Rome was introduced. Of the ninety-two entries in the code, number 53 was assigned to *"lascibo"* (lustful, lecherous) and number 54 to *"amistad de muchachos"* (friendship with boys).[64]

The second factor limiting information about Catholic priests in China comes from the Chinese obsession with violations of female chastity. With their more tolerant attitudes toward same-sex activity, the Chinese re-garded its occurrence as unworthy of serious attention, reserving instead their ire for any instances of priestly adulterous affairs with women.[65] Consequently, the few sex scandals that we do know about involved male priests seducing female parishioners. Nevertheless, the Catholic theologi-cal explanations of sexual sin, whether heterosexual or homosexual, were similar. Sexual sins were thought to be the result of a type of subtle mad-ness or temporary insanity caused by diabolical forces. When they oc-curred among Italian missionaries in eighteenth-century China, they were referred to as "madness" (*mattia*), "filthiness" (*sozzetto*), and "diabolical things" (*cose diaboliche*).[66]

To date, even less has been uncovered about same-sex relations involv-ing Protestant missionaries in China than about their Catholic counter-parts. Protestant missionaries did not enter China until 1807, and many Protestant mission boards preferred that male missionaries be married before going into the mission field. Moreover, the growing number of female missionaries in the late nineteenth century changed the dynamics of the mission field in China. An 1890 survey found that among Protes-tant missionaries, women surpassed men by 707 to 589, with 316 of the women being unmarried.[67] Same-sex relations between women (lesbian-ism) were far more problematic than between men, since in Anglo-Saxon cultures, the physical touching of affection between women was consid-ered normal, unlike with men. The German penal code was typical of many Western countries in prohibiting sexual relations between men, but not women. In short, the experiences of gay Protestant missionaries in China are yet to be uncovered and told.

3

Establishing Friendships
in Imperial China

"A VERY HUMAN AFFECTION, AND CONTRARY TO RELIGIOUS DETACHMENT"

For men with same-sex desire, friendships with Chinese men were one way of realizing their attraction to China. Because of the absence of romantic relationships with women, "special friendships" with other men played an important role in the lives of these men. This was particularly true of Catholic priests who had taken vows of celibacy. Their friendships with Chinese men were diverse in their emotional intensity. Some of these friendships had a sexual component which was usually more latent than realized, but it was a driving force in the allure China held for them.

The modern history of relations between China and the West dates from the arrival of the Jesuit missionaries in 1579 in Macau. The Jesuits were not only pioneers in traveling thousands of miles on a dangerous sea voyage to reach China, but they were also leaders in establishing a connection between Europe and China by learning the Chinese languages and acquiring a degree of understanding of Chinese culture. Other Christian missionaries followed who deepened that connection by serving as intermediaries between the Chinese imperial court and the papacy in Rome. The connection was further deepened by missionaries who brought Chinese to visit and live in Europe. Although the distance in time and the sexually repressive techniques of Catholic religious life obscure any attempt to identify men with same-sex attraction among these missionaries, the lives of two men offer some evidence of that attraction.

When Europeans first began entering China in the sixteenth century, they soon noticed the pervasiveness of male homosexuality. One of the earliest reports to appear in Europe was written by the Portuguese merchant Galeote Pereira, who had been imprisoned by the Chinese in 1549–1553 for illegal trading along the Fujian coast of southern China.[1] The Jesuits first published an abridged Italian version of Pereira's report at Venice in 1565, and it was later republished in other languages. In his report, Pereira condemned the practice of sodomy by the Chinese as "a filthy abomination" and a "sin of unnatural vice."[2] Pereira reported that the Chinese expressed surprise that sodomy was a sin because it had never been condemned in China. The situation was, of course, more complicated than that.

Shortly before his death in 1610, the famous China Jesuit Matteo Ricci wrote a history of the introduction of Christianity into China. In a chapter entitled "Concerning the Superstitions and Certain Excesses of China," Ricci included, following brief descriptions of Chinese polygamy and prostitution, a one-paragraph description of "sodomia" and "pederastia."[3] The famously accommodating Ricci refers in very unaccommodating terms to Chinese same-sex male "lust as unnatural as perverted, neither prohibited by law nor regarded as illegal or shameful." He speaks of streets in Beijing where boys who are "elaborately dressed and colored with rouge" and trained to dance and sing may be purchased as "whores" (*putti*).

Whereas the gay secrets of a scholar, aesthete, or refugee are individual secrets guarded by friends and colleagues, the gay secrets of (especially Roman Catholic) missionaries are guarded by institutions that are protecting their reputation. When that secrecy is broached, it is usually done by personal enemies of individual clerics or by groups whose hostility tends to distort the facts. Since their founding in 1540, the Society of Jesus has attracted some of the most brilliant men of any religious order. The Jesuits played a particularly important role in the history of Christianity in China. In the years between 1579 and 1807, Catholics were—apart from a few Russian orthodox priests—the only Christian missionaries in China, and the Jesuits were (until the temporary dissolution of their order in 1773) the leading force among them. Their remarkable success in converting eminent Chinese and in getting close to several emperors produced two things: arrogance among Jesuits and jealousy among their critics. These two factors color any attempt to discuss Catholic missionaries in China with same-sex attraction.

The most prominent China Jesuit to be accused of indiscretion with other males was the German Adam Schall von Bell (Tang Ruowang) (1592–1666). Schall established connections to the Chinese at the highest political levels. His remarkable adaptation to China and his mathematical knowledge caused the Chinese court to appoint him to head the Bureau of Astronomy, which was responsible for producing an official calendar (figure 3.1). He was on very close terms with the first Manchu to rule in the Qing dynasty and came the closest of any missionary to converting an emperor. During his youth, the Shunzhi emperor (r. 1644–1661) frequently visited Schall in his residence and sat on Schall's bed, looking at pictorial Christian books and talking about religion. The emperor called him by the affectionate name of "*mafa*" and gave Schall a house in which he lived in an elevated style apart from his Jesuit confreres. All of this imperial favor along with his arrogant manner of dealing with people earned Schall numerous enemies who began to spread rumors. One of these was Gabriel de Magalhães (1610–1677), a fellow Jesuit, but a Portuguese whose dislike was sharpened by intraorder nationalistic rivalries. In 1649 he and four other China Jesuits wrote a letter to the Jesuit vice provincial in which they accused Schall of provoking a scandal in chastity by his excessive affection for a servant.[4]

Figure 3.1. Father Adam Schall von Bell, SJ (1592–1666), portrayed by the engraver Wenzel Hollar (1627–1677). The astronomical instruments and crane insignia on his chest signify his high rank as a Chinese scholar-official (since 1658) in the Bureau of Astronomy. Hollar seems to have made the engraving from other portraits of Schall. The engraving first appeared in Athanasius Kircher, *China Monumentis . . . illustrata* (Amsterdam: Jacobum à Meurs, 1667), between pages 102 and 103.

The servant in question was Pan Jinxiao who served as Schall's majordomo (chief steward). Pan was a Christian, semieducated, and very capable in managing Schall's household. Schall trusted him, perhaps too much, and confided in him, sharing his personal views of others.[5] Pan was very devoted to Schall and began imitating his cheeky manner with guests. Their relationship was unusually close, but it is difficult to know if it was sexual. Magalhães did not accuse Schall of homosexual relations per se, but rather of indiscreet behavior toward his servant that gave rise to suspicions of homosexuality. For example, one night when he was returning from a banquet, Schall had Pan ride pillion (behind him) on his horse, which was the custom among Chinese homosexuals. Schall often treated Pan with an equality which was very untypical of Chinese relations with their servants. When Schall became distant, Pan complained, in the manner of a rejected lover, that Schall had abandoned him for someone else. Magalhães also gossiped that Schall had said Pan once had a homosexual affair with a mathematics student.

Not surprisingly, Jesuit historians have consistently defended such an eminent member of their society from accusations of sexual impropriety. Nevertheless a charge appeared in 1758 in a posthumous work by Giovanni Marcello Angelita (Ning Dacheng), who died at Rome in 1749. Angelita had accompanied the papal legate Maillard de Tournon to China from 1705 to 1711 as his lay secretary and treasurer.[6] Tournon had intense disagreements with the Jesuits, who saw him as a threat to their tenuous position in Beijing. Angelita had picked up a story that during his last years, Schall had invited a woman into his house and had fathered two children with her.[7] The Jesuit historian Joseph Brucker, SJ, explains this rumor to be based on a misperception of Schall's son as illegitimate when in fact he was adopted.[8]

Although Angelita's story has been largely discredited as baseless, the Jesuit historian George H. Dunne noted that "other tales were believed, tales of the who-knows-what-might-be-going-on-behind-closed-doors type of gossip."[9] Dunne dismissed the rumors about a sexual relationship between Schall and Pan as attributable to Schall's "democratic nature," which made him friendly to both servants and emperors. Dunne claimed that Schall's indiscretion lay not in sexual matters, but rather in voicing his blunt and unflattering views of people, including other Jesuits, in front of Pan. Pan repeated the rumors to others and incurred enemies for Schall.

Dunne's explanation is plausible, but there are other equally plausible explanations. A same-sex attraction may or may not be acted out. It is plausible that Schall felt a sexual attraction to other men that was merely latent and that he remained celibate. In fact, the Catholic priesthood has traditionally been a fulfilling life for such men. The view of the Jesuit historian Louis Pfister seems closer to this possibility in writing that Schall had for both Pan and Pan's son "a very human affection, and contrary to religious detachment."[10]

The Shunzhi emperor was concerned that Schall's celibacy would prevent him from having a son to care for him in his old age and to carry on his famous name after his death. In response to his concern, Schall adopted his majordomo's son Pan Shihong (baptized John) who took Schall's Chinese surname Tang. However, because of the age difference between Schall and Shihong, the boy was adopted as a grandson rather than as a son. According to this type of adoption (*qiyang*), the adopted person had no claim on the inheritance of the adopter.[11] Nevertheless, the Xunzhi emperor bestowed privileges on both the boy and his father. Moreover, this adoption had the effect of making the majordomo Pan Jinxiao appear to be Schall's adopted son.[12] This close relationship with Schall would bring Pan both benefits and trouble.

After the premature death of the Shunzhi emperor in 1661 and the enthronement of the Kangxi child emperor, the government was run by four regents. The Jesuits' superior computations in the Bureau of Astronomy had enabled them to displace Muslim scholars. In their resentment, the latter conspired with a fellow Muslim named Yang Guangxian to bring down the Jesuits. In 1664 Yang accused Schall of making several computational errors which were linked to subversive activities.[13] Yang used xenophobic tones to accuse the Christian missionaries and their "million followers" (a blatantly exaggerated number) throughout China of conspiring to overthrow the state. One of the most important duties of the Bureau of Astronomy was the production of an annual calendar with auspicious and inauspicious days designated to allow for planning important events. The most damaging accusation lodged against Schall was that he had deliberately chosen an inauspicious day in 1658 for the burial of an infant prince in order to cast spells on the Shunzhi emperor and the empress which led to their deaths. Since the Manchus came from a shamanistic culture which believed in such spells, Yang's accusation had a certain credibility.

Schall and several other missionaries as well as Pan Jinxiao and his son were arrested, placed in chains, and jailed in November 1664. In the midst of these stressful circumstances, the elderly Schall suffered a stroke and lost the ability to speak and to defend himself against these charges. On April 15, 1665, Schall and his jailed associates were condemned to dismemberment and decapitation. Then nature intervened with an earthquake, meteor, fire, and thick fog. These events shook the shamanistic-minded regents enough for them to suspend the death sentence for Schall and several others, including Pan Jinxiao, and they were released. However, five Chinese Christian astronomers were executed.[14] Once again, Christian churches throughout China were closed, and all missionaries, except for four in Beijing, were expelled to Macau. Later, when the Kangxi emperor dismissed the regents and took control, Schall and his associates were pardoned. A Chinese court document from 1671 records that Schall's adopted grandson Tang Shihong was also pardoned.[15]

On July 21, 1665, Schall made a deathbed confession to his Jesuit brothers for his "excessive indulgence towards this servant [Pan Jinxiao], of the scandal he had caused in adopting as his grandson the son of [Pan]," and for occasional gifts he had made to both Pan and his son in violation of his vow of poverty.[16] None of these lapses necessarily mean that Schall had sexual relations with Pan, but they are quite in harmony with the explanation that Schall's lapses were caused by same-sex attraction.

"THE GREATEST AFFLICTION OF MY LONG AND AGITATED LIFE"

Eighteenth-century European Catholic priests went to great efforts to suppress any mention of same-sex desire except to condemn it. Their attitude was expressed in the Latin legal term for same-sex male love—*peccatum illud horrible inter Christianos non nominandum* (that horrible sin unmentionable among Christians). Unlike during the first millennium when the Church had been more tolerant of same-sex desires, hostility was formalized in the thirteenth century when the influential philosopher Thomas Aquinas developed a natural law theology that viewed same-sex desires as unnatural.[17] Later the Counter-Reformation intensified this hostility by including sodomites (along with witches, Jews, and Protestants) in the broadened category of heresy.[18] Nevertheless, the Church inevitably contained (then, as today) many priests who felt a same-sex attraction. The official hostility of the Church toward these feelings created many cases of a conflicted personal morality of self-hatred in priests, which intensified the condemnation of these innate feelings in themselves and others.

Father Matteo Ripa (Ma Guoxian) (1682–1746) was responsible for fostering many friendships between Europeans and Chinese through his work with Chinese boys whom he brought to Europe for seminary training in Naples. The plan was based on two judgments by Ripa: first, that only native Chinese could effectively proselytize China and, second, that such priests could be effectively trained only in Europe. Ripa's latent same-sex attraction to boys and young men seems to have played a role in his forging of these two judgments. Admittedly, the evidence for this claim is circumstantial and tied to his unusually close relationship to Chinese boys whom he cultivated as seminarians. Two of these boys became involved in a sexual relationship with one another. Ripa was not very tolerant of weakness, either in himself or in those around him. In his memoirs, he recalled that moment on the streets of Naples in 1700 when he was convicted of his sinfulness and called to serve God.[19] Although only eighteen at the time, he described his vices as shocking. Ripa does not specify what his vices were, and because of the horror with which the Catholic Church officially condemned sodomy, it is unlikely that he would have been specific if sodomy had been involved. On the other hand, not all same-sex activities were covered by sodomy. There was a certain amount of ambiguity surrounding the word, and usually only anal penetration was punished. Mutual masturbation and frottage (rubbing the penis against another person's body to the point of ejaculation) were usually treated differently and were punished less severely, if at all. This left a lot of maneuverability for the pervasive sensuality of Neapolitan culture in which numerous forms of physical touching between males has been commonplace and natural. There is reason to believe that Ripa's "shocking" vices involved same-sex activities such as mutual masturbation and frottage, if not sodomy.[20]

Whatever temptations Ripa might have succumbed to in his youth, after becoming a priest he repressed those feelings. Later, in the classic pattern of someone closeted for God, he became harshly critical of his pupil Lucio Wu who failed to repress similar feelings. Ripa was chosen to be trained as a missionary to China by Propaganda and arrived there in 1710. The Kangxi emperor was particularly interested in having Europeans at his court who were trained in technical arts. In Ripa's party there were missionaries who were skilled in mathematics (Fr. Guillaume Febre Bonjour, OSA); music (Fr. Teodorico Pedrini, CM); and painting (Fr. Ripa). Although not highly trained, Ripa had artistic talent and was a quick learner. In his memoirs, Ripa expressed disappointment that he was forced to serve in China primarily as an artist rather than a missionary.[21]

In June of 1719, Ripa was following the Kangxi emperor's entourage beyond the Great Wall to Renhe in Manchuria for his summer retreat. While en route, he went to the town of Gubeikou (Ku-pe-cchieu), where the Christians pressed him to receive three boys for training in the priesthood, including Huang Batong (Filippo Huang) (1712–1776). These three joined a fourth youth from Gubeikou who had been with Ripa since 1714.[22]

After arriving at Renhe, Ripa had a room divided into five partitions, each of which contained a bed and a curtain in front for these four youths. The fifth partitioned area was for a Chinese teacher. Ripa then undertook a program of instruction, and although it resembled a novitiate more than a school, Ripa initially had no thought of continuing it after leaving China. However, he later became convinced that the advancement of Christianity in China required native Chinese priests because the difficulties of learning Chinese were too great for Europeans to overcome. Although Ripa received considerable support from some Europeans, others joined with Chinese to oppose the school. In his memoirs, Ripa makes frequent references to his "enemies," who included several Jesuits. He was accused of keeping the boys for "abominable purposes." Efforts were made to raise doubts in the minds of the parents about Ripa's intentions with these boys, but the parents remained steadfast in their support. When this opposition intensified, Ripa decided to move the school to Europe.

Ripa also agreed to take the son of his scribe and catechist Tommaso Wu (Wu Duomo). Lucio Wu (Wu Lujue) was born in 1713 in the town of Jinshan in southern Jiangsu province, just southwest of present-day Shanghai, and he was baptized in 1720. The boy arrived in Beijing after a long forty-day journey, and although Ripa wanted to send him away, he hesitated to do so. So began the relationship that Ripa described many years later (in 1744) as "the greatest affliction of my long and agitated life."[23]

They departed from Beijing on a bitterly cold and windy day on November 15, 1723, with the two youngest boys (ten-year-old Lucio and eleven-year-old Filippo) in one litter and Ripa in a second litter, while the two older boys, the Chinese teacher, and two servants rode on horseback.[24] On the day of their departure from Beijing, the winds were so fierce that the litters were overturned several times. After the first day, the weather turned calm, and thirty-five days later they arrived at Nanchang and then transferred to a boat. After a journey of fifty-six days, they arrived at Canton on January 10, 1724.

At this point, Ripa once again considered leaving Wu behind, not only because his body was frail and sickly, but Ripa felt that his intelligence was weak and his temperament unsuitable.[25] Consequently, he arranged to take only four Chinese and to leave Lucio in Canton with a Signore Appiani, apparently another missionary, to be educated at Ripa's expense.[26] However, when he began to say mass one day, he heard the words of an inner voice: "Have I given him to you to abandon him? Do everything that you can to take him, and if you fail, then leave him."[27] The next day when he said mass, the voice spoke to him again in similar words. In one of the rare cases that Ripa allowed himself to be influenced by such signs, he changed his mind and the next day arranged with the captain of the ship to include Lucio. Given the disastrous results of his decision, one wonders if it was God or Ripa's own attraction to Lucio that was speaking.

Ripa embarked with his five Chinese companions on January 23, 1724, from Canton on a ship of the British East India Company bound for London. The journey took four months and was made more difficult by the taunting hostility of the crew. This hostility appears to have been a mixture of anti-Catholicism, prejudice against the Chinese, and antagonism to Ripa's strong personality. They were all forced to sleep together in the captain's cabin, but when Wu lost control of his bowels two nights in a row, the captain evicted all of the Chinese from his cabin, and they were forced to sleep on the open deck.[28] The Chinese were so exposed to the rain and cold on the deck that the ship's callous surgeon suggested to Ripa that the Chinese be thrown overboard because it would be impossible to keep them alive in such conditions, but Ripa answered that they should leave their fate in God's hands. Ripa praised the remarkable patience of all five Chinese and most particularly their teacher for enduring these harsh conditions with cheerfulness.

The English crew tended to treat the Chinese as exotic animals, and there appears to have been a sexual curiosity. One day at the Cape of Good Hope, when the entire crew and passengers were spending several days ashore at an inn, a group of Englishmen and Dutchmen (probably bored and possibly drunk) teased the Chinese youth Giovani Yin by pushing the landlord's daughter against him in the hopes of arousing him sexually.[29] But Yin was very pious and responded with trembling and tears, climbing under a bed to escape them. Ripa arrived to extract him, but Yin was very shaken and begged to be taken back to the ship.

When they arrived in England in September of 1724, Ripa and his five Chinese were treated very hospitably by the British court. King George I showed great interest in them, and their first and last audiences with him both continued for three hours.[30] The second was an evening event with dinner and lasted from 9 p.m. until midnight. In October they sailed for Livorno and then traveled on to Naples in November. Ripa was then called to Rome where he met with Pope Benedict XIII. The pope approved his plan to establish a religious community and school, although the project was not to be funded by Propaganda. The Chinese pupils took their first vows on September 22, 1725 (figure 3.2).[31]

It took Ripa seven years (1725–1732) and protracted negotiations with Propaganda (who opposed having the school in Naples instead of Rome), with the Bourbon monarchy in Naples, and with Emperor Charles VI in Vienna. The Congregazione della Sacra Famiglia di Gesù Cristo (Congregation of the Sacred Family of Jesus Christ) was formed, and the Collegiò de'Cinesi (Chinese College) was opened in 1732.

The younger boys, Filippo Huang and Lucio Wu, had greater difficulty adjusting to life in Europe than the older boys. In 1731, when Ripa was traveling in search of funds to establish the Chinese College, he received frequent letters from Huang expressing his unhappiness and wish to leave.[32] In September 1736, the twenty-four-year-old Huang and the twenty-three-year-old Wu went through a very disturbed period in which they were thought to be possessed by Satan.[33] Demonic possession in the clerical world was often used to explain illicit sexual relations, in this case probably involving mutual masturbation and perhaps even frottage and sodomy. For several months Huang and Wu had engaged in sexual play

Figure 3.2. Father Matteo Ripa, ca. 1725, reading the Gospel to his first four Chinese pupils, Naples, oil on canvas, dated 1818, by Giovanni Scognamiglio. Ripa is surrounded by the four young Chinese males (aged 10 to 22) whom he brought to Europe in 1723–1724. The four youths were ordained at the seminary for Chinese in Naples, which Ripa had founded in 1732. In 1818, when this painting was made, French forces had withdrawn, and the Congress of Vienna restored the Bourbons to the throne in Naples. This probably explains the emphasis given to the Bourbon royal palace on the top of the hill Capodimonte, visible through the window. During this period, the priests of the Congregation of the Sacred Family emphasized the Bourbons' patronage of the Chinese College and idealized Ripa's role as the college founder by portraying the youngest boy, Lucio Wu, in a kneeling position with his face reverently raised toward Ripa. Permission of the Rettore dell'Università degli Studi di Napoli "l'Orientali," Naples.

in bed and were undetected by the Chinese College staff.[34] After being discovered, they planned to flee the college together, but they then had a disagreement in which Huang, with the aid of another student, struck Wu some heavy blows. Huang ran away from the Chinese College twice. When he was brought back from the second flight, he was stripped of his college attire, dressed in rags, and locked in a room. His isolation might have prevented Wu's own flight. Ripa assigned one of their fellow students at the college to watch them.[35]

In April of 1739, Huang and Wu made their vows, and they were ordained as priests on March 18, 1741.[36] In the spring of 1744, in response to a request from Propaganda that a student of the Chinese College and a congregant of the Holy Family be chosen to go to China, Ripa chose Wu and Domenico La Magna. However, something very serious went wrong because on June 25, 1744, Ripa wrote to Propaganda asking that Wu be withdrawn as a nominee to go to China because of immaturity. Wu appears to have set his heart on returning to China and was devastated by this change on Ripa's part.

The exact cause of Ripa's change of heart is hard to discern because documents that might have explained the change are missing.[37] Ripa listed a litany of "so many offenses, incorrigible acts" (*tanti delitti, fattosi incorrigibile*) of which the young seminarian was found guilty.[38] These included damaging the door lock to his room so that it could not be opened by his superior and making unauthorized keys to gain access to the room of his fellow students and using these keys to steal nine shirts, five soutanes, six pairs of shoes, and "lustful clothes" (*vestiva lussuosamente*). In addition, he disgraced the Chinese College by saying that he was kept in a constant state of hunger and was forced to wear disreputable clothing to prevent him from carrying out his threats to flee. On July 3, 1744, ten days after Ripa wrote to Propaganda withdrawing Wu as a candidate for going to China, Wu fled the Chinese College.[39]

Nothing was heard about him until the spring of 1745 when Ripa learned that he was at the monastery of Monte Cassino, about sixty miles north of Naples. He was brought back to Naples on May 3.[40] However, the punishments inflicted on him by Ripa were severe. In a later interrogation, Wu claimed that he was unable to endure the punitive treatment and mortifications which included eating bread and water, and sometimes a dish of dog and cat, and using whips of self-flagellation (the Discipline) in the refectory.[41] The penance of eating dog and cat was still widespread in Italian colleges, monasteries, and seminaries at the end of the eighteenth century.[42] Unwilling to accept this punishment, Wu decided to flee again. Twenty days before leaving the college, he forged two documents that he planned to use in establishing his credentials as a priest.[43]

Wu fled a second time on July 14, 1745. He remained in the area of the Pontifical States and finally came to Senigallia on the Adriatic Sea and east of Florence.[44] He celebrated mass in churches in these cities. When he showed his forged documents to the vicar general at Senigallia, he was arrested on September 12, 1745.[45] The transcriptions of two interrogations (September 25 and 28) at Senigallia describe him as a thirty-six-year-old man (he was actually thirty-two) of short stature, squalid appearance, almost beardless, very black hair cut in the style of a tonsure, and wearing dark clothes.[46] In response to questions, Wu identified himself as Giuseppe Lucio Wu. He said that he had resided at the Chinese College in Naples for twenty years and had studied Latin, philosophy, and theology.

Ripa was filled with despair, aggravated by his own failing health. On October 19, 1745, he wrote to the vicar of the bishop of Senigallia, Ferdinando Giuliani, lamenting that he had supported Wu with room and board for twenty-six years since taking responsibility for him on April 22, 1720, in China.[47] Wu was sentenced at Senigallia on October 29, 1745, to a year of confinement and atonement in the Chinese College at the discretion of the rector.[48] Ripa ordered Giuseppe Andrada, an elderly member of the congregation, to go to Senigallia to bring Wu back to Naples. On November 22, while Andrada was en route, Ripa died and was succeeded as rector of the Congregation of the Sacred Family by Gennaro Fatigati, who shared Ripa's negative attitude toward Wu.[49]

On December 6, on the return journey to Naples, Wu escaped from Andrada. An eyewitness at Macerata on December 20 described him as being short in height and as having black hair, olive skin, a long face, and a bruised nose; he was wearing a black habit and speaking a dialect part Neapolitan and part Illyrian.[50] He was arrested by constables at Foligno on January 11, 1746. There had been a marked deterioration in Wu's clothing and appearance in the four months between his first interrogations at Senigallia on September 25 and 28, 1745, and his interrogation at Foligno on February 1, 1746.[51] His shoes had become worn and had lost their buckles, while his clothes had become filthy and threadbare. In the later interrogation at Foligno, Wu gave his age as "about thirty" (he was actually almost thirty-three) and declared that his father, Tommaso Wu, was deceased.

Up to that point, Ripa's comments about Wu had been relatively restrained, in part to protect himself and the Chinese College from the damage that Wu was inflicting upon their reputations, but also because he had made an emotional investment in the young man. Now something changed, and a rancor entered into Ripa's attitude toward Wu, akin to that of a spurned lover. He realized that Wu's misbehavior amounted not only to a rejection of the Chinese College, but also of him personally.[52] The intensity of Ripa's response suggests that Ripa's feeling for Wu might have been like Schall's feeling for his servant Pan, amounting to "a very human affection, and contrary to religious detachment," that is, a same-sex attraction. In a letter to Monsignor Lecari, secretary of Propaganda, Ripa expressed great bitterness toward this "perfidious Judas" (*perfido Giuda*) whom Ripa recalled taking into his care at the age of six when Wu was too young to care for himself.[53] With his anger causing him to lose a sense of proportion, Ripa called for the most severe punishment for Wu's misbehavior, namely that he be sentenced to servitude as a galley slave on the pontifical ship at Cittavecchia.

In Rome, calmer heads prevailed. Ripa's cousin, Father Giuseppe Ripa, conveyed to him that his recommendation that Wu be sent to the galleys had been rejected by the cardinal prefect of Propaganda as overly harsh. At the bottom of the page of his cousin's letter, Ripa added a marginal note, desperate in its intensity, expressing his wish that Wu at least be imprisoned for life and expelled from the Chinese College.[54] This notation was dated March 29, 1746, the day of Ripa's death, and indicates that his obsession with Wu continued to trouble him into his final hours.[55]

The cardinals of Propaganda decided on April 4th to imprison Wu in Castel Sant'Angelo (Castro Sancti Angeli) near the Vatican in Rome.[56] Wu's fate was sealed by the unrelenting hostility of the Chinese College as conveyed by the new rector, Fatigati, who shared Ripa's fear that Wu might disgrace the college if he was allowed to return to China as a missionary. Consequently, Wu was sent from the Foligno jail to the Castel Sant'Angelo, where in the roll of Easter 1746 he was listed as one of only seven prisoners.[57]

During his first month in Castel Sant'Angelo, Wu appears to have been a model prisoner in the hope of securing an early release, but when no release was forthcoming, he had a letdown. He loved to play cards, but he lost control of his temper when he lost. He became enraged and aggravated his opponents with curse words until they pushed and punched him. The jailers described Wu's behavior as "scandalous" (*scandalosa*) for a priest.[58] It is unclear whether Wu learned that Filippo Huang, with whom he had shared a litter on their departure from Beijing thirty-seven years before, was sent back to China in 1760. Huang served as a missionary in his native Zhili province, which included Beijing, and died in 1776.[59] Wu died in Rome in August of 1763.

4

Establishing Friendships
in Post-1911 China

FRIENDS FROM AFAR

The opening lines of Confucius' *Analects* (Lunyu) praise the importance of having friends who come from afar. Over the years, the relationship between friendship and the cultivation of Confucian virtue became a fundamental principle of the Chinese literati. The Jesuit missionary Matteo Ricci was well aware of the importance of friendship in China and incorporated it into his famous method of accommodation by writing a book in Chinese devoted to the subject. The *Jiaoyou lun* (Essay on Friendship) (1695) along with the *Mappamondo* (Map of the World) were the first works in Chinese that Ricci wrote. This is ironical because although there is very little mention of God in either work, Ricci regarded these works as essential to establishing relationships with the literati, which would ultimately allow him to convert them to Christianity.[1]

From the outset, men with same-sex desire who were attracted to China realized the importance of establishing friendships with the Chinese. Father Schall's close association with Pan Jinxiao and Father Ripa's relationships with several Chinese boys were among the earliest friendships in Sino-Western history. The American poet Witter Bynner had significant friendships with at least two Chinese. His relationship with the Chinese scholar Jiang Kanghu during the years 1918 through 1929 was based on their intellectual collaboration in translating the Chinese poems in *Jade Mountain*. His friendship with the student Nie Shizhang, who served as his guide on several journeys in China, was more complicated. It began in Hangzhou but continued throughout his stay in China in 1920–1921.

There seems to have been an element of physical attraction on Bynner's part. It is difficult to know if their relationship became sexual, but it may have been an early manifestation of a pattern of relationships that Bynner had later in New Mexico. In this pattern, Bynner was a paternalistic and supportive older partner ("daddy") to younger males, such as Lynn Riggs and Robert Hunt, who served as both lovers and secretaries.[2]

Harold Acton established friendships with several Chinese men during his stay in Beijing in the 1930s. He collaborated with Dr. H. H. Hu in translating the drama *Changsheng dian* (The Palace of Eternal Youth) by Hong Sheng (1645–1704), and he collaborated with Yan Yuheng in translating the novel *Jinghua yuan* (Romance of the Mirrored Flowers) by Li Ruzhen (ca. 1763–1830).[3] Acton was physically attracted to Chinese young men. Some of his friendships with them were sexual, but others were more intellectual, such as with the scholar Chen Shixiang (Ch'en Shih-hsiang) (1912–1971). After leaving China, Acton and Chen renewed their collaboration by translating one of the greatest *kunqu* dramas, *The Peach Blossom Fan* (Taohuashan), a southern-style play by the scholar Kong Shangren (1648–1718), a sixty-fourth-generation descendant of Confucius. The plot focuses on events in the southern Ming court of the Ming pretender after the Manchu conquest of 1644–1645. After the suicide of the emperor in Beijing, the Ming court fled south to Nanjing and attempted to reestablish a Ming emperor. The romantic hero of this drama sought to revive Confucian ideals, and he was supported in this effort by a beautiful sixteen-year-old singsong girl who displayed great strength of character. Kong completed the drama in 1699, and it immediately became popular.

The setting for this collaborative effort was the Berkeley Hills. In 1948 Acton came to California to visit Chen who was homesick for Beijing and caught in a difficult period between marriages.[4] Acton proposed that they make a "spiritual return" to a Chinese past that seemed to be slipping away by translating *The Peach Blossom Fan*. The parallels between the imminent fall of Nationalist China to the Communists and *The Peach Blossom Fan*'s portrayal of the fall of the Ming to the Manchu conquerors were painfully obvious. During those weeks Chen and Acton completed draft translations of thirty-four of forty scenes and then stopped. The uncompleted typescript lay among Chen's papers in his Berkeley hillside home when he unexpectedly died of a heart attack in 1971 at the age of fifty-nine.[5] Chen's widow Grace found the incomplete translation among his papers and passed the manuscript to Chen's colleague Cyril Birch who completed the work for publication.[6] This translation has been highly praised and represents Acton's most lasting contribution to Chinese studies.

The allure of China in the early twentieth century was so strong that it attracted several famous homosexual authors in search of material for their books. These were authors with no particular knowledge of Chinese culture. Among them was William Somerset Maugham, one of the most successful writers of his time. He wrote dramas as well as novels and short stories. His success, however, was measured in popularity and financial rewards rather than critical acclaim, and his fame is confined more to his own age than to posterity. He was so deeply closeted as a homosexual that he went to great efforts in his old age to destroy all of his personal correspondence.[7] He also asked friends to destroy any of his letters in their possession, and he instructed his literary executors to refuse to cooperate in any effort to write his biography.

Maugham was born in Paris in 1874, the fourth son of an attorney to the British embassy. His mother died the day before his eighth birthday, and his father died when he was ten. He was sent to live with an uncle and aunt in England who offered him a stable home but little affection. It was in England that he began to stammer, a social disability that afflicted him for the rest of his life. He was educated at King's School, Canterbury, but instead of attending university, he trained as a physician. He never practiced medicine but turned instead to writing fiction and dramas. He had a passion for writing and for living the good life. Aside from the memory of his mother, his relations with women were unhappy. He was slow to recognize his homosexuality, and the one woman he wanted to marry refused his proposal. He ended up being drawn into a disastrous marriage out of a sense of honor to a woman he had impregnated, but also out of a fear of being blackmailed by her for his homosexual affairs.[8]

When World War I began, Maugham volunteered to serve in the Red Cross, and it was in France in October 1914 that he first met his longtime companion. Gerald Haxton (1892–1944) was a handsome and gregarious man eighteen years younger than Maugham. To some, Haxton's charm was "delightful," and to others it was "disreputable."[9] One year after meeting Maugham, he was arrested in a London hotel for "gross indecency" with another man and, although acquitted, was expelled from Britain. Thereafter Maugham was forced to go abroad to meet him, and this partly explains Maugham's love of overseas travel, which ended shortly after Haxton's death.

Maugham and Haxton were a symbiotic pair. Maugham's stammer had created a reticence that prevented him from talking with people, something that was crucial to the conception of the characters in his novels. Haxton's charm and verbal facility provided Maugham a guide in going to strange places and meeting new people. Since Maugham's fiction was based on a study of personalities, Haxton became crucial to his art and income. Haxton came from a middle-class background and lacked the means to support his expensive tastes. Maugham's wealth provided him with a lifestyle that he could not otherwise have afforded. Haxton was undisciplined, addicted to both alcohol and gambling, and aggressively promiscuous in his pursuit of sex.[10] Although he and Maugham probably ceased being sexual partners early in their relationship, he procured sexual partners for Maugham, who was too prim and fastidious to procure them for himself.

Maugham had long planned on a trip to China. In 1919 China was not only at the opposite end of the world physically from England, but it also constituted an antipode of traditional culture to Europe's modern, industrialized world dominance. China's serious reform efforts were just getting under way, and much of the past still lingered. Many Westerners were fascinated by this ancient culture, and Maugham, highly attuned to popular tastes, wanted to mine its treasures for his writings. Maugham's journey there from August 1919 until April 1920 resulted in a travel journal called *On a Chinese Screen* (1922), which consists of fifty-six vignettes, mainly about individuals, but also two short stories.

Maugham began his journey to China by departing from Liverpool in August 1919 and sailing to New York, then traveling by train across the United States to California (figure 4.1). In Chicago, he reunited with Haxton, who would accompany him for the rest of the journey. They traveled to Hong Kong, Shanghai, Tianjin, Beijing, and Manchuria.[11] They journeyed 1,500 miles, spending five days on a sampan, up the Yangtze River to Chongqing. They returned via Japan and the Suez Canal to Europe. Maugham's interest in China was not in China per se, but what China

Figure 4.1. The novelist W. Somerset Maugham (1874–1965) at approximately the time of his trip to China with his companion Gerald Haxton in 1919–1920. George Grantham Bain Collection, Library of Congress Prints and Photographs Division, Washington, DC.

meant to Westerners. For this reason, most of his interviews were with Western expatriates living in China. He focused on their attitudes toward China because he realized that this is what would interest his readers. Although Maugham was imbued with the prejudices of the Victorian professional classes, he was quite harsh in criticizing the narrow-minded and superficial attitudes of the foreign expatriate community. In the short story "The Taipan" (a term for the leading foreign merchant in China), Maugham drew a blunt and scathing portrait of a self-centered man who had risen from the lower middle class in England to great wealth and power in Hong Kong.[12] Although he had made his wealth from the Chinese, he despised them and refused to learn their language.

Maugham's commercial interest (in selling his books) dictated the contents of *On a Chinese Screen*. It is not a profound book, and had it not been written by such a famous author addressing a subject very much in vogue, it is unlikely that it would have received the attention that it did. Today it reads like a period piece, filled with insightful observations into mostly Western individuals and mostly anonymous Chinese by a perceptive writer. But while Maugham saw a great deal on his journey, he lacked the knowledge of Chinese culture needed to interpret what he had seen. His overconfidence led him to dispense with a translator in interviewing three educated Chinese, who were probably chosen in the first place because they could speak English. Of these three, "The Cabinet Minister" was corrupt, "The Philosopher" was a reactionary Confucian, and "A Student of the Drama" was a pedantic and narrow-minded "Professor of Comparative Modern Literature." These three were hardly representative of the most creative thinkers in 1919–1920 China, and yet they are the only sophisticated Chinese featured in Maugham's work.

Although Maugham does not identify the three Chinese by name, the "Philosopher" was in fact Gu Hongming (1857–1928). Gu belonged to an overseas Chinese family that had migrated from Fujian province to Kedah on the Malay Peninsula.[13] Gu's father was the manager of a British-owned rubber plantation. At the age of about ten, when his father died, Gu was taken to Edinburgh by a Scottish family friend. After studying the classical university curriculum and earning an MA degree in 1877, he went on to study at Leipzig, obtaining a degree in civil engineering before returning to Penang around 1880. Being abroad seems to have intensified his Chinese identity, and he began wearing a queue and Chinese clothes and studying classical Chinese. Gu's knowledge of Western affairs made him useful to Zhang Zhidong, a conservative reformer of the Self-Strengthening school, and Gu served as a member of his personal staff in from 1885 to 1905.

Maugham astutely recognized that Gu was far more of a polemicist than a philosopher. In fact, at the time of his interview, Gu had become a Confucian reactionary, attacking all forms of Westernization, including the emerging literary renaissance led by the American-educated student of John Dewey, Hu Shi. Maugham insightfully captured a prominent Chinese attitude of that time in quoting Gu Hongming, saying, "We sought to rule this great country not by force, but by wisdom. And for centuries we succeeded. Then why does the white man despise the yellow? Shall I tell you? Because he has invented the machine gun. That is your superiority."[14]

Maugham presented Protestant missionaries in a very unflattering manner. He portrayed them as rigid and uncompassionate ("God in Truth"), smug and ignorant of Chinese history and culture ("The Seventh Day Adventist"), and simple minded ("The Missionary Lady"). He was somewhat more favorable to Catholic missionaries because of their greater commitment to remaining in China ("The Servants of God"). He displayed genuine sympathy for "coolies" (Chinese laborers), a term that has since passed into history. In the vignette "The Beast of Burden," Maugham applied his medical training to evaluate the plight of these workers. As they rested in a crouched position, his trained eye observed "the poor tired heart beating against the ribs: you see it plainly as in some cases of heart disease in the out-patients' room of a hospital."[15] And he noticed on their backs hard red scars and sometimes open sores caused by rubbing against the wood of their pole and sometimes even "an odd malformation . . . arisen so that there is a sort of hump, like a camel's, against which the pole rests."

The depth of Maugham's interest in China lay somewhere between the superficiality of foreign expatriates who exploited it in colonialist style and the deeper study of scholars and aesthetes who devoted themselves to it. Maugham was not particularly fascinated with Chinese culture and art. Although he spent hours in art museums throughout the world studying Western art, his interest in Chinese art was incidental. Even the sexual attraction of Chinese men was not viewed by Maugham as special, but merely as one of the many varieties of male sex available in Asia.

As was typical of Maugham's writing, *On a Chinese Screen* avoids any reference to homosexual experiences with Chinese. Haxton, who was criticized for introducing Maugham to some of the most sordid areas of homosexual life, would have been aware of the male brothels in Tianjin and the boy brothels in Shanghai that were popular with Europeans.[16] Given the months they spent in China and Maugham's promiscuity, it is hard to believe that Haxton did not procure Chinese boys for him. It was well known among gay colonials that the lands east of the Suez Canal were far more fertile for same-sex activities than Britain. China merely represented one of the many varieties. From Cairo to Karachi to Siam to Beijing, boys were available, and given Haxton's abilities as a guide to homosexual haunts, the amount of time he and Maugham spent traveling in these areas, and Maugham's ability to pay for these boys, it is likely that they were sex tourists in a grand style who enjoyed the varieties of pleasure available to them.

Maugham claimed that his most memorable sexual experience was with a boy in Malay on a sampan under the moon.[17] This claim reveals a remarkable innocence about the nature of his sex life. In spite of his promiscuity and numerous sexual experiences throughout the world, Maugham's sexual tastes were surprisingly unsophisticated. The gay writer Glenway Wescott remembered that once when they were observing a nude painting of a man and woman making love in the "missionary position" (man on top), Maugham expressed regret that two men could not do the same thing.[18] Wescott was too embarrassed to explain that they could.

THE SEARCH FOR BOYS

W. H. Auden (1907–1973) was one of the greatest poets of the twentieth century. Christopher Isherwood (1904–1986) was a famous writer of fiction who is best remembered for his *Berlin Stories* set in the 1930s when the permissive culture of Weimar Germany clashed with the rise of Hitler and from which the musical and movie *Cabaret* were generated. Auden and Isherwood had gone to the same prep school in England, and they shared a passion for writing and trusted each other as critics. They also shared an attraction to men rather than women. They were perhaps onetime lovers who evolved, in a manner common to gays, into close friends. In their youth, the same-sex friendliness of Berlin provided an escape for them. Auden first discovered it and told Isherwood to go there.[19] Isherwood went, lived in the poorest neighborhoods, and ate the cheapest food to survive as a writer.[20] The result was the *Berlin Stories*. However, when the Nazis came to power in 1933, the sexually free life of Germany was shut down.

In 1937, the publishers Faber and Faber of London and Random House of New York commissioned Auden and Isherwood to write a travel book about the East. They were chosen because of their reputation as rising young writers, not because they had any special knowledge of the East. They chose to go to China where the Sino-Japanese War had just broken out.[21] As for China, they were both amateurs who had never been east of Suez. And certainly neither one of them knew any Chinese. They were young and gay in all senses of the word, and the book they wrote is an impressionistic, amusing take on a serious subject. Although they met some of the most significant people in wartime China, Auden and Isherwood, like Maugham before them, focused on personalities and surroundings rather than ideas or politics.

They left England in January 1938 and returned at the end of July (figure 4.2). Their wartime itinerary began in south China, going from Hong Kong to Canton by boat, then on by rail northward to Hankou, Zhengzhou, Suzhou, and Xian, then south again to Nanchang and Lake Tai, and then finally to the coastal city of Wenzhou and by boat from Wenzhou to Shanghai. They did not go to Beijing. They interviewed a large number of people and were apolitical in their treatment of Nationalists and Communists. (The Nationalists and Communists were then cooperating in an uneasy united front against the Japanese.) They visited W. H. Donald, an Australian, who had begun as a London *Times* correspondent in Harbin

Figure 4.2. Portrait of novelist Christopher Isherwood (left) and poet W. H. Auden by photographer Carl Van Vechten, 1939, one year after their trip to wartime China in 1938. Carl Van Vechten Photograph Collection, Library of Congress Prints and Photographs Division, Washington, DC. Isherwood and Auden were regarded at this point in time by many of their British compatriots as cowards who ran away to the United States to escape the war in Britain.

and then became an adviser to the Manchurian "Young Marshal" Zhang Xueliang, and finally to the Nationalist leader Chiang Kai-shek. Donald warned them off Chinese food, which he himself never ate.[22]

They had tea with Madame Chiang Kai-shek (Soong Mei-ling) who was in the process of sending the gift of her two-foot-high birthday cake to the refugee children of Hankou. She did not like birthdays. They described her as "vivacious rather than pretty," remarkably skilled in handling all types of visitors, and wearing "the most delicious" perfume either of them had ever smelled.[23] When they interviewed the Communist supporter Agnes Smedley, her cold exterior warmed in the face of Auden's untidiness. She asked them ironically, "Do you always throw your coats on the floor?"[24]

Imperialism produced all kinds of "boys" in China at that time. In Hankou, the British consul found them a "Number One Boy" named Chiang.[25] Chiang was middle aged, did not cook, knew little English, and had "the manners of a perfect butler." He accompanied Auden and Isherwood as a servant throughout the rest of their journey in China. There were other types of boys. Auden and Isherwood encountered some at Guling (Ox Ridge), a summer health resort located less than ten miles south of the Yangtze River city of Jiujiang. There, 3,500 feet above sea level, was the Journey's End Inn. As they arrived at the inn by car, "a drilled troop of house-boys in khaki shorts and white shirts, prettily embroidered with the scarlet characters of their names," ran out to greet them.[26] The proprietor, Mr. Charleton, trained each boy for three years at the inn—as a servant, gardener, carpenter, or painter—taught them a smattering of servant's English, and then placed them in jobs with foreign businesses or consular offices. The boys were taught boxing as well as the manner of speaking in lowered voices and were allowed to use the swimming pool daily. One boy was assigned to each inn guest.

Of course, given the standards of the late 1930s, it is not surprising that Auden and Isherwood made no mention in *Journal to a War* of any sexual liaisons with these boys. However, Ye Junjian (C. C. Yeh), who translated for Auden and Isherwood on this wartime journey, described Auden's behavior with boys in China as "careless" and "indiscreet," whereas Isherwood was "sensible" and "a gentleman."[27] Auden and Isherwood do note in their book that both girls and boys in Shanghai were available "at all prices, in the bath-houses and the brothels."[28]

The sexual atmosphere in Shanghai was different than in Beijing. Shanghai was a more modern, less traditional city. While Beijing was political and cultural, Shanghai was commercial. It was a more international city, geared to foreign interests. These differences were reflected in the theaters where actresses began to replace female impersonators and in restaurants where singsong girls (*hei guanyin*) replaced the singsong boys (*xiaochang*) of Beijing.[29] There was also more racial segregation in Shanghai. Although commerce was conducted on an interracial basis, recreation was more racially segregated.

According to the 1932 Chinese guidebook *Shanghai menjing* (Key to Shanghai), there were three classes of male prostitutes.[30] The first-class male prostitutes lived in houses on Third Street (San Malu) in the same area where female houses of prostitution were located. As with their female counterparts, male prostitutes were available to clients in these houses, or they could come to clients in their hotel rooms. However, while female prostitution was legal, male prostitution was not, and so the male houses were operated clandestinely. New clients were not admitted to the houses for fear of police entrapment. However, male prostitutes from these houses could be ordered through attendants in upscale hotels. Once a client became known, he would be received at the houses. The first-class houses were visited by warlords, high-ranking officials, and wealthy businessmen. Presumably foreigners of means could also order these male prostitutes. The cost was considerable, since the houses were richly furnished.

Northern Chinese ran downscale male prostitute houses in Shanghai that catered to less affluent northerners. The prostitutes were *dan* (female impersonator) actors in Peking Opera who tended to have effeminate mannerisms. They solicited men on the street and took them to their squalid houses and attic rooms. Finally, at the bottom of the scale were male prostitutes who offered their services for the lowest fees of all; however they had no place to host their clients. They were identifiable by their cosmetics and clothing, which consisted of a small jacket over a long Chinese-style robe (*changpao*) and a Japanese peaked hat. They congregated in theaters and amusement centers, such as "Great World" (Dashijie).[31]

It is unlikely that most foreigners in Shanghai had contact with these cheaper male prostitutes because of the linguistic barrier. The more expensive male prostitutes were available through hotel attendants who could speak pidgin English and who were attuned to providing prostitution services to guests and were eager to do so since they earned commissions in the process. In contrast, the cheaper male prostitutes operated on the streets, and it would have been a daunting experience for a foreigner without the ability to speak Chinese to negotiate with them. However, longer-term gay residents with proficiency in Chinese, like Rewi Alley, could have availed themselves of their services.

MIXING BOYS AND POLITICS

Rewi Alley was, in contemporary gay slang, a "rice queen," which means that he was particularly attracted sexually to East Asian males. His attraction to Chinese young men led him to Shanghai, where in the 1930s he established numerous friendships with Chinese males in their late teens and early twenties. His relationships were both paternal and sexual, in a pattern similar to Witter Bynner. Alley adopted two Chinese boys who became his functioning family in China, although he later became estranged from them.[32]

Rewi Alley (Luyi Aili) was born in New Zealand and was named after a famous Maori chief, Rewi Maniapoto, who had made a heroic last stand against the British in 1864. At the time of his death in 1987, Alley had spent most of his life in China and had worked closely with the Chinese Communists. He was one of the small group of famous foreigners who were portrayed as great friends of Communist China. He was one of the few among the foreign friends of China to be referred to with the most honorable title of "internationalist" (*guoji zhuyizhe*).[33] And yet few people realized that the driving force leading him to China was not politics, but his homosexuality. Alley was born a middle child of six children in a rural village of New Zealand in 1897. The children were all overachievers, except for Alley, who was the only one not to excel in athletics and academics. He was baptized and raised in the Anglican Church, but later in China he turned to Buddhism and Daoism.

Alley's father was an idealistic schoolteacher with progressive views about education, but he was conservative about sexuality.[34] In the latter, he was merely reflecting the social environment of New Zealand. Homophobia was strong there, and homosexual acts were not decriminalized until 1987, while discrimination based on sexual orientation was not outlawed until 1993. To protect himself, Alley developed a pattern of disguise that would cloak his homosexuality. He continued to cultivate this pattern throughout his life, creating a myth about himself that had little basis in fact. When he died, many of his closest associates in China had no inkling that he was gay.

In 1917, Alley joined the New Zealand Expeditionary Force and went to Europe to fight in World War I. From the outset, he was sexually attracted to Chinese males, and it is no accident that his first sexual experience in March 1918 was with Chinese men. When the New Zealand forces were fighting alongside the Chinese Labor Corps, Alley and another New Zealander met and spent the evening with two Chinese from Shandong. He later described them as "tall men, dressed in blue and with fur hats."[35] In 1919, Alley returned to New Zealand. His political views at the time were conservative, and he joined other ex-servicemen in the Legion of Frontiersmen, which was dedicated to perpetuating the British Empire.[36] However, after six years of hardship trying to farm a remote area on the North Island of New Zealand at Moeawatea, he resigned.

In April 1927, Alley went to Shanghai, a place that fit his colonialist sympathies. An acquaintance from another regiment of the New Zealand Legion of Frontiersmen helped him find work at the Hongkou fire station in the International Settlement of Shanghai.[37] Initially Alley disliked the chaotic lifestyle of the Chinese and much preferred the highly organized Japanese. Although Chinese reformers were criticizing certain long-established homosexual traditions in China, including the female impersonators of Peking Opera, the sexual atmosphere in China did not become homophobic until after the Communists took control in 1949. In the 1920s and 1930s, there was an active homosexual life in Shanghai, and many foreign travelers came to the city as sex tourists.[38] During his years of residing in Shanghai, Alley was able to freely explore his sexuality.

As long as one practiced a degree of discretion, sex in China at that time was regarded as a private matter. The Confucian values of age-based relationships involving mutual nurturing and respect pervaded Chinese society. Even the names of siblings—*gege* (older brother) and *didi* (younger brother) or *jiejie* (older sister) and *meimei* (younger sister)—reflected these complementary roles. In Fujian and Guangdong provinces, this pattern had been extended to homosexual relationships in which the elder male was called "elder brother partner" (*qixiong*), while the younger male was called "younger brother partner" (*qidi*).[39] A similar age-based relationship was also found among samurai in Tokugawa Japan.[40] The hierarchy of elder brother and younger brother was an essential part of all forms of Japanese male love. The elder brother was the top, and the younger brother was the bottom in sexual intercourse. Alley formed numerous relationships of this sort with younger males, although not all of these were sexual.

During the years 1930 to 1938, Alley and another gay man, Alex Camplin, shared a house in the International Settlement in Shanghai.[41] They were more friends than lovers. Both were mainly attracted to Chinese males. Both adopted orphans, although Alley's sexuality was characterized by ephebophilia (love of adolescent males) rather than pedophilia (love of preadolescent males). He was attracted to Chinese males in their late teens and early twenties. He adopted the orphans Li Xue (Mike) and Duan Shimou (Alan). Alley led a double life by encouraging speculation about his girlfriends. Sometimes the rumors served a double purpose. When the American YWCA official Maud Russell attended a left-wing discussion group with Alley, a rumor began about their mutual love interest, which Alley did not deny.[42] Actually, Maud Russell was a lesbian who was also living a double life.

Alley had a short, muscular body and an outsized personality. His charisma impressed the American social worker and author Ida Pruitt as well as Auden and Isherwood. While in Shanghai, Auden and Isherwood met Alley. Shanghai was a large city, and one suspects that their shared same-sex affinities somehow brought them in contact. At the time, Alley was working as a factory inspector and official of the Public Works Department to improve working conditions in the hundreds of Chinese factories around Hongkew.[43] Most of the workers were young boys who had been bought from their parents for a small sum and who would die early of malnutrition, tuberculosis, or industrial poisoning. Some children had the blue line in their gums which is a symptom of lead poisoning. Alley was genuinely concerned with helping these boys, but we also know that he slept with some of them.

When the Japanese bombing of Shanghai in 1937 disrupted the coastal factories and created a refugee crisis, Alley joined with a group of Chinese and foreigners to establish the Chinese Industrial Cooperatives (CIC) to offer employment to Chinese in the inland regions.[44] Alley became field secretary to the CIC while his two adopted sons joined the Communist forces in Yenan. He fostered rumors that he had "a woman in every town" as a smoke screen for his homosexuality.[45] Initially he was opposed to diverting CIC funds into education, but he changed his mind when he became involved with the Bailie School.

The Bailie School was first established in Shuangshipu, Shaanxi province, in 1941 under the leadership of George Hogg.[46] It was a pioneering effort in seeking to teach practical and technical skills to Chinese children. When the Japanese invaded and Nationalist forces tried to conscript staff and older Bailie students into their ranks, the school was moved westward to the more remote Shandan in Gansu province. Because of the remote location, many of the teachers were foreigners. When Hogg died of an accident in 1945, Alley assumed the headmastership, even though he had little formal education. However, Alley had a lot of ideas that he wanted to implement, including nudity. As soon as the weather was warm enough, the students wore short clothes, and in the swimming pool nothing at all.

Homosexual activity was quite common at the school. Many of the boys slept together, especially on sauna night (Saturday), when bed partners were carefully chosen. Alley and some of the other teachers also slept with the boys. Though not a pedophile, Alley did have sex with some of the older students. All of this was widely known at the Bailie School but was politely ignored in the traditional Chinese manner. If it had become known in New Zealand and other Western countries, it would have been shocking and would have disrupted foreign financial contributions for humanitarian work in China, but Alley was able to keep it secret from unsympathetic people.

The victory of the Chinese Communists in October 1949 caused a sudden change in the atmosphere of China. Not only were Western capitalists and missionaries condemned, but foreign homosexuals also became un-welcome.[47] The sex tours to Shanghai were over. Aesthetes like Harold Acton were gone from Beijing and unlikely to return. A foreigner like Vincenz Hundhausen stayed until he was expelled. The Communists ad-opted a puritanical outlook, except for the leaders like Mao Zedong who continued to have a prolific sex life with his young attractive nurses.[48] Instead of the traditional Chinese point of view of tolerance, the Com-munists adopted the dominant Western point of view of homosexuality as a sickness that required treatment, or a crime that should be punished. It was categorized under the legal category of "hooliganism" (*liumang*). In certain cases, men who acted out their same-sex desires were executed.

Alley felt the cold wind of change blowing. Just before the Communist takeover, he called a meeting of homosexual teachers at the Bailie School and warned them to be more discreet. He had a personal decision to make. He was almost fifty-two years old and had lived the last twenty-two years of his life in China. He decided to stay. He had never been a Communist, but now he decided to become a supporter. His public announcement of support for the Chinese Communist government was widely reported in Western newspapers. During the early 1950s, he struggled with depres-sion and with the antiforeignism aroused by the Korean War.[49] In Janu-ary 1951, he and the foreign teachers at the Bailie School wrote a public letter of support for American prisoners of war in Korea, claiming that the United States had invaded Korea. He also supported the Chinese allegations that the United States was using germ warfare in Korea and north China. These allegations were very harmful to the United States in the Cold War propaganda battle, although later research conclusively disproved them.[50]

Soon afterward, the Chinese government closed the Bailie School. Alley regarded his years at Shandan as a golden time. Although he had to fight accusations that he was a foreign agent, reactionary spy, and antirevolu-tionary, he was never criticized for his homosexual affairs, even later dur-ing the Cultural Revolution. This probably indicates that the traditional Chinese tolerance of homosexuality continued on a private level.

In later years, Alley was part of a small contingent of foreigners who were allowed to stay on in China. His lifestyle was fairly indulgent, with a driver and car, secretary, and cook to serve him.[51] When he was hospitalized for his ailments, he stayed at the hospital used by Chinese leaders. He had enough extra money to assemble a valuable collection of Chinese antiques. He was not an admirer of revolutionary art. Alley survived by always supporting the dominant political line, whether the Great Leap Forward of the fifties, the Cultural Revolution of the sixties, or the condemnation of the Gang of Four in the late seventies.[52] He was anti-intellectual, in part due to his New Zealand upbringing and in part due to his unwavering following of the Communist party line. He did not support the demands of many Chinese intellectuals for greater freedom.[53] Ultimately, his loyalty was to himself. He became estranged not only from his natal family in New Zealand, but also from his adopted Chinese children. He died of cerebral thrombosis and heart failure in 1987. According to his Chinese physician, he died from a fit of rage when several Beijing hotels informed him that the internal Chinese currency, renminbi, was no longer acceptable to pay for afternoon tea and that he would have to pay in Chinese currency used by foreigners (foreign exchange certificates).

FRIENDS BUT NOT LOVERS

Perhaps the strangest friendship of a foreign homosexual and a Chinese woman involved the marriage of David Kidd and Aimee Yu in 1949 for political reasons. The political and sexual mix of this situation is reminiscent of the marriage in 1935 of the homosexual poet W. H. Auden and Erika Mann to save the latter from becoming stateless when the Third Reich was on the verge of revoking her citizenship.[54]

Kidd's family descended from Virginia and Kentucky pioneers. He was born in the Appalachian town of Corbin, Kentucky, in 1926, but he was raised in Detroit where his father was an executive in the automotive industry. He attended the University of Michigan at Ann Arbor and was unhappy there. World War II was ending, and campuses were being flooded with practical-minded veterans who were studying on the G.I. Bill. Post–World War II American culture was triumphant, hypermasculine, and not very interested in foreign cultures, except to teach them the American way of life and to nurture them as allies in the Cold War. The American postwar occupation of Japan tried to re-create Japan in an American image. The auto industry in Detroit epitomized that can-do culture. Men with same-sex attraction were marginalized in that triumphant culture, and this may explain why some of them swam against the tide by turning to China. As a sensitive young gay man, Kidd wanted to escape from that American triumphalism. He chose one of the most exotic foreign languages to study—Chinese. When an escape was offered through a university exchange student program to China, he enrolled.

Kidd arrived in Beijing in the autumn of 1946, two months before his twentieth birthday. Armed with the elementary Chinese that he had learned from Mr. Tian (T'ien), his instructor at Michigan, he entered the life of Beijing. As an aesthete, he saw the beauty of Beijing while showing little interest in its revolutionary turmoil. He studied Chinese poetry at Yanjing (Yenching) University and taught English at nearby Qinghua (Tsinghwa) University. He lived in a house on the Qinghua campus, six miles outside of Beijing, but he also rented a small house in Beijing for weekends and holidays. He made friends with the international set of foreigners who lived in Beijing, and he felt at home.

The British author John Blofeld (1913–1987), who married a Chinese woman and had two children, lived in Beijing from 1934 to 1937 and visited later, becoming friends with Kidd; he also wrote a book about that now-lost atmosphere. Apart from the missionaries, Blofeld divided Westerners in Beijing into two categories.[55] The larger group contained diplomatic officials, businesspeople, and professionals (like Josef Schedel) who lived within the walls of the Legation Quarter. Although physically free to leave the quarter at will, they had an insular/ghetto mentality that was out of touch with events in Beijing and China at large. The other group consisted of people who loved Beijing and lived in scattered *hutongs* (back alleys) throughout the city. This group consisted of research scholars, university lecturers, writers, and visual artists, like Thomas Handforth. A few of them, like Harold Acton and George Kates, had private means of support. Some, like Alan Priest and Laurence Sickman, depended on institutional and foundation grants, while others, like Vincenz Hundhausen and David Kidd, survived independently on meager teaching salaries and entrepreneurial activities. Germans were the most numerous of this second group, but there were also many British, American, and French nationals.

Kidd liked Peking Opera and frequently visited the theater district in the Outer City, just south of Qianmen. In the summer of 1947, he was sitting in an open booth at the balcony railing, watching the performance while drinking tea and eating watermelon seeds.[56] He was waiting for the last performance of the evening in which the *dan* actor Xiao Cuihua (Hsiao Ts'ui-hua) would appear. Xiao was one of the last actors in China who could perform in toe shoes to imitate the gait of upper-class women with bound feet. Suddenly in the next booth a young Chinese woman made a dramatic entrance with her two maids both dressed in blue. The elaborate treatment of the waiters indicated the woman's high status. Perhaps she was not Chinese at all, but rather Manchu. The writer Nien Cheng in reviewing Kidd's account makes this suggestion in noting that many Manchus remained in Beijing during the Japanese occupation because the Japanese treated the Manchu nobility with greater deference than the Chinese.[57] She also notes that this woman later wore the high platform shoes of the Manchu nobility at her wedding.

Aimee Yu did not display the typical reserve of an upper-class Chinese woman. In a striking display of audaciousness, she had a pot of her special tea sent to Kidd, introduced herself, and asked if he would like to accompany her backstage to meet Mr. Xiao. Kidd, a bit overwhelmed, accepted. Gone were the days of the boy-actors who impersonated women and doubled as prostitutes. In his dressing room, Mr. Xiao was revealed to be an old man whose makeup had created the illusion of youthful female beauty.

This wealthy woman wrote out her address for Kidd and invited him to tea a few days later. It was not a case of love at first sight, but a calculated effort by an upper-class Chinese/Manchu woman. Her aim was to provide herself, through marriage to an American, with an escape route from the Communists, who were threatening not only Beijing, but also her family's privileged way of life. Yu's father had been the chief justice of the Chinese Supreme Court and a noted collector of antiques. Legend claimed that he had once traded an entire country estate in the hills west of Beijing for a pair of antique porcelain wine cups.[58] The family lived in a compound whose one hundred rooms, outbuildings, and garden occupied nearly fifty-thousand square feet.[59] Twenty-five members of the Yu family occupied this compound. Aimee, the fourth Miss Yu, was the fourth eldest of nine sisters, and there were two brothers. She could play the violin, knew classical Chinese dance, and had majored in chemistry at the university. Kidd met her father only once.

The marriage of Aimee Yu to Kidd was expedited by the imminent death of Yu's father whose mourning rites would have delayed any marriage for one year. The marriage was also expedited by Beijing's surrender to the Communist Army in January 1949. The American consulate would not recognize their marriage if it was conducted by a Buddhist priest, and so the Yu family quickly located a Christian clergyman in the form of a Chinese Assembly of God minister named Joseph Feng. After only two days of preparation, the ceremony took place secretly and was attended only by members of the family, a few friends, and a consular representative who had to maneuver through the Communist troops camped in the front yard of the family compound. The next morning Kidd went to the consulate to pick up the coveted "U.S. Consular Service marriage certificate" which was locked among the couple's most valuable documents.[60]

Soon after their marriage, old Mr. Yu died. He was given an impressive funeral, but that was the last grand act the family could afford. After the funeral, their servants were reduced to two in number. Other than his collection of antiques, whose sale the Communist government restricted, he left behind the Beijing mansion, the family's ancestral temple in the Inner City, and a trunk filled with obsolete currency and worthless stock. The father's death delayed Kidd's move into the family compound by a forty-day mourning period. The newly married couple had no honeymoon, but it was not missed. The marriage was a practical arrangement. At times, Kidd expresses fondness for his wife, but never passion. Since he did not initiate the marriage, he can hardly be accused of misleading her. The apparent lack of a sex life seems to have made for one less responsibility that Yu had to fulfill. In "post-Liberation" China, Kidd was no longer allowed to teach English. While his feelings for his wife were tepid, his love of the beauty of the Yu family compound was passionate. However, Communist China was not interested in accommodating apolitical foreign aesthetes.

Kidd and his new wife obtained their exit visas and left China in 1950. After arriving in New York in 1951, Yu took courses in chemistry at Columbia University while Kidd taught the history of Chinese art at the old Asia Institute.[61] When the Asia Institute closed, Kidd was unable to find a new position. Whereas Americans viewed Yu sympathetically as a refugee from Communism, Cold War McCarthyism made them suspicious of Kidd who had chosen to live for two years under a Communist Chinese regime. Yu still had access to family jewelry that could be sold if she needed money. So while Kidd felt alienated living in the United States, Yu felt comfortable and decided to make a new life there. She and Kidd separated. He states that neither of them remarried, but he does not clarify whether they were divorced. They continued over the years to be friends.

With China removed as a welcoming land for homosexuals, Japan became the closest substitute. Several of the world's most eminent gay Japanologists chose to live there—and still do. This situation probably was the source of a joke still circulating among academics that while Sinologists are drunks, Japanologists are queers. (One troubling implication of this joke is that with the loss of a welcoming land to escape to, queer Sinologists turned in frustration to alcohol.) In 1956, Kidd went to Japan, where he worked as a lecturer and became a dealer in Chinese and Japanese art and antiquities. In 1976 he founded the Oomoto School of Traditional Japanese Arts in Kyoto.

In 1981 after an absence of thirty-two years, Kidd was able to return to Beijing alone. Yu chose not to accompany him. Perhaps a homecoming in such a changed world was more than she could bear. However, she gave him Second Brother's address.[62] Aesthetically, Beijing had suffered enormously. On the drive in from the airport, Kidd realized that the countryside looked different because all the graves and tomb enclosures had been removed. The city wall around Beijing had been dismantled as a feudal relic. A six-lane highway had been built over the moat that had surrounded the city wall. Identifiable old buildings had grown shabby. New buildings were built in blocks of ugly utilitarian structures. Gray was the predominating color—the buildings were gray, the people were dressed in gray, and the sky was gray due to air pollution. The food in the Peking Hotel dining room consisted of mounds of different kinds of meat cooked in brown sauce—a feast for peasants.

Kidd knew that the old Yu mansion in the West City had been converted to a clinic in the 1960s and then into the residence of Lin Biao, who during the Cultural Revolution had become Mao's heir. After Lin's disgrace and death in 1971—allegedly dying in a plane crash in Mongolia after a failed coup d'état—the mansion had been opened to the public so that the people could see how a traitor lived. However, when Kidd arrived at the site on Crooked Hair Family Lane in 1981, the mansion as well as the courtyards and gardens were gone, replaced by a multistoried brick building housing the secret police. Kidd's driver warned him not to get out of the car. Later he met Second Brother who had been unemployed since 1956 when he had begun serving ten years of hard labor as a form of "reeducation." The heavy rocks he had carried on his back damaged his spine and left him hunchbacked, but the Yu family had survived.

Kidd returned to Kyoto where he had a wonderfully aesthetic traditional Japanese house, Togendo, which he left to the University of Hawaii. After he died of cancer in 1996, the house was dismantled piece by piece and put in storage in Japan. Unfortunately the University of Hawaii chose not to fund the shipment of the house to Hawaii, and there is little awareness of the bequest among faculty on the campus today.[63]

SPECIAL FRIENDS

Most of the men with same-sex desires who went to China befriended Chinese "boys," to use the word in its widest meaning. These friendships varied enormously, but there were two elements that were almost always present: physical attraction and (a sometimes fleeting) tenderness. The journalist Michael Davidson expressed this in a description of his relationship with a Chinese boy in 1950:

> In Hong Kong I made friends with a sweet slender Chinese boy, like a porcelain figure, named Chou. His little pinched underfed face was made beautiful by a prefect nose; it's the nose, as well as the hooded eyes and the alabaster skin, that makes the Chinese the loveliest people in the world. . . . Chou was a studious boy, and I sent him to school; tenderly faithful he needed a mother's affection. I saw him last in the huge grandiose Peninsula Hotel on the Kowloon-side, like Euston Station, when I came back from Korea; he used to write to me after I had gone for good.[64]

For Schedel and Soulié de Morant (and perhaps also Acton, Kidd, and Backhouse), a Chinese boy might be a teenage actor who played women's parts. For Auden, Isherwood, and Alley, a boy might be an ephebe from a poor background. Alley was particularly prone to feel fatherly toward boys in need. For Ripa, a boy was a pliant and obedient acolyte. Bynner's and Hundhausen's taste in young men ran a bit older, preferably young men in their twenties who were a bit intellectual and eager to serve as assistants and aides in return for room and board. Schall inclined toward a more mature companion, like Pan Jinxiao, who could serve as a confidante. Acton also liked male intellectual companions only slightly younger than himself who could evolve into professional colleagues, such as Chen Shixiang. For Schedel, the singsong boys were just evening companions, but Soulié de Morant sought someone like the Belted Jewel for a long-term "special friendship." In sum, the friendships that these men made with Chinese were a rich mixture of male relationships, each as much a reflection of the man's personality and tastes as of his sexual desire.

5

Establishing Intellectual Connections with China

THE PERSISTENT RUMOR

While special friendships with Chinese males could be initiated fairly quickly by foreign men with same-sex desires, intellectual connections were much more time consuming. They required a long period of Chinese language study or a long period of residency in China. The process frequently involved establishing a working relationship with Chinese scholars, although collaboration was often limited by physical distance and political obstacles. The fruits of these intellectual connections fostered a cultural encounter between China and the West on many different levels, from the popular to the scholarly.

For a century, a rumor has persisted in the university community of Leiden that the Sinologist Johannes Jacobus Maria De Groot was a homosexual. The rumor is based on De Groot's lack of interest in women, his special friendship with Josef Marquart, and his obsessive concern with expressions of homosexuality in the Leiden student fraternity. The evidence is by no means conclusive, but the lack of clear evidence of same-sex attraction is typical of many closeted men of De Groot's time.

De Groot was born into a prosperous and pious family in Schiedam (near Rotterdam) in the Netherlands. His father was a distiller and prominent local businessman, while his family was Roman Catholic and was devout to the point of naming six of their thirteen children Maria.[1] Throughout his lifetime, he remained deeply devoted to his parents, and when he received an attractive offer to move from Leiden to Berlin (first declining in 1902 and later accepting in 1911), one of the main obstacles was being separated from his family. His education was shaped by Dutch colonialist opportunities. He studied at Leiden for service as an interpreter in Chinese. In 1877 he went to Amoy in Fujian province for a year of "practical Chinese."[2] During this time he invented his own field method and gathered material on popular religion in Amoy.[3] This was followed by service in the Dutch colonies of the East Indies. After a period of sick leave in the Netherlands, he returned to China and stayed from 1886 to 1890. He again went to Amoy, which was the main area of interest to the Dutch because of the Chinese immigration from there to the Dutch East Indies. De Groot was always more comfortable with the Fujian dialect than with the Mandarin dialect of northern China.

Dr Groot was a pioneer in the development of ethnographic Sinology. This involved the use of the social sciences and the application of a sociological method to the study of Chinese religion.[4] This approach contrasted with the then-dominant philological study of China, which focused on the Chinese language. His major work was *The Religious System of China*, in six volumes (1892–1910). Throughout his lifetime, De Groot was a dedicated and hard worker. However, as an interpreter, he was limited to a second-class status in the colonial civil service. He hated the insensitivity of the Dutch colonials to Chinese customs and attitudes. He was sometimes abrasive in voicing his differences, as when he published a criticism of their dancing at official balls and became a social outcast for doing so. While alienated from the colonial establishment, he established close relations with the Chinese.

Back in Holland, he was appointed to the chair in ethnography (*Land- en Volkenkunde*) at Leiden University and taught Chinese. There he trained about seventy future colonial civil servants.[5] However, when Gustav Schlegel died in 1903, De Groot was appointed to succeed him in the chair in Sinology. De Groot accepted the new chair out of duty but would have preferred to continue working in ethnography and in training students for colonial service.

A taint of frustration and loneliness ran through De Groot's life. Apart from his family, he had few close friends. Toward his predominantly male students, he was kind and approachable.[6] However, toward women he was less warm. The traditional view at Leiden that De Groot was a homosexual stems in part from his cool relations with women and in part from his sexual prudery and hypersensitivity toward homosexual innuendos. Although De Groot became agnostic, he always retained the puritanical sexual attitudes of his pious Catholic upbringing. When he studied at Leiden, Schlegel's salacious comments in his lectures on China had offended him. In his youthful diary, De Groot wrote that Schlegel "always makes us swallow filthy and erotic anecdotes during this lectures" and is full of "smutty jokes and vulgarities about sexual life."[7]

De Groot's puritanical attitudes led him to neglect the sexual elements in Chinese culture. Marcel Granet's *La pensée chinoise* (Chinese thought) criticized De Groot for not giving proper significance to the phallic elements in Chinese writing.[8]

R. J. Zwi Werblowsky, in his study of De Groot, claims "there is not a shred of evidence" that De Groot was homosexual.[9] However, for those familiar with the signs of closeted homosexuality, there are several indicators. One was De Groot's special friend and collaborator, the Iranist Josef Marquart (1864–1930). Marquart was keeper at the Museum of Ethnology and an unsalaried lecturer (*privaat-docent*) in Armenian and Syrian at Leiden University. De Groot's insistent requests for a university appointment for Marquart at Leiden were spurned by the university.[10] Finally, in 1910, the university offered to appoint him an assistant lecturer, but the University of Berlin wanted De Groot so much that they sweetened their invitation by offering to create a new chair in Iranian philology for Marquart. The offer has the air of a contemporary spousal appointment offered to attract certain desired scholars. The Berlin offer was accepted, and both De Groot and Marquart moved to Berlin.

De Groot's painful departure from family and friends was eased by his bitterness over the Dutch ministry's decision that he was not entitled to a pension, in spite of thirty-seven years of work in the colonial service and his regular contributions to the pension plan. The move came for De Groot at fifty-seven years of age. He was the first occupant of the Berlin university chair in Chinese. However, his contribution to the development of Sinology is questionable. His knowledge of Chinese was good, but his linguistic skills surpassed his ability to do critical scholarship.[11]

One wonders if Berlin might have offered De Groot something else. There is little evidence that he ever had a romantic relationship with a woman. At that time many men who were not interested in marriage went into the colonial services. De Groot was close only to the women in his family, especially his mother. In formal relationships with women, such as his tutoring of the young queen Wilhelmina in 1899–1900, he was cordial, but he never married, and he expressed a degree of misogyny.[12] His estate went to his nephews while his many nieces were completely ignored. An elder sister served as his housekeeper in Leiden for twenty years but did not accompany him to Berlin in 1912.[13]

Berlin was then in the process of developing the most tolerant attitudes toward homosexuality of any city in Europe. The campaign on behalf of homosexual rights was led by the physician Magnus Hirschfeld, the son of a prominent Jewish physician, who moved to Berlin in 1896. This campaign was strengthened by Hirschfeld's reputation as a scientific investigator of sexuality. He published several widely read books, beginning in 1904 with *Berlins dritte Geschlecht* (Berlin's Third Sex). In 1919 he opened the Institut für Sexualwissenschaft (Institute for Sexual Science) and appeared as a sexual therapist in one of the first sympathetic films about homosexuality, *Anders als die Andern* (Different than the Others). Given that De Groot's special friend, Marquart, accompanied him to Berlin, one wonders if this move to Berlin represented an opportunity for cracking open, ever so slightly, the door of his sexual closet. At the very least, Berlin, known as the city of the *warme Brüder* (warm brothers, i.e., homosexuals), would have offered De Groot an accommodating atmosphere for engaging in a discreet and secretive homosexual life. Whether he actually did so is unknown.

In Berlin, De Groot shifted his loyalties to Germany. When he made his last visit to the Netherlands in 1921, shortly before his death, he made no effort to seek an audience with his former student, Queen Wilhelmina. He knew that she had voiced her displeasure over his move to Berlin. He had sealed his alienation from his homeland when on October 4, 1914, he joined ninety other prominent German academics in signing the "Es ist nicht wahr" manifesto.[14] Formally known as the *Aufruf an die Kulturwelt*, this document rejected as foreign slanders the assertions that Germany was the aggressor in World War I, claimed that Germany's violation of Belgium's neutrality had been for defensive rather than offensive reasons, and denied accusations of German war atrocities.[15] For his support, the German government awarded De Groot a *Verdienstkreuz* (Service Cross), a national decoration awarded for community service.

The major incident of De Groot's life that suggests a closeted homosexuality was his famous attack on freshman hazing at Leiden University that culminated in the *"ontgroen"* (degreening) scandal of 1911. Degreening referred to initiation rites imposed by upperclassmen on new (i.e., green) students at the beginning of their *Groentijd* (freshman year).[16] De Groot's animosity to the degreening process dated from his own experience at Leiden in the 1870s when he was initiated into the Leiden student fraternity—the Student Corps. In the hazing process, one of his fellow students was soaked with water, causing an illness that led to his death.[17]

In 1904 he anonymously published a pamphlet in Dutch entitled *The Green Path: A Serious Word to Parents and Guardians of Forthcoming Students, by a Professor*.[18] In shrill and colorful language, De Groot described the initiation process that was inflicted on Leiden freshmen. He described sadistic behavior with sexual overtones; however, the language of his portrayal was puzzling in its intensity and out of proportion to the acts of youthful foolishness that he was describing. Had the publication of this pamphlet been an isolated act, it could more easily be disregarded, but actually it was part of a continuing obsession with De Groot. Although there were others who shared his criticism of the degreening process, the intensity of De Groot's feelings eventually isolated him.

In addition to the Green Cabaret (*Groenencabaret*), a newer "reception revue" or "green revue" had developed and took place in 1911 for only the seventh time.[19] This was a reception for the senior members during the hazing period of the council of the Student Corps. Five of them were commissioned to write a libretto for a revue, with satirical skits to be performed by the freshmen. The previous year had featured "The Night-mares of Professor Le Groo or the freshmen period horrors in China," containing lustful fantasies, naked seductions, and blood revenge by castration—all done in the spirit of humorous satire.[20]

There was a rivalry between the students of Utrecht and Leiden universities, and the 1911 Leiden green revue satirized the Utrecht Student Corps' masquerade festival of the summer of 1911. The Utrecht production had featured an open-air performance, "Willem van Holland," with verse and music. The theme of the open-air production was the founding of the federation of the Netherlands.[21] The unification was symbolized by the love affair between the Lady Johanna van Renesse and a nobleman from the army, Count Gerrit van Herlaer van Poederoijen. The Utrecht production romanticized their love as overcoming the enmity of their separate regions and thus enabling the fourteenth-century birth of the Dutch nation.

The Leiden Student Corps libretto of the green revue performed on October 12, 1911, was a pornographic parody of this love affair. Had it not been for De Groot, all copies of the libretto might have disappeared. However, the Leiden faculty was divided on reforming the degreening process.[22] When the university merely posted a reprimand of the Student Corps on the door of the academy without mentioning names, De Groot became so angry that he had the libretto printed and sent copies in a "*Gesloten Brief*" (confidential letter) to both houses of the Dutch Parliament, with the demand that they take action against the degreening process.[23] Because of De Groot's prominence, the Dutch Parliament met in closed session to consider his demand. However, they declined to act favorably. The Netherlands was a small country, and many of the Parliamentarians were fathers and uncles of the Leiden Student Corps members. They were disinclined to tarnish the reputations of their young relatives in order to respond to De Groot's exaggerated claims of horror.

One can understand the Parliament's reaction when one reads the outlandish words of the libretto text. The Student Corps published an open letter in the national newspapers in which it claimed that their green revue had contained only allusions and that nothing obscene had been practiced or graphically presented in their production.[24] But De Groot was obsessed by the fact that the Leiden fraternity had already for several years imposed on new members a hazing rite in which the freshmen performed scenes of a homosexual character, clothed as women wearing low-necked gowns.[25] It is worth noting that the Student Corps' parody had been stimulated by passage in the previous year of legislation criminalizing homosexual behavior in the Netherlands.[26]

THE ECCENTRIC SINOLOGIST

The most widely read English translation of a classical Chinese novel today is probably *Monkey*, Arthur Waley's abridged version of *Xi you ji* (Journey to the West). The adventure story of this uppity monkey who seeks salvation through enlightenment has been for many their introduction to Chinese culture. It is a work that has delighted generations of readers, although its blending of the Three Teachings (Confucianism, Buddhism, and Daoism) of Ming syncretism makes for confusion. Still, this translation provides one of the best introductory level connections between Westerners and China.

The translator of *Monkey*, Arthur David Waley, was one of the great eccentrics of modern Sinology. He never received formal language training in Chinese or Japanese, he never visited East Asia, and he participated in a very minimal way in academic life. And yet some regard him as the greatest translator of Chinese works in the first half of the twentieth century.[27] Many aspects of his life contributed to his uniqueness. He was born in 1889 into an agnostic Jewish family of German ancestry in England at a time when anti-Semitism was far more prevalent than today. His father was David Frederick Schloss, an affluent civil servant in the Board of Trade.[28] His maternal grandfather, Jacob Waley, was an academic and a leader in the Anglo-Jewish Association.[29] This association included Jews from the entire British Empire, and it was particularly concerned with the plight of Jews in Russia, Romania, and Turkey.

Young Arthur attended Rugby School and studied Classics at King's College, Cambridge. The atmosphere that he encountered at King's was homoerotic and included homosexuals like G. L. Dickinson, a tutor who introduced Waley to China.[30] He spent a year studying in France and Germany, one of the few times, other than skiing in Norway and Switzerland, when he left Britain. In 1910, he suffered a cornea problem that led to the loss of sight in his left eye and disqualified him from military service. When World War I was declared in 1914 and anti-German feeling was strong in England, he followed his mother in changing his surname from the German-sounding Schloss to the more English-sounding Waley, although he was already twenty-five years old.

It was not until 1913 when he was appointed assistant keeper of Oriental prints and manuscripts at the British Museum and transferred to the Oriental Section that he began to study Chinese and Japanese. He worked in the Oriental Section under the poet and translator Laurence Binyon. A friend described him at that time as "a haughty young man with a high, thin cutting voice and a refined and intellectual face."[31] Waley had a remarkable talent for foreign languages and a wonderful feel for translating poetry. In 1916 he printed his translations of forty short Chinese poems and had them sent out as a type of Christmas card.[32] Some of his friends who received copies were Laurence Binyon, G. L. Dickinson, T. S. Eliot, Ezra Pound, Leonard Woolf, Bertrand Russell, and W. B. Yates.[33] He was a prolific author and left the British Museum in 1930, when he felt that he could survive on income from his publications. He published three dozen books and numerous articles and reviews. He was a poet as well as a scholar, and this led him to aim his works more at a popular audience than at academics. He disliked systems and theories and regarded them as "boring."[34]

Although he is frequently associated with the Bloomsbury Group, he was really too individual to have been more than a peripheral member.[35] He was reclusive, eccentric, and very private (perhaps closeted) in his habits. Virginia Woolf called him "a little demure and discreet."[36] The Bloomsbury Group was famous for its challenging of Victorian repression, particularly in terms of love and sexuality, but it also advocated leftist political philosophies, feminism, and pacifism. According to Waley's longtime female companion Beryl de Zoete, the Bloomsbury Group "exchanged beds like musical chairs."[37] Waley seems to have felt comfortable with their attitudes, but not with their intense socialization, and he limited his involvement. As for Waley's sexuality, not much evidence is available.[38] There were two women in his life to whom he formed emotional attachments, but it is questionable whether he had sex with either one of them.

The first of these women was the English writer, Asian dance enthusiast, and dance critic Beryl de Zoete (1879–1962), who was ten years older than Waley. She was attractive and as eccentric as Waley, but not well liked. She had been one of the first women to study at Oxford and retained into her sixties a strikingly attractive figure through the practice of eurhythmics.[39] She and Waley met in 1918 and out of mutual admiration developed a long-term relationship, which is difficult to characterize since it did not involve marriage, children, or even, at times, a shared flat.[40] Zoete had been married but seems to have been sexually frigid, and the marriage ended. The consensus was that Waley and Zoete shared an affectionate bond, but not a sexual relationship. A friend wrote this about them: "There was something so ascetic about him and so emotically equivocal about her that many people believed there was no physical link between them."[41]

In fact, the reasons that Waley liked her were a mystery to his friends. Initially they shared a very small flat at the top of a house in Russell

Square, although they also lived separately. Waley occupied a small flat at the top of 50 Gordon Square—the same street where most of the Blooms-bury Group lived—for a long time.[42] Presumably they lived separately because Waley's mother would have objected to them living together, and Zoete refused Waley's proposals to marry. A friend suggested that she "suffered from a fastidiousness very common in those days among women, which made normal sexual relations repugnant to her."[43]

At the Russell Square flat, the staples of their diet were Ovaltine and dry biscuits.[44] They sometimes invited friends to an austere meal that was always the same: a heated can of beans with apples and grapes. (Zoete was an uncompromising vegetarian.) But the austerity of these meals seems to have been driven mainly by Waley, who was reluctant to spend money on food and was notorious for inviting friends to cheap restaurants. This was done not out of poverty, because after his mother's death, he was well off financially. It was simply due to his asceticism and unwillingness to spend money, time, or energy on material things. He once invited Hu Shi, the eminent Chinese philosopher, cultural reformer, and ambassador to the United States (1937–1939), to dinner. Dr. Hu ar-rived at the flat in evening dress to find Waley in shirtsleeves preparing dinner over a gas ring. Waley proceeded to quiz him about the sources of certain Zen Buddhist texts.[45]

Harold Acton described how when he visited and rang the doorbell, Waley's head would pop out of a top-floor window. Sometimes he would throw out a key, and at other times he would race down the stairs to open the door. Waley was agile and fit and could race up and down the steep stairs without losing his breath. Up until the end of his life, he rode a bicycle as a means of transit all over London. He was intense, cryptic, and obsessed with Chinese poetry, which he introduced into most of his conversations even though his comments were often beyond the under-standing of non-Sinologists. And yet he was loyal to his friends, although his shyness and inability to make small talk often left him standing alone in a corner.

The second woman in Waley's life involved an equally bizarre relation-ship which overlapped with the first relationship by thirty-three years. In fact, both relationships were variations on Waley's pattern of seeking female companionship rather than romance. Together they support the conjecture that Waley was a latent homosexual. Alison Grant was born in New Zealand in 1901 and came to London for a visit in 1929. She was so entranced by its literary and artistic culture that she remained, cashing in the return portion of her ticket back to New Zealand.

According to Grant's narrative published fifty-three years later, she met a kindly stranger at a Soho café who befriended her.[46] He was of medium height, carelessly dressed with an open shirt, cotton trousers, and dirty tennis shoes. His jacket was crammed with books, a pipe, and a beret, and he had a battered green bicycle. Although she did not learn his name until later, that first encounter was the beginning of her thirty-seven-year romantic obsession with Arthur Waley. Alison Grant married Hugh Ferguson Robinson in the following year and gave birth to a son in 1932. From 1929 to 1942, the family was in Australia and New Zealand before returning to London. She met Waley again in 1943 and divorced her husband. She and Waley continued to meet at irregular intervals. She was always available for him, but the reverse was not true.

In her very strange memoirs, where she relates her long relationship with Waley in a romanticized, impressionist tone, Alison Waley almost, but not quite, states that on one occasion they made love.[47] However, Hilary Spurling notes in an introduction to Alison Waley's memoirs that there is some discrepancy between certain events related by the author and the recollections of eyewitnesses. Much of the book's narrative belongs to "an inner landscape of the emotions rather than to the biographer's world of documentation."[48] As a result, some of the events described in the book seem to have been shaped by the author's wishful thinking. Given the role that the imagination plays in sex, it is possible that the intimacy she experienced as sexual was viewed by Waley merely as affection.

Unlike Zoete, who was a member of the Bloomsbury Group, Grant Robinson was too naive, impetuous, and devoted in her adoration of Waley to be accepted by this sophisticated literary circle. Waley himself tried to keep her apart from his friends, taking her to Kew Gardens for a picnic during the noon hour, when it tended to be deserted. He seems to have been embarrassed by her. Grant Robinson was aware of this and wrote, "I—my presence—is, as usual, ignored. I do not exist."[49] While Zoete was ten years older than Waley, Grant Robinson was two years his junior. Although Zoete and Waley were not married, Zoete was jealous of Grant Robinson and treated her cruelly. Grant Robinson tried to convey the impression that Waley loved her while Zoete was still alive, but it is more likely that he simply needed her for emotional support during the years when he was trying to cope with Zoete's long-term illness.

Toward the end of her life, Zoete suffered from a rare but fatal degenerative disease of the nervous system called Huntington's chorea.[50] It causes involuntary tics and tremors and inevitably ends in dementia and death. Waley was very faithful in caring for her, even reading Chinese poems to her night after night. The Japanologist Carmen Blacker visited them a few weeks before Zoete died. She described Zoete as a pathetically shrunken woman, unable to make coherent sounds, lying in bed "like a withered doll, with no teeth, hardly any hair, her face skeletally thin, one arm making convulsive movements round her head."[51] Blacker was touched by Waley's gentle treatment of her, even though he had suffered an accident and lost the use of his right arm. Toward the end, she had screaming fits and had to be watched constantly by a nurse. Zoete died in 1962 at eighty-six years of age.

Grant Robinson replaced Zoete as a live-in companion. In 1963, when the University of London forced the tenants of the Bloomsbury houses on the east side of Gordon Street to vacate so that they could be converted to academic offices, Waley bought a house at 50 Southwood Lane in Highgate. On the morning of February 17, 1966, Grant Robinson was driving Waley somewhere in a small Morris when a much larger car ran a red light and crashed into them. Grant Robinson was unhurt, but Waley's back was broken. When he was hospitalized, it was discovered that an advanced cancer had caused the deterioration of his spine. Surgery failed to halt the progression of a debilitating paralysis. A home nurse lifted him carelessly and caused a second fracture to his back. Blacker remarked on Grant Robinson's care of Waley in his last days: "I have never seen anyone so loving, so single-mindedly and imaginatively devoted."[52] One month before he died, he proposed to Grant Ferguson, and they were married. Waley died at his house in Highgate and was buried in the famous Highgate Cemetery under a beautiful tree from China where the two of them had often shared a picnic lunch.

Throughout his life, Waley had contact with numerous homosexuals. He had many friends among the Cambridge Conversazione Society, a secret society more commonly known as the Apostles, or simply the Society. Because the membership lists were secret, it is difficult to exclude the possibility that Waley was a member, but the Society seems to have been too socially intense for someone with Waley's reclusive tendencies. It was founded at Cambridge in 1820. The poet Alfred Tennyson was a member, as was Arthur Hallam, who seems to have felt same-sex desires. Hallam's death inspired Tennyson's famous poem *In Memorium* (1849). The extent to which the relationship between Tennyson and Hallam might have been sexual is still subject to speculation, but this poem clearly marked the beginning of a "sublimated homosexual cult within the Society."[53]

G. L. Dickinson (affectionately known as "Goldie") was elected to the Society in 1884. Dickinson developed an enthusiastic sympathy for the plight of China, then suffering under the yoke of Western imperialism. He expressed this sympathy in an anonymously published book entitled *Letters from John Chinaman*, in which he included letters from an imaginary Chinese official.[54] Dickinson's homosexuality was marked by extreme frustration. Throughout his life, he fell hopelessly in love with heterosexual men. He had a shoe fetish and masturbated to sexual fantasies of domination by men in boots. After visiting his good friend E. M. Forster in India in 1913, he went on to China, which he found far more to his liking.

In his autobiography, Dickinson describes the Saturday-night meetings of the Apostles in which a paper was read and then members commented in turn, drawing lots to determine their order of speaking.[55] By the end of the nineteenth century, the Apostles' homoeroticism, grounded in certain Platonic dialogues, surfaced in more explicit and physical form. A theory emerged, becoming an Apostolic tradition, that love between men occupied a higher emotional and intellectual plane than love between a man and a woman.[56] This was referred to in the Apostle's secret terminology as the "Higher Sodomy."

The period from 1905 to 1910 was the high tide of flamboyant same-sex attraction among the Apostles. Waley attended Cambridge for three years (1907–1909) during this period. The prominent homosexual author E. M. Forster was a member. The homosexual Duncan Grant, later a prominent painter and part of the Bloomsbury Group, claimed that homosexuality had become so fashionable that even womanizers pretended to be gay.[57] There were open displays of affection between male couples. The leadership of the Apostles during this time was dominated by Lytton Strachey and John Maynard Keynes of Keynesian economics fame. In 1908, Waley delivered a paper to a group at Cambridge (possibly to the Fabian Society) on the passionate love of comrades. Keynes thought the paper was offensive.[58]

Tensions within the Society came to a head when Ludwig Wittgenstein was nominated in 1912 for membership. Wittgenstein appears to have been a conflicted homosexual who opposed the idea of the Higher Sodomy.[59] Thereafter the influence of homoeroticism among the Apostles ebbed and flowed, although it continued to have an elitist appeal. By the 1930s, the Apostles' homosexuality was more subdued than twenty-five years earlier, but Marxist influence grew, led by Julian Bell, Guy Burgess, and Anthony Blunt. The Apostles Burgess and Blunt later incurred a great deal of negative publicity when it was revealed in 1979–1982 that they had been communist agents of the Soviet Union. This homosexual faction within the Apostles has evoked criticism and led to the charge that it was a manifestation of the "homosexual mafia," part of a recurring homophobic attack on the tendency of gays to support one another.[60]

Beginning in the 1930s, homosexuals in the arts were widely viewed as an international threat with conspiratorial undertones. They were referred to as members of the "Homintern"—an artistic counterpart of the Comintern (Communist International).[61] The term seems to have originated in England in the thirties by W. H. Auden, Cyril Connelly, and others as a mocking response to the accusations of queer power in the fine arts. It was later applied in the 1950s and 1960s to the threatening power of queer Americans in the arts who included Aaron Copland, Leonard Bernstein, Lincoln Kirstein, Tennessee Williams, James Baldwin, and Carson McCullers.

The poet Rupert Brooke (1887–1915), another Apostle, embodied the homoerotic ideal of striking good looks, athleticism, and intelligence. His early death in World War I fostered a romantic Adonis myth, although his famous war poems with their sentimental patriotism compare unfavorably to the more serious war poems of homosexual World War I soldiers like Winfred Owen and Siegfried Sassoon. Brooke seems to have been heterosexual, but ambiguously so. He had very close associations with numerous men with same-sex attraction and did not mind being an object of their flirtatiousness. His very queer fellow Apostle, James Strachey, once serenaded him.[62] Waley met him at Rugby School where Brooke's father was a housemaster. They both moved on to King's College, Cambridge, whose atmosphere was so homoerotic that it was affectionately known at that time as "Queen's."[63]

Until the very end of his life, Waley held very sentimental memories of Brooke. In May 1966, one month before he died, his companion Grant Robinson asked if she would have liked Waley when he was a student at Cambridge. He answered, half joking, "Oh, not in the least, I expect. Or certainly, you'd have liked Rupert better . . . because everybody did. He was beautiful and so gay. . . . I did cry when he died. . . . Half the world did. . . . With me it was a teeny bit more personal than that because my half-brother had known him in Tahiti. . . . He got the strangest impression of a creature 'in flight.' *From* something. I was in flight too. *From* something."[64] Whatever these comments mean, Waley felt he shared something very important with Rupert Brooke. Their sensibility was in many ways homoerotic.

The intensity with which Waley pursued his translations of Chinese texts may have been a sign of this flight. Certainly the material pleasures of this world (wealth, food, clothes, and sex) were not things that absorbed him. Unlike Harold Acton, Julian Bell, or even his King's College tutor G. D. Dickinson, he never traveled to China. Even his longtime companion Baryl de Zoete traveled frequently to India and Southeast Asia. Waley knew that the China he sought could be reached only through his imagination. So clearly did he enter into this imaginative Land of Oz that he created an additional chapter to the *Journey to the West* (Xiyouji) that was, according to Harold Acton, "so true to the style of the original that even a Chinese scholar might be hoodwinked by it."[65] This chapter seems not to have been included in *Monkey*.[66]

While this created chapter sounds to Western ears like a clever forgery, it was in fact exactly how the historical kernel of the journey of the Chinese monk Xuancang (Hsüan-tsang) to India in 629–645 was expanded into one of the greatest literary works of China. Over the years, elaborations were added by itinerant storytellers until these stories were finally organized into a long, popular work by Wu Chengan in the seventeenth century. So, although Waley encountered China through his imagination, it was one sure way of gaining entry to a culture that no longer existed in modern China.

The homosexuals at King's College with whom Waley had contact were the art critic Clive Bell, the painter Duncan Grant (who later did the illustrations for Waley's *Monkey*), the economist John Maynard Keynes, the writer Lytton Strachey, and the journalist Leonard Woolf. Strachey, in particular, was interested in the topic of sex, especially sex between men. These Kingsmen would provide a nucleus for the Bloomsbury Group, a group of British artists and writers who gathered in the decaying section of London at 46 Gordon Square from around 1904.[67] The more prominent women in the group were the sisters Vanessa Bell and Virginia Woolf and the painter Dora Carrington. The group later facilitated the literary work of the Chinese woman author Ling Shuhua (1900–1990), who had the adulterous love affair with Vanessa Bell's son, Julian Bell (1908–1937).[68]

Waley had an affinity with queers that extended beyond Kingsmen and the Bloomsbury Group. Once when he and Grant Robinson were preparing for a party, she was making up a guest list and having trouble getting "the men sexually balanced."[69] On a block pad she had made a list of the male party guests divided into columns marked "NORM" and "QUEER." The first column had three names, with the third name followed by a question mark. The queer column extended the entire length of the page in smaller and smaller script and then continued along the margin. Waley looked at the imbalanced lists, made a typically terse comment, "No buggers—no party," and then returned to correcting galleys of a book on the Chinese poet Li Bo. Clearly homosexuals formed a mundane part of his life. Exactly how mundane is difficult to determine. After Waley's death, his papers disappeared in mysterious circumstances.[70] It is hard to believe that his new wife had no role in their disappearance, but the question of why they disappeared is more difficult to answer.

Harold Acton belonged to a younger generation than the Bloomsbury Group, and he was a good friend of Julian Bell. Although it is unclear exactly when they first met, Acton and Waley shared an interest in translating Chinese texts. Acton's references to Waley occur in the second volume of his memoirs, which cover the years 1939 to 1969.[71] Waley and Zoete were the only friends who took an interest in Acton's translations of Chinese dramas that were being printed by Kelly and Walsh in Shanghai.[72] Unlike Acton, who excelled in small talk, Waley communicated his thoughts with "staccato directness." Given the brevity of Acton's comments on their friendship, it is surprising that Waley dedicated *Monkey*, his abridged translation of the famous Chinese novel *Xiyouji* (Journey to the West), to both Acton and Beryl de Zoete. This became Waley's most widely read work.

One of the few cases in which an affinity for men with same-sex desire appears in Waley's scholarship is his biography of the eminent poet and essayist Yuan Mei (1716–1798). Yuan was a precocious scholar who passed the highest literati exam, the *jinshi*, in 1739 at the age of only twenty-three. He was appointed a fellow of the prestigious Hanlin Academy in Beijing, but when he failed an exam in Manchu in 1742, he was demoted to district magistrate.[73] After a series of tours as provincial magistrate, he withdrew from official life in 1749 and retired to a historical site in Nanjing called "the Garden of Contentment" (Suiyuan). With the income he made as a writer, he reconstructed the neglected site into a beautiful villa where he maintained a large household and entertained friends.

In his private life, Yuan appears to have been a classic Chinese bisexual who fulfilled his obligation to procreate and continue the family life while enjoying the company of male actors. As was typical of many aspiring scholar-officials, Yuan married in the same year that he attained the *jinshi* degree—1739. Miss Wang, to whom he had been betrothed since childhood, was twenty-two, eight years older than the typical marrying age of a women at that time. The marriage produced no children, and Waley speculated that it was because Yuan did not find her physically attractive.[74] However, at this same time, Yuan was cultivating an effusive friendship with a young actor, Xu Yunting. They were on affectionate terms, and Yuan penned elaborate poems to him as well as to one or two other boy-actors. However, Waley adds the rather defensive comment that Yuan was not "exclusively interested in men."[75] Yuan fulfilled his filial obligation by later taking a Miss Tao as a concubine with whom he was able to produce children.

Yuan's interest in actors seems to have continued throughout his life. In 1774 he went to Hangzhou for a vacation in the company of a young actor named Gui Lang.[76] When the actor left after five days to fulfill an engagement at Nanjing, Yuan was so miserable that he could not sleep. However, Yuan's sorrow was not long lived. A poem by Yuan reveals that another actor, Cao Lang, had soon replaced Gui Lang as a companion.

Waley does not explain why he chose to devote a book to Yuan, but perhaps he found a kinship with Yuan's eccentricities and his willingness to violate social conventions. The great philosopher Zhang Xuecheng (1738–1811) attacked Yuan for perverting youth by interpreting the Confucian classics in a way that supported his hedonistic views, and he also criticized him for accepting female students, thereby violating the ideal Confucian division between males and females.[77] Waley was far more ascetic than hedonistic, so what he admired in Yuan probably was related to Yuan's individuality and possibly his bisexuality. This might explain why Waley had portrayed Yuan with a surprising resemblance to the Bloomsbury figures, who of course prized individuality and bisexuality.[78]

FOREIGN EXPATRIATES AND CHINESE INTELLECTUALS

Beijing was built upon a flat, empty plain in the early 1400s. It was transformed into a majestic city by human hands. Its political fortunes ebbed and flowed for five hundred years, but it remained a work of art created by Chinese civilization. In the 1930s, it became a magnet for foreign aesthetes. It was, in the words of the art historian Laurence Sickman, who lived there at the time, "the only city in the world where physical and social traditions a millennium old had survived into the twentieth century."[79] Beijing's attractiveness at that time was enhanced by contrast with Europe, whose depressed economic conditions had given rise to ugly political extremism of both the left (Communism) and the right (National Socialism).

In Beijing, Harold Acton began to temper his youthful dandyism in favor of a more serious and scholarly existence, although he remained an aesthete and a Roman Catholic. He was able to live in a fairly grand manner because of the generosity of his American uncle, Guy Mitchell. He eventually bought a Chinese house at number 2 Gong Xian *hutong* and began living in Chinese style, including Chinese clothing. He hired a Chinese language tutor who knew no English and would teach by pointing at objects and having Acton repeat his pronunciation.[80] Beijing in the 1930s had a large expatriate community. These Europeans and Americans who were estranged from their homelands found in Beijing an inexpensive, profitable, and exotic environment where they could rent luxurious homes from impoverished Manchus and hire servants who could communicate in Pidgin English. Most of these foreign residents refused to learn the Chinese language. Such people were too philistine for a high-culture figure like Acton, and he delighted in satirizing them in his novel *Peonies and Ponies* (1941). He avoided them, and they in turn mocked him for "going native." Instead, Acton cultivated the friendships of Chinese intellectuals and foreign residents who shared Acton's enthusiasm for China and its young men.

Acton chose his friends carefully. He had a few select Chinese women friends, some of whom traded on their exoticism. One of the more colorful of these women was Rong Ling (Madame Dan Paochao), who was the elder sister of the more famous Der Ling (1885–1944).[81] Their father was Yu Geng, a high-ranking Manchu bannerman who served as minister of the Qing government in Tokyo (1895–1899) and Paris (1899–1903). In Paris the sisters learned French and studied dance with Isadora Duncan from 1899 to 1903. Upon their return to China, the two sisters and their mother were invited by the Dowager Empress Cixi to live at the imperial court to assist Cixi in learning about foreign cultures. They spent two years (1903–1905) at the court, and each assumed the honorary title of "princess," which is how Acton refers to them. Der Ling later wrote a famous book about their experiences at the court.[82]

When Acton met Rong Ling in the 1930s, she was married to a wealthy Chinese general, Dan Paochao, whom Acton describes as "a General by courtesy, . . . Cantonese, very bland and formal."[83] Rong Ling spoke fluent French and idolized the dowager empress. Acton said that she and her husband lived in the past, while her sister Der Ling tried to be more contemporary. Unlike Rong Ling who remained in China, Der Ling married the American consul in Shanghai, Thaddeus Cohu White, in 1907 and moved to the United States in 1928. She had a flair for self-promotion and a tendency to exaggerate. Between 1911 and 1935, Der Ling wrote eight books in English on China, all of them published in New York. During the last two years of her life, she taught Chinese on the University of California, Berkeley, campus. She lived in the Hotel Carlton, the same hotel where Witter Bynner had lived in 1918–1919.

While Acton enjoyed female company, he regarded women as akin to the beautiful artworks of Beijing. For serious friendships, he sought out male company. In his memoirs, he published a picture of a stag birthday party that reveals how aesthetics and same-sex attraction blended in Acton's world (figure 5.1). The photograph features four Western friends and nine Chinese friends, largely Beijing University (Beida) students.[84] Most of the students wore traditional Chinese robes. Acton commented with pity on the married state of his young Chinese friends: "Most of my Chinese cronies were cramped by premature marriage and its attendant burdens; there was an astonishingly high rate of mortality among their infants; they were hen-pecked by their wives, bullied by their parents and plagued by their mothers-in-law. They came to me with their woes, all due to matrimony, yet they pitied me because I was unmarried."[85]

The birthday picture shows the scholarly quality of Acton's friends in Beijing. It includes (in a Western suit) the youthful Chen Shixiang who came from a distinguished literary family. His grandfather, Chen Shaowu, was a poet, and two of his uncles had attained the prestigious *jinshi* and *zhuren* degrees before the classical examination system was abolished in 1905. Chen was educated by private tutors in the classical tradition and entered Beida in 1929. Chen and Acton met when Acton was invited by Wen Yuanning to lecture in English literature at Beida.[86] They began their literary collaboration, which would continue for many years. Chen went to the United States in 1941 to study and teach at Harvard and Columbia. He moved to the University of California at Berkeley in 1945 and remained there for twenty-six years until his death.

Acton also collaborated with Li Yixie (Lee Yi-hsieh) to translate a group of popular Chinese novellas (short fictional narratives) from the seventeenth century.[87] These were lively "prompt-book stories" used by

Figure 5.1. Harold Acton's birthday party in Beijing, 1930s. On the back row from left to right is Desmond Parsons, Harold Acton, unidentified Chinese, and Laurence Sickman. On the front row from left to right is Li Yixie (Lee Yi-hsieh), Chen Shixiang (Ch'en Shih-hsiang), and Alan Priest. Apart from Cecil Taylor in the second row, the others are Beida students. From Harold Acton, *Memoirs of an Aesthete*, facing page 276.

professional storytellers. They were published in a limited edition in 1941 under the title *Glue and Lacquer*, a metaphor for physical intimacy.

Two of the men in Acton's birthday picture were in the early stages of their careers as American museum curators of East Asian art. Both were homosexual, although quite different in personality. One was Laurence Sickman (1906–1988), who became the director of the Nelson-Atkins Museum in Kansas City. The other was Alan Reed Priest (1898–1969), who became the curator of Far Eastern Art at the Metropolitan Museum of Art in New York.

Of the two, Priest was the far more flamboyant. He was born in Massachusetts, and after graduating from Harvard in 1920 he worked as an assistant in fine arts at the university.[88] He first went to China in 1924 as part of the second Fogg Museum expedition to north China and to the ancient Silk Route site of Dunhuang, which is rich in antiquities. He stayed on in Beijing, supported by Carnegie and Sachs fellowships from Harvard. He concentrated on studying the Forbidden City and Beijing temples. Priest had a flair for drama. He became a Buddhist monk. Acton described him in Beijing wearing priestly robes and serving cocktails in "a dreamy house on the moat by the Forbidden City where he played non-stop records of *Pelléas and Mélisande*, an opera of which he never wearied."[89] He was one of the few non-Chinese knowledgeable enough to warble *kunqu* opera lyrics along with a fat Manchu named Fu.[90]

As curator of Far Eastern Art at the Metropolitan from 1928 until 1963, Priest was a memorable figure, with his florid complexion, sandy hair, glasses, and a cigarette holder constantly hanging from his lips. He wore a cape or long overcoat that reached to his ankles and sometimes walked his dog through the museum at night. He had little patience with the detailed concerns of art historians and was not really a scholar. But he excelled in organizing fine arts events and even tours of Buddhist temples in northern Shanxi, especially when wealthy matrons were involved. He was rewarded when they bequeathed their artworks to the Metropolitan. But while Acton developed a friendship with Sickman, his feelings toward Priest were less than warm. Acton characterized him as very un-Chinese in his tendency to lose his temper, which he did frequently. He said that Priest "inspired terror in his colleagues." Once when Acton visited him at the Metropolitan, Priest (who mistakenly thought Acton was looking for employment) greeted him by giving his trash can a fierce kick and using a tone to which the patrician Acton "was not accustomed."[91]

Acton's birthday photograph also includes Desmond Parsons, who some friends claimed was the one true love of Acton's life. Parsons was a younger brother of the sixth Earl of Rosse.[92] Acton's description of Parsons presents him as a restless upper-class Englishman, in short, someone of the same class and background as Acton. In Acton's eyes, Parsons was "tall, fair and nordically handsome" but suffered from chronically poor health.[93] He had endured an "unhappy period" at Sandhurst.[94] Possibly he was compelled to go there because of a military tradition in his family. After Sandhurst, Parsons began to travel. He was good at foreign languages and had archeological interests. He seems to have known Acton before joining him in Beijing in 1934. He took a house near Acton in Chuihua *hutong* and followed him in having a fully Chinese household and began studying Chinese, but his restlessness led him to travel to the Caves of the Thousand Buddhas at Dunhuang, on the border of northwest China.[95] Parsons climbed through the dark caves, taking pictures of the frescoes of the Buddha's life. His passport was not fully in order, and he was suspected of looting the caves. He sent a frantic telegram to Acton after he was arrested at Anxi in Gansu province, and most of his luggage was confiscated, but he was finally released.

Acton had taken a serious interest in Chinese drama, and Parsons was one of the few foreign friends who enjoyed accompanying him to Chinese theaters to watch Peking Opera. Parsons suddenly fell ill and had to return to London; however, he intended to return because he continued to maintain his house and servants in Beijing.[96] He died of Hodgkin's disease in 1939 at the age of twenty-six.[97] The news of his death hit Acton hard. He regretted letting Parsons return to London because Parsons could not resist the temptations of his former dissolute life: "He should never have returned to London. He was so young that the night-club world still had a charm for him, and even when he was ill he was dragged out of bed to dance in some foetid *boîte* [nightclub]."[98] Acton reproached himself for not accompanying Parsons "to Zurich on his last journey." Apparently Parsons went to Switzerland in a final, desperate search for a cure.

But what of Acton's Chinese male lovers? Literary conventions of that time prohibited published expressions of same-sex relations, but Acton was quite candid in conversations with friends. One of these friends was the poet Julian Bell (1908–1937). Bell had studied at King's College, Cambridge, and was connected to the Bloomsbury Group through both his mother and his aunt, Virginia Woolf. From 1935 to 1937, Bell taught at National Wuhan University, where he carried on his scandalous affair with the woman writer and painter Ling Shuhua (1900–1990). She was married to the prominent historian and literary critic Chen Yuan, who received his PhD from the London School of Economics and who was the dean of humanities at Wuhan. Bell visited Acton in Beijing and described him as "very chi-chi and homo, but high culture to the hilt."[99] Bell described Beijing as "the nicest town in the world: the only great capital besides Paris—full of queers."[100]

The heterosexual Bell regarded Chinese men as an "inferior race" and wrote, "An intelligent Tamerlane would introduce mass castration into this country and cross the women with Nordic and Aryan stocks—you might get something good. Certainly there's a much higher average of looks than the Western women."[101] The pervasiveness of this sort of racist thinking is shown by the fact that Bell was very far from being a Fascist rightist. He was a second-generation member of the wildly unconventional and politically leftist Bloomsbury Group who died in July 1937 serving a leftist cause as an ambulance driver in the Spanish Civil War.

Acton had a very different view of Chinese men. He found young Chinese men sexually exciting. Opposite physical types often attract, and this seems to have been a driving force in Acton's attraction to Chinese men. In contrast to his physical bulkiness, their bodies and penises were exquisitely delicate, and their skin was silken.[102] Moreover the widespread poverty and sexual tolerance in China made such young men readily available to a wealthy and charismatic foreigner like Acton. While the love of his life (Parsons) may have been "tall, fair and nordically handsome," Acton had sophisticated sexual tastes that included other types of men, and this may be one reason why he chose to live most of his life in places (China and Italy) where such fair types did not predominate.

In Beijing, Acton lived an openly homosexual life that would have been impossible in Europe. In regard to the Chinese, the racial attitudes of Bell and Acton reflected their different sexuality. Bell's love affair with Ling Shuhua modified his racist views toward the Chinese in regard to women, but not to Chinese men. In contrast, Acton's same-sex attraction to Chinese men led not to one passionate affair, but to sexual liaisons with numerous Chinese men, as well as more long-lasting and substantive friendships with other Chinese, like the scholar Chen Shixiang. While class prejudices taint Acton's memoirs, there is very little racism. In experiencing the sensual delights of China, he also indulged in the ecstasy of opium and became a careful smoker—a habit that he continued periodically for the rest of his life.

Acton's interest in the classical drama of China had a homoerotic component. He was particularly fascinated with the tradition of *dan* actors who played female characters. He believed that the role of heroine was best played by males who created an illusion of ultrafemininity, which he called "a genuine triumph of art over nature."[103] Foreigners had to develop an appreciation for it because the shrill music that accompanied the falsetto singing of the actors offended the uncultivated ears of non-Chinese. Desmond Parsons had been one of Acton's few friends who did not shrink from attending.

When Acton had first arrived in Beijing in 1932, and before he found his own house, he stayed at Tom Handforth's house on Ganyu *hutong*. Handforth (1897–1948) was a talented (apparently homosexual) American artist who was living in Beijing on a Guggenheim fellowship.[104] His most famous work is *Mei Li* (1938), a beautifully illustrated story of a little girl who sneaks away from home to follow her older brother to a Chinese New Year's celebration in the walled city (figure 5.2). The story was based on Handforth's personal experiences in China. It won the Caldecott prize for children's literature in 1939. Handforth's house was a gathering place for artistic Americans, and Acton met several who surprised him with the depth of their understanding of Chinese art.

Figure 5.2. Title page from the award-winning illustrated children's book by Thomas Handforth entitled *Mei Li*. Copyright © 1938 by Doubleday, a division of Random House, Inc. Used by permission of Doubleday, a division of Random House, Inc. Handforth lived in Beijing in the 1930s and was part of the circle of homosexual aesthetes that included Harold Acton and Laurence Sickman.

The name-dropping, narrative style of Acton's memoirs obscures the fact that he had a keen artistic sensibility. The two Chinese painters he knew happened to be among the outstanding artists of that period. One was a Manchu of imperial blood whom Acton refers to as Prince Puru (Pu Xinyu) (1896–1963).[105] When the Guangxu emperor died in 1908, Puru was one of the candidates for the throne, but his cousin Puyi was chosen instead. Puru lived in a crumbling old palace that had once belonged to the Qianlong emperor's notoriously corrupt prime minister, He Shen (1750–1799). Yet Acton saw a charm and dignity in the flaking paint and weed-choked tiles of this palace of Prince Gong (Gong Wang Fu). He described how every spring Puru opened his palace with a social event, inviting the tottering survivors of the Qing dynasty, with their queues and long fingernails. Even the aging palace eunuchs attended. Puru was a landscape painter in the tradition of the Song dynasty painters, such as Li Longmian (1046–1106). For a time, Acton was a pupil of the prince, and he was able to watch how he painted. Seated at a table with the loose paper or silk before him, he moved the brush spontaneously as the vertical scene was transferred to paper without hesitation.

The second painter Acton knew was Qi Baishi (Ch'i Pai-shih) (1863–1957), whom some regard as the greatest artist of twentieth-century China. Unlike the princely Puru, Qi was born to peasants in Hunan. As a child, he was sickly and frail and was forced to drop out of school.[106] He became a carpenter, but finally at the age of twenty-seven he was able to study painting with a qualified teacher. Civil disturbances caused him to move to Beijing in 1917, which is where Acton encountered him. When Julian Bell and his mistress Ling Shuhua, whom he called Sue, visited Beijing in January 1936, they met and became friends with Harold Acton. Ling Shuhua found Acton very amiable and admired his good taste in literature and painting.[107] So she invited him to come along when she and Bell visited the painter Qi Baishi and bought paintings.[108] Qi lived a very simple life in a back-alley house in the western part of Beijing. Acton spoke of having to pass through several wild-looking urchins, probably Qi's children by his concubine, who cluttered the doorstep.

Qi's unique style was based on the early Qing dynasty painters Zhu Da (Ba Da Shan Ren) (1626–1705) and Shi Tao (Tao Qi) (1630–1707). Whereas Pu Ru specialized in landscapes, Qi painted fish and flora, such as crabs, shrimps, lotuses, and persimmons, in a very distinctive style. He is said to have painted more than ten thousand paintings in his lifetime, though he was widely imitated, and perhaps half the pictures ascribed to him are fakes. His pupils sold their works, ascribing them to their teacher. Sometimes Qi would even sign their works for them. He was too eccentric to be regarded as a man of culture, and his works were not held in high esteem by Chinese collectors. Nevertheless, his works were more famous in Europe than those of Pu Ru.

As the Japanese occupied Beijing and inflicted suffering on the populace, Acton was impressed by the prominent Chinese who did not flee but worked in the hospitals and cared for the needy. One of these was Madame Lo Chang (Kang Tongbi), the daughter of the famous Confucian reformer Kang Yuwei (1858–1927). She cared for the old and the sick and tried to raise the spirits of Acton and others with her paintings of birds and blossoms. In 1939 she made a painting of Acton in which he is portrayed as a Buddhist *luohan* in search of enlightenment (figure 5.3). Luohans (lohans) are Buddhist saints who are said to have been enlightened and charged with saving the world. They often combine Buddhist insight with physical ugliness. Usually spoken of as eighteen in number, they are sometimes increased to five hundred. Although the luohan was Hinayana in origin (in Sanskrit, *arhat*), it was expanded by Mahayana influence in China where it incorporated elements of the mountain-dwelling Daoist immortals.[109]

The vertical scroll painted by Madame Lo Chang contains a clearly identifiable picture of Acton wearing the robes of a Buddhist monk and seated in a lotus position under a pine tree, a stock image of Daoism in Chinese landscape paintings. Acton's bald-headedness echoed the luohans, who were also portrayed as bald, commonly with shaved heads. The scroll also contains an inscription in the form of a *zan*. This is an ancient verse form consisting of four characters per line and commonly inscribed on the portraits of great men, particularly on those who could be characterized as luohans. It reads,

> To a man learned in both East and West,
> the world calls you a venerable poet.
> Using both spirit and resonance,
> your poetry rises to the level of Qu Yuan[110] and the *Book of Odes*.
> A follower of both Jesus and the Buddha,
> you harmonize their different teachings in yourself.
> Real and illusory phenomena,
> are grasped in your mind.
> As one of the enlightened Five-hundred Luohans,
> that is how the world should view you.

The inscription contains very conventional phrases and is not great poetry, but it does represent a very literate honor paid to Acton and shows the status in which he was held. He was the Confucian "friend from afar" whose knowledge was respected by the Chinese.

In 1939 the Japanese occupation forced Acton to depart China in such haste that he had to leave his Chinese art collection behind. Without Acton's knowledge, Laurence Sickman crated and shipped Acton's collection to the United States, thereby saving it from probable dispersal or destruction. Acton first learned of this in 1954 when he visited Sickman

Figure 5.3. Portrait of Harold Acton as a Buddhist *luohan* (arhat), by Kang Tongbi (Madame Lo Chang), 1939, frontispiece of Harold Acton's *Memoir of an Aesthete*.

in Kansas City and was moved to see his best pieces again, especially the Tang horse with its "lush Devonshire cream color" (figure 5.4).[111] When Acton first learned about this, he was angry, but his anger apparently dissipated because all the comments about Sickman in his memoirs are very positive. He allowed the pieces to remain in the Nelson-Atkins Museum because he felt they would be out of place among his father's collection at La Pietra. After leaving China in 1939, Acton returned to London and pulled strings with his many prominent contacts in Britain to be accepted as an officer in the Royal Air Force in May 1941. He was ecstatic and was assigned to the Intelligence Service. He wrote about his feelings in the second volume of his memoirs:

> Absurd as it may sound in retrospect, I had a sense of vocation that was almost mystical: I could almost compare my experience to Joan of Arc's voices. In my case the voices urged me to Chungking as, if even in a humble capacity, I could clear the air of suspicion and mistrust that seemed to clog our relations with the Chinese. In China I was certain to justify myself in the struggle against the *samurai*. And the R.A.F. would enable me to reach my goal.[112]

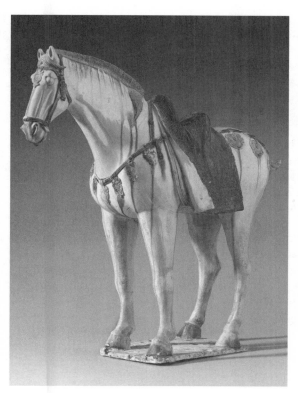

Figure 5.4. *Figure of a Horse*, Tang Dynasty (618–906). Earthenware with lead glazes, 29½ × 33 × 11¾ inches (74.9 × 83.8 × 29.8 cm). The Nelson-Atkins Museum of Art, Kansas City, Missouri. Purchase: William Rockhill Nelson Trust, 51–52. Photo credit: John Lamberton. This piece was possibly part of Harold Acton's personal collection that he left behind in Beijing when he departed in 1939 and which was later shipped, without Acton's knowledge, to Kansas City by Laurence Sickman.

However, reality caught up with Acton, and he never made it to the Nationalist wartime capital, Chongqing (Chungking). He was sent to an obscure post near Calcutta called Barrackpore where his waiting and frustration grew. He was not assigned important duties, and he began to feel a sense of distrust from his superiors. Then "by chance" he came across a file written anonymously by an embassy official, which Acton referred to as a "gross libel" on his character.[113] This would prevent him from being allowed to serve in China. The "gross libel" consisted of a report on his homosexual activities in Beijing.[114] Acton never got over this "malicious slander" and brought it up (without mentioning details) in the introduction to his second volume of memoirs.[115] He felt that his friendship with numerous Chinese gave him a certain credibility that would have enabled him to contribute to the war effort. With a sense of entitlement and privilege, Acton believed that his fate during the war made him comparable to one of "Senator McCarthy's victims."

Acton was never able to return to Beijing. Peace did not come to China after the Pacific War ended. Civil War between the Nationalists and Communists followed in 1945 and ended in 1949 with the Communist victory. Foreigners were no longer welcome to live in Beijing in the prewar style. Many upper-class Chinese, including the painter Puru, fled to Taiwan. Aesthetes tend to be oblivious to politics, and Acton was no exception. The magnetic force of Beijing's beauty was dismantled by a revolution that glorified the practical values of peasants and workers. It was no longer fertile ground for an aesthete. After leaving China, Acton returned to La Pietra and spent more of his time in Naples. Naples was the old family home of the Actons, and he devoted himself to writing histories of the Bourbon rulers there.[116]

While Naples replaced Beijing as the object of Acton's attention, he never lost his interest in Chinese drama. Before leaving China, he had collaborated with L. C. Arlington in editing and translating a book entitled *Famous Chinese Plays* that was published by the famous French publisher Henri Vetch in Beiping in 1937.[117] Acton had a particular interest in the earlier *kunqu* form of musical drama which had dominated the Chinese stage from the mid-sixteenth to the early nineteenth century, peaking during the reigns of the Kangxi emperor (1662–1722) and the Qianlong emperor (1736–1796).[118] The *kunqu* dramas excelled at presenting romances. The singers and other instruments followed the lead of the main accompanying instrument, which was a long, horizontal bamboo flute. The melodic low buzz of this instrument contrasted with the shriller string and percussion instruments of the later Peking Opera. *Kunqu* drama emerged in the late Ming dynasty at Suzhou. During that time, actors and singers flocked to Suzhou, which was a center of both commercial prosperity and fashion. However, its culture was largely destroyed in 1853 by the Taiping Rebellion.[119]

VIRGIL AND AN UNFINISHED POEM

With the Communist victory and the flight of the Nationalist government to Taiwan in 1949, U.S.-China relations entered into a difficult period. The Cold War and American support for the Nationalists as allies against the Chinese Communist government led to a thirty-year diplomatic break. The hostility was intensified in 1950 by the Korean War in which Communist Chinese forces entered the battlefield to stave off a feared American invasion. Mao Zedong's son was killed in the fighting.[120]The ideological peak of the hostility came with the Vietnam War and the Chinese Cultural Revolution that began in 1966. A thaw began with President Nixon's visit to China in 1972, and diplomatic relations were finally reestablished in 1979.

During this thirty-year period, American visitors, scholars, and students were excluded from the Chinese mainland and were largely limited to Hong Kong and Taiwan. Nevertheless, the study of the Chinese language, history, and culture continued in foreign academic institutions. China research was able to proceed using the valuable collections of Chinese books that had been amassed in foreign libraries and the collections of art objects and historical artifacts in museums, such as the Nelson-Atkins Museum in Kansas City.

Harvard University was one of the leading institutions in this study as John King Fairbank became the doyen of China historians in the United States. However, very few homosexual China scholars have been identified at Harvard, even though same-sex attraction there has been the subject of more than one book. *Harvard's Secret Court* is a tragic account of the campus purge of homosexuals in 1920.[121] A more positive treatment of the subject is *The Crimson Letter: Harvard, Homosexuality, and the Shaping of American Culture*, although its author, Douglas Shand-Tucci, is unaware of any gay China scholars at Harvard.[122] The China art historian Laurence Sickman attended Harvard as an undergraduate from 1928 to 1930 but was deeply closeted. A gay scholar who obtained his doctorate in history and East Asian languages at Harvard in the early 1980s initially responded with enthusiasm to my query about gay China scholars at Harvard by writing that he "would be happy to work with [me] on this project," but after thinking about it, he fell silent. Perhaps closeted fear lingers in the air at Harvard.

Nevertheless, the Harvard China scholar Glen William Baxter was surprisingly open about his sexuality during the homophobic period of the sixties and seventies. He is remembered as a genial associate director of the Harvard-Yenching Institute. Because the directorship is a part-time position that frequently rotates, Baxter as the assistant and associate director became the face of the institute during his twenty-five years of service. He was born in Sherman, Texas, in 1914 and graduated from Stanford in 1947 at the age of thirty-three, possibly delayed by military service in World War II. He studied in the Far Eastern Languages Department at Harvard, completing his MA in 1949 and his doctorate in 1952. His dissertation was a study of the first anthology of *ci* (lyrics).[123] *Ci* were lyrics set to musical tunes and constituted one of the main poetic genres of the Chinese. It was an obscure topic, even by academic standards.

Baxter's entire career in the China field was linked to Harvard. He, like Laurence Sickman two decades before him, was awarded a Harvard-Yenching Institute traveling fellowship from 1952 to 1954. The limited research that he did concentrated on the history and literature of the Three Kingdoms period (220–265) and the Tang dynasty (618–907). He collaborated with two other scholars by editing a translation of ten chapters from Sima Qian's annalistic history *Zizhi tongjian* (Comprehensive Mirror to Aid Government) (1067–1084).[124] Although he was for a time a lecturer in East Asian Studies from 1956 to 1961, he did relatively little research and teaching, preferring administrative work instead. He was the assistant director of the Harvard-Yenching Institute from 1956 to 1961, the acting director from 1961 to 1964, and the associate director from 1964 to 1980. During these years he was also a member of the editorial board of the *Harvard Journal of Asiatic Studies*.

Those who knew him describe him as personable and helpful. He delighted in telling good-natured anecdotes about his colleagues. One of his favorites was about an anti–Vietnam War demonstration. When stone-throwing protesters marched up Divinity Avenue in search of the Center for International Affairs, the Harvard-Yenching Institute director became so afraid that the protesters might break the institute windows by mistake that he briefly considered planting a sign on the front lawn pointing the way to the center. Baxter was also a gay man of some courage. In an age when most homosexuals at Harvard were closeted, Baxter introduced his partner Aki Shimizu to colleagues. Their relationship was well known and respected, and they frequently entertained guests, including colleagues, in their Boston townhouse and at their home in Honolulu. In 1998, Baxter suffered a concussion when he slipped and fell in Boston. After being hospitalized, he fell again and died. A memorial service was held at the Harvard faculty club, and because Baxter was a man with few enemies, his colleagues remember it as a joyous celebration.[125]

AIDS was the great leviathan that crashed open the secrecy of the closeted gay lifestyle. For fifteen years (1980–1995), it not only destroyed the lives of gay men but also stripped away the carefully hidden secrets of their sexuality. On top of fighting a debilitating illness with declining energy, AIDS sufferers were forced to defend their denials. Nevertheless, this illness played out in very different ways in the lives of Howard

Wechsler and Marston Edwin Anderson. They were both gay scholars for whom China played a crucial role in their lives, but there the similarity ends. Wechsler was an ambitious and active personality who tentatively started to come out of the closet after securing tenure, while Anderson was an extremely private person who tried to carry the secret of his sexuality to the grave.

Wechsler was a New York Jewish intellectual who used China as a ladder to climb to recognition and success. Inspired by his academic mentor's blending of academic success, wealth, and gentility, he combined application with a genial personality, rising to professional prominence with the success of his second book. He pursued his sex life with the same forceful drive, but AIDS ended his career at the age of forty-four.

The AIDS plague was a watershed in the development of the gay sensibility. By the time retrovirals were introduced in 1996 and vastly reduced mortality, the catastrophic effects of the disease had fostered a greater assertiveness among gay men and a greater willingness to make public declarations of their same-sex orientation (outing). However, prior to 1996, pervasive homophobia combined with the ominous death sentence imposed by the diagnosis of someone as HIV-positive caused all but the most defiant to hide their illness, and nearly everyone agreed on the advisability of suppressing any reference to AIDS in their obituaries. One could, however, often guess that the cause of death was AIDS when the deceased was a relatively young, unmarried male. Wechsler lived at a time of this secretive mode of public denial, such that his obituary published in the *Journal of Asian Studies* omitted any mention of AIDS.[126] Certainly the authors of the obituary were not only colleagues, but also friends of Wechsler. In omitting the cause of death from his obituary, they were performing what was then seen as an act of kindness. The problem, of course, was that omission of the cause of death perpetuated a pattern of self-loathing that homosexuals had borne for years. Homophobia was felt by not only the enemies of gays but—what was far more destructive—by gays themselves.

Wechsler came from modest origins. He was born into a nonobservant middle-class Jewish family in the Bronx, and he remained close to them. He would later dedicate his first book to his parents, Melvin and Gertrude Wechsler. His climb up the ladder of academic success began humbly at Brooklyn College and then on to Yale where he studied under the eminent China historian Arthur Wright. Wechsler's same-sex desire was not as important in shaping his life as his open personality and drive for success. He was a hard worker and genial. He was extroverted, he liked to talk, and he projected confidence in a likeable way. He specialized in the history of the Tang dynasty (618–907) and had good rapport with students.

Wechsler's entire teaching career was spent at the University of Illinois at Champaign. He first went there in 1969 and by 1984 had been promoted to professor. His first book, *Mirror to the Son of Heaven: Wei Cheng at the Court of T'ang T'ai-tsung* (1974), was met with a mixed reception. His mentor, Arthur Wright, had first suggested the orphan, scholar-official, general, and high-ranking politician Wei Zheng (580–643) as a dissertation topic in 1965, and he later directed Wechsler's dissertation from 1966 to 1970. Wright's contacts probably also played an important role in the book's publication by Yale University Press. However, in 1976, Wright collapsed on a golf course and died, leaving Wechsler without a patron.[127] Undeterred, Wechsler prepared for his second book by studying anthropological theories of ritual. *Offerings of Jade and Silk: Ritual and Symbol in the Legitimation of the T'ang Dynasty* (Yale University Press, 1985) met with a more positive reception than his first book and was praised as both sound and original. Conscious of his debt, he dedicated his second book to his "three *lao-shih*" (teachers), one of whom was Wright. He was doing research for a third book involving a portrait of the T'ang capital of Changan when he fell mortally ill.

Initially Wechsler was cautious about revealing his same-sex attraction. He preferred to socialize with nonacademic types who were gay. But after receiving tenure in 1975, he felt secure enough to come out of the closet a bit and lived with a gay partner named Edward Winslow, who was a furniture refinisher. They moved from an apartment in Urbana and bought a house. In the acknowledgements section of his second book, he made this revealing and affectionate reference to his partner: "Edward F. Winslow humored, consoled, and loved me during the long years of research and writing. His support made all the difference."

Wechsler became a follower of the *est* movement developed by Werner Erhard and attended self-actualization seminars in the San Francisco area, which were taught from 1971 to 1984. Erhard had studied Zen with Alan Watts in the 1960s, and it became the basis for the concept of personal transformation that he developed in the *est* teaching. Wechsler liked to share his *est* insights with friends and colleagues, but he was not aggressive in his proselytizing. He told one friend that he learned from the *est* seminars that one should not focus simply on the end product, but also enjoy the process. It sounds like a lesson that would have special meaning for a hard-working Bronx boy who had come far and was now trying to learn how to slow his hectic pace and enjoy his success. Unfortunately, he didn't realize how little time he had left.

Physically, Wechsler was under six feet, very muscular, and worked out regularly in the gym. He went bald early. He was described by a gay colleague and friend at Illinois as very genial and more experienced in gay life. Wechsler was "a good friend" who was "open and candid about his sexual proclivities." Once they visited San Francisco together and visited a gay bathhouse. The friend said, "Howard was my Virgil for my tour of the gay inferno." Of course, gay bathhouses were the spawning grounds of the gay plague, and Wechsler was not immune.

Wechsler's illness began with flulike symptoms around the end of 1984. Feverishly high temperatures followed. During the last year of his life, he spent a lot of time in the hospital. A core of friends visited him there. He and his partner continued to travel, and they visited his former colleague at his home in Sarasota, Florida. In January of 1985, he traveled to Hawaii, and in August he visited Israel, where he stayed in another colleague's apartment. Later that colleague discovered that Wechsler had AIDS and was alarmed by the possibility of the illness being transmitted to him. (Unfounded rumors about AIDS transmission were rampant in the eighties.) The friend whom Wechsler had guided Virgil-like through the San Francisco bathhouse last heard from him when he called from the hospital so weak that he could barely talk. He died shortly thereafter. His partner inherited their house and died of AIDS two years after Wechsler.

The exact details of Wechsler's suffering are not known, but AIDS inflicted a common core of appalling misery upon many young gay men like Wechsler. Prior to the development of antiretroviral therapy in 1996, the median time of progression from HIV infection to AIDS was nine to ten years, with death following less than one year after developing full-blown AIDS. As the immune system was suppressed by the AIDS virus, the body became vulnerable to opportunistic infections, including the intestinal parasite *Cryptosporidium*, which radically reduces body weight; to blindness caused by the herpes infection cytomegalovirus (CMC); and to cryptococcal pneumonia and cryptococcal meningitis, which were commonly found in AIDS sufferers in the 1980s and which were very painful.

The leading cause of death in terminal AIDS patients at that time was respiratory failure due to *Pneumocystis* pneumonia (PCP). This involved a yeastlike fungus that filled the air sacs of the lungs, causing suffocation. The suffering from AIDS was so devastating and so concentrated in a relatively small segment of society—sexually active young gay men, especially "bottoms" (receptive partners in sexual intercourse)—that a new genre of literature developed to describe this experience. Paul Monette's *Borrowed Time* (1988) and Randy Shilts' *And the Band Played On* (1987) are two of the most notable. Both authors themselves later died of AIDS.

Twenty-five years after Wechsler's death, the trauma of his dying had still not been laid to rest among his colleagues in the History Department at the University of Illinois at Champaign. Although several former colleagues claimed friendship and admiration for Wechsler, photographs of him had disappeared. There were none in the departmental files or in the university archives. One person, the wife of a colleague, was known to possess snapshots of Wechsler, but she refused to share them on the grounds that they had "too many personal associations to be included in a book for the general public."[128]

Marston Edwin Anderson (An Mincheng) not only came from a very different background than Wechsler, but he also had a very different personality. His attempt to remain deeply closeted was the dominating pattern of his entire life, and also explains his flight to Chinese studies. He was born on October 2, 1951, in the upper Midwest to Swedish-American parents, Marbury and Sylvia Anderson. His father was a Lutheran pastor in Minneapolis, and Anderson went to high school in south Minneapolis. He majored in Chinese at the University of Minnesota. He tried to fit into a heterosexual mold and had a daughter out of wedlock in 1972 at the age of twenty-one. However, he never married the child's mother, and he wanted to get away from his old life. This is a common experience of gay men who are unable to come out to their family and friends. They solve the problem by going far away and establishing new lives that have no connection to their former lives. Anderson did this by going two thousand miles away to Berkeley to study a subject—Chinese literature—whose exoticism gave it added appeal. What could be farther away from the blond, Lutheran culture of Minnesota than China?

When Anderson entered graduate school at the University of California at Berkeley, he drew a curtain across his former life. Neither friends nor colleagues knew about the existence of his daughter until she appeared at his memorial service in 1992. It was generally recognized by friends that he was gay, but not because Anderson told them. Today some of his straight friends express dismay that he never came out to them. He seems to have had a very few close gay confidantes, and it was understandably easier for gay men to come out to other gays. Anderson looked Nordic—he was tall, thin, and blond with a wispy moustache and fair complexion. A friend once remarked that Anderson would have easily won a "Max von Sydow look-alike award," in reference to the famous Swedish actor and director. Three fellow Berkeley women students—Suzanne Cahill, Wendy Larson, and Jocelyn (née Nash) Marinescu—who went to China in the same group with Anderson in 1980 on US Academy of Sciences fellowships have remarkably similar memories of him (figure 5.5). They were impressed by his mental powers and exquisite manners but didn't really know him because he never shared details about his personal life. He was a passive personality. Friends remember him as soft-spoken, calm, kind, and approachable, with a sense of humor.

For his master's degree, Anderson studied in the Oriental Languages and Literatures Department, which was still dominated by the philology and traditional Sinology of such eminent scholars as Peter Boodberg

Figure 5.5. Photograph of Marston Anderson with three Berkeley graduate school class-mates in a Guangzhou hotel room, the night before separating for Beijing and Shanghai, late August 1980. Left to right: Marston Anderson, Suzanne Cahill, Jocelyn Nash, and Wendy Larson. Courtesy of Dr. Jocelyn (Nash) Marinescu.

(1903–1972) and Edward H. Schafer (1913–1991). (The department has since been renamed East Asian Languages and Cultures.) His 1978 MA thesis dealt with the fiction of Wu Zuxiang (b. 1908), a socially conscious but non-Marxist writer whose novels of the 1930s and 1940s had been largely neglected by orthodox mainland Chinese critics.[129]

For his doctorate, Anderson transferred to the Comparative Literature Department because he was very attuned to the new literary theories that were then emerging in the academic field. This interest in literary theory is reflected in his dissertation (1985), which dealt with the construction of social reality in modern Chinese literature.[130] He did dissertation research in 1980–1982 at Fudan University in Shanghai on a grant from the Committee for Scholarly Exchange with the People's Republic of China and was able to interview three of the Chinese authors he treated in his book—Ai Wu, Sha Ting, and Wu Zuxiang. Friends remember Anderson visiting in Beijing at the time and worrying about whether he would be safe if he were trying to make contact with the underground gay community.

Anderson's dissertation adviser was Cyril Birch, one of the leading scholars in Chinese literature and an unwitting link to another gay man who was fascinated by China—Harold Acton. Anderson also studied with Misao Miyoshi and others who regarded themselves more as comparativists than

Sinologists. His dissertation became a book in 1990, which gave a new interpretation of realism in Chinese literature from 1900 through the 1930s. Rather than seeing Chinese realism as essentially a cultural transfer from the West to China, Anderson described how realism adjusted to its new cultural and historical context in China. The work received an unusual amount of praise for a first book. It contains a nordically uneffusive dedication to his parents, thanking them for their support and love through "what must have seemed an interminable process of education."[131]

After finishing his doctorate, Anderson taught Chinese language and literature at the University of Tennessee, Knoxville, but his star was rising and he was actively recruited by several senior scholars on behalf of their departments. One friend, while conceding that Anderson's book was the best scholarly monograph to come out of their field in a generation, also wondered if his physical attractiveness had played a role in Yale hiring him. In any case, Anderson went to the Department of East Asian Languages and Literatures at Yale, where he was, in the view of one colleague, "adored" by his students.

His descent was almost as precipitous as his ascent. By 1990, colleagues at an academic conference noted that he had become visibly ill, and some suspected AIDS. A friend recalls seeing him for the last time at a conference in June 1992, where he looked so ill that the news of his death two months later was no surprise. Nevertheless, new medicines for the treatment of AIDS were being developed, and this enabled him to continue teaching until four days before his death. A rumor circulated that Yale had given him tenure on his deathbed in order to secure better benefits for him.

Kang-I Sun Chang was chairing the Department of East Asian Languages and Literatures when Anderson died in the early morning hours of August 23, 1992. She organized a memorial service that took place in Dwight Chapel on campus on October 3. It was at this service that Anderson's twenty-year-old daughter and her mother made their surprise appearance. Sun was very moved by Anderson's death and later wrote a poem, "Final Words," in Chinese which was published in Taiwanese and mainland Chinese journals.[132] The poem was based upon an incident that happened in August 1992. Four days prior to his death, Anderson walked over to the department office to deliver a required Chinese exam for a second-year graduate student. However, after the student took the exam, Anderson was dead, and Professor Sun graded it on his behalf.[133] Tellingly, two of the lines of her poem repeat a lament that characterizes Anderson's entire closeted life. She wrote, "In my memory he is always like an unfinished poem."

6

The Reorientation
of Western Aesthetics

FRENCH HOMOEROTICISM

The establishment of intellectual connections with China and the reorientation of Western aesthetics to include Chinese models were related efforts. These efforts sometimes overlapped in the same individuals, although the more creative-artistic mentalities tended to have less facility in the Chinese language than the scholars. From the late nineteenth century through the early twentieth century, France was the center of Sinological studies in the Western world, with leading scholars like Stanislas Julien (1797–1873), Edouard Chavannes (1865–1918), Paul Pelliot (1878–1945), Henri Maspero (1883–1945), and Marcel Granet (1884–1940).[1] This high tide of scholarship reflected a broader French interest in China and a fascination with what the historian Jonathan Spence called the "cult of the Chinese exotic in France."[2] Spence defined this Chinese exotic as combining four elements: grace and delicacy, sensuality, violent impulses, and an opium-induced longing for something lost. However, Spence omitted any mention of homoeroticism, which was also part of the Chinese exotic in France. French homoeroticism, in fact, played an important role in reorienting Western aesthetics toward China.

During his lifetime, Victor Segalen was an obscure figure, out of step with his own age. He exalted the indigenous Asian and Pacific cultures and condemned the "civilizing" process of Western colonialism that was destroying them. In the years since his death, he has been rediscovered as an apostle of diversity. But like Edmund Backhouse, Segalen is one of the great mystery figures of early twentieth-century Sino-Western history.

Much of the mystery of both men is entangled with their fictionalizing of court life in the last days of the Manchu dynasty. But while Backhouse's fictions were deceptions for personal profit, Segalen's fictions were more imaginative and artistic in blurring the line between fantasy and reality.

Among the different interpretations of Segalen's novel *René Leys*, one school emphasizes his same-sex attraction.[3] The homoeroticism of Victor Segalen was, in part, deeply buried in his personal frustration, but it was also sublimated into an aesthetic form that was blended with Chinese culture. The mystique of repressed same-sex desire was entangled with the erotic elements of the imperial inner court of the Forbidden City in Beijing. Segalen created parallel fantasies in which the untouchable nature of sex with an imperial dowager empress was a mirror image of the untouchable nature of sex with the youthful male character René Leys. Both metaphors faded—the imperial institution dissolved in history, and René Leys died—which was Segalen's figurative way of saying that neither fantasy was nor could be realized, except in the imagination. Given the deeply closeted nature of Segalen's life, it is likely that his same-sex desires remained fantasies that were rarely, if ever, realized.

Segalen was born to an obscure family of teachers in Brest, France, in 1878. He was educated at a Jesuit school and later trained as a naval physician in Bordeaux, but he had strong interests in literature, music, and archeology. His psychological problems first manifested themselves in 1899 and coincided with his infatuation with a young woman, a relationship his mother strongly opposed.[4] In the following year, he had a more serious love affair with another young woman which coincided with a period of severe depression. His relationships with women were fraught with problems. After a long convalescence, he had his first of many experiences with opium.

After completing his training as a naval physician, he embarked in 1902 for Tahiti by way of the United States. In San Francisco he fell so gravely ill with typhoid fever that he was given the last rites. While convalescing, he discovered Chinatown and became entranced with China. He proceeded on to Tahiti where he served as a ship's physician. He later wrote an ethnographic novel, *Les Immémoriaux* (1907), lamenting how European influence was destroying native Tahitian culture. During his long journey back to France in 1905, he was initiated into Buddhism in Ceylon (Sri Lanka). He was so deeply influenced that he tried to interest Claude Debussy in collaborating on an opera inspired by the life of the historical Buddha Sakyamuni. Debussy instead proposed an opera about Orpheus on which they collaborated in producing a libretto *Orphée-Roi* (1921). Segalen was attracted to the poetry of Arthur Rimbaud (1854–1891), an artistic radical who openly celebrated homosexuality in his relationship with the married and older Paul Verlaine. Meanwhile Segalen became engaged and married the daughter of a physician. In 1908 he began studying Chinese at the Collège de France in Paris with the noted Sinologist Edouard Chavannes and went to China the following year. In China he made a long journey from Beijing to the southwest, traversing the provinces of Shanxi and Shaanxi to Sichuan and then sailing down the Yangtze River.

In June 1910 in Beijing, Segalen met Maurice Roy, the young man around whom he would construct the literary character of René Leys. At the time, Roy was nineteen years old, the son of the director of the French postal service in Beijing. As Roy related his incredible tales of intimate relationships, which extended into the Manchu imperial family, Segalen became infatuated. From June 1910 to October 1911 he compiled a secret account of his relations with Roy entitled "Annales secretes d'après Maurice Roy." Segalen saved these pages from his private diary before destroying the rest of it in December 1918, several months before his death.[5] Also during this period in Beijing, Segalen began writing his *Stèles*, a collection of creative prose-poems based on ancient Chinese stone monuments.[6] This work was first published in Beijing in 1912, the same year in which Segalen was appointed personal physician to the son of the military strongman Yuan Shikai.

After a brief visit to France in 1913, Segalen began work on the first version of the novel *René Leys*. In the spring of 1914, he interrupted work on the manuscript to participate in the excavation of the tomb of Madam Bao Sanniang in Sichuan province (figure 6.1). With the outbreak of World War I, he returned to France. In 1915 he was hospitalized with acute gastritis, a condition often related to emotional stress. He worked on the second version of *René Leys*, which he finished in 1916. In 1917, when he was named military physician responsible for examining Chinese volunteers who applied to work in the French armament factories, he visited Beijing for the last time. Back in France, his health declined, and shortly after World War I ended, he was hospitalized for acute depression. After being released from the hospital, he took a leave of absence and vacationed with his wife. However, one day when he was alone, he went for a walk and never returned. Two days later his body was found in the forest where he had played as a boy, with blood on his heel. The mystery of his death has never been resolved, but his closest friends believed it was a suicide.

In the early twentieth century, it was extremely difficult for any Western author of respectable status to write about male same-sex love in a positive way. Those who did so, like Rimbaud and Verlaine, were bohemian types who rebelled against the conventions of society. André Gide's *Corydon* (1924) was one of the first books by a respectable author that defended homosexuality, portraying it as an identity that went deeper than merely having sex with other men.

Figure 6.1. Victor Segalen (1878–1919) (center, with moustache and hand in pocket) at the excavation of the tomb of Madam Bao Sanniang, Sichuan province, April 1914. Photograph by Jean Lartigue. Musee des Arts Asiatiques-Guimet, Paris, France. © Reunion des Musees Nationaux / Art Resource, New York. The other European dressed in black is Augusto Gilbert de Voisins, and the Chinese official is the subprefect of Zhaohuaxian. Segelan interrupted the writing of his novel *René Leys* to participate in this excavation.

In this repressive cultural atmosphere, someone like Segalen was forced to express his same-sex feelings in sublimated ways. Segalen was no social rebel. He made the thoroughly bourgeois choices of becoming a naval physician and marrying a woman. Forcing himself into these conventional roles seems to have contributed to his psychological problems and led ultimately to his early death at the age of forty-one. He escaped from his unhappiness by going to China. China was an escape—a Land of Oz—not only because it was remote and exotic, but also because it provided the ingredients which his imagination transformed into an inspired work of art called *René Leys*.

Segalen seems to have become emotionally obsessed over Roy. It is the sort of obsession that gay men commonly experience, especially very young or very closeted gay men, and it is often hopelessly directed at a heterosexual male. The obsession simultaneously generated a great deal of emotional attachment and frustration. Because Maurice Roy was heterosexual and unable to return Segalen's love, Segalen re-created Roy as the fictional René Leys. Beijing in the last days of the Manchu dynasty provided the exotic ingredients for this re-creation.

The decline of the once-great Qing dynasty (1644–1911) was reflected in the virility of its emperors. While the great Kangxi emperor (r. 1661–1722) had produced fifty-six children from thirty consorts, the late Qing emperors had difficulty supplying the throne with a single male heir.[7] The Xianfeng emperor (r. 1851–1861) produced two sons (one of whom died in infancy) and one daughter. His successor, the Tongzhi emperor (r. 1862–1875), died without producing a male heir. Unconfirmed rumors circulated that he died of a sexually transmitted disease contracted from his visits to (male?) brothels.[8] The Guangxu emperor (r. 1875–1908) was childless. The infant Puyi, the last Manchu monarch, who ruled from 1908 to 1911, grew to manhood afflicted by impotency with women and homosexual tendencies.[9] He admitted that he had not consummated a sexual relationship with any of his four wives or his concubines.

René Leys is portrayed in Segalen's novel as having an affair with the Empress Dowager Long Yu (Longyu Huangtaihou). She was a daughter of a maternal uncle of the Guangxu (Koung-Siu) emperor and a cousin three years older than the emperor.[10] Guangxu felt no affection for her but was forced to accept her as a wife in 1889 when the Dowager Empress Cixi selected her as someone who could be used to control the emperor after Cixi's retirement. According to the text of *René Leys*, at the end of the imperial wedding ceremonies, the clueless emperor asked a friend what he should do. The friend advised him to climb on top of the empress and let nature take its course. But when the emperor climbed on top of the empress, he fell asleep![11] Because of all the wine he had drunk during the eight to ten days of the marriage ceremony, the emperor "forgot to act," but knowing of the emperor's lack of interest in women, the inability to act is understandable. Leys, by contrast, did act. At the time of Leys' affair with the empress, he is said to have been eighteen while she was between thirty-eight and forty years old.[12] In contrast to the impotency of the emperor, Leys claimed to have conceived a child with the empress that—blessed by supreme Chinese good fortune—was a boy.[13]

Of course, this is not a historical narrative of factual events. Although the characters in the novel are based on historical figures, they are manipulated by Segalen to weave together an imaginative story. Just as the Dowager Empress Long Yu was real, so was the regent, Prince Tch'ouen (Chun Qinwang). His given name was Zaifeng (Tsai-feng), and he was the younger brother of the Guangxu emperor. In 1901 he had led a mission to Berlin to apologize for the Boxer murder of the German ambassador. When his son Puyi was elevated to the throne in 1908, Zaifeng was designated regent (*shezhengwang*).[14] He was completely incapable of dealing with the contending factions of reactionaries, reformers, and revolutionaries, so he presided over the demise of the Qing dynasty.

In telling the story of René Leys, Segalen shows that same-sex feelings are a manifestation of something far deeper than physical desires. Because of this sublimation of sexual desire into something more subtle, the story of René Leys is homoerotic in sensibility rather than explicitly homosexual in action. The aberrant sexuality is disguised by the exoticism. Much of the homoeroticism centers around Leys, who is an object of both physical and emotional attraction. He is described as very good looking.[15] In a bizarre scene, Segalen describes how, after Leys died, he stripped the clothes from the body of the dead youth to make a physical examination. He rhapsodized over the strength and beauty of Ley's body.[16] In fact, time sharpened the difference between fantasy and reality. When Segalen returned to Beijing for the last time in 1917, the Manchus were gone from the throne, and Roy had become a prosperous, well-fed, boring European expatriate who had little contact with the Chinese.[17] He was now an entirely conventional figure who worked in a bank and no longer had any interest in the Manchu imperial family. When Segalen's widow sent him a copy of *René Leys*, he did not even reply.[18] He died a prosaic death in an elevator accident in 1941 in Shanghai.

MOVING THE MUSE OF POETRY FROM EUROPE TO CHINA

In classical Greek antiquity, the poet Homer (ca. ninth century BC) invoked the muse at the beginning of the *Iliad* and the *Odyssey*. Thereafter, Greek poets viewed poetry as being inspired by one of nine muses, who were goddesses of literature and the arts.[19] Over time, a muse evolved into the person or thing that inspired a writer's creative work.

Traditionally, Europe had provided the sources of inspiration for American writers. However, Witter Bynner, unmoved by Europe and losing momentum among the leading American poets, was one of the first American writers to turn to China for inspiration. Bynner's contact with China was stimulated by World War I. He opposed the war and refused to fight in it. He was in a fluid state, looking for answers, when his good friend Arthur Ficke proposed that they make a trip to East Asia.[20] Ficke was trained as an attorney, but he rarely practiced law and was far more interested in writing poetry. He was not homosexual and so was free from any sexual entanglements with Bynner. However, he had a genuine concern for Bynner's welfare. Ficke and Bynner and the poet Edna St. Vincent Millay all shared an emotional attachment to one another that involved a love triangle of sorts. Millay was deeply in love with Ficke and remained lifelong friends with him and his two wives. But while Ficke never proposed marriage to her, Bynner did. However, since Bynner was homosexual and Millay was also inclined toward lesbianism, the marriage proposal was never accepted.

Bynner, along with Ficke, his wife Evelyn, and several other friends, departed from Vancouver on the RMS *Empress of Asia* on March 15, 1917.[21] Evelyn Ficke's attraction to Christian Science, which was then a new religion in vogue among certain educated Americans, reflected the spiritually open and experimental outlook of this group—they were searching. Bynner traveled to Japan, Korea, and then on to Beijing. He expressed his fascination with China in a letter to a friend: "Korea was exciting—but Peking is almost everything. I can't get my breath from the wonder of it. Japan is but bothersome dust in the nostrils of the dragon."[22] In a second letter, he added, "China still stirs me to the depths."[23] In this same letter, Bynner expressed opposition to the entry of the United States into World War I and wrote that his remote location in China enabled him to form a better perspective on the war and "a clearer view of its large aspects and better find my own place." Bynner arrived back in the United States in July of 1918.

That same summer, Bynner decided that he would perform his war service by teaching public speaking to the men in the Students Auxiliary Training Corps at the University of California at Berkeley.[24] He lectured in the open-air Greek theater on campus, and after the armistice of November ended hostilities, he switched in January 1919 to teaching a verse-writing class. He was unconventional in his teaching methods, requiring no texts or tests, meeting outside on the lawn, and allowing the students to smoke. He fostered the development of several poets who later became quite prominent in the California school of literature. At the semester's end, the class honored him by publishing their poems in a book called *Witter Bynner in California* and held a dinner in his honor for eighty people.

Bynner lived in two rooms at the Hotel Carlton, at the corner of Telegraph and Durant Avenues, where he had a "shrine to the mysterious Orient" (figure 6.2). When his unconventional ways led him to serve liquor to freshmen in his hotel rooms, he was reprimanded by the university.[25] It was at this time that Bynner, visiting in New York, met and fell deeply in love with Paul Thévenaz (1891–1921), a Swiss artist-decorator whose open acceptance of his homosexuality left a lasting impression on Bynner.[26] His affair with Thévenaz caused Bynner to accept his own same-sex attraction, a debt that Bynner expressed in his autobiographical poem *Eden Tree* (1931). Bynner was deeply affected by Thévenaz's early death from a ruptured appendix. Four years after his death, he dedicated a poem to him which indicated the depth of his feeling. Bynner was active in the social life of Bay Area artists and was a member of the Bohemian Club, which had been founded in 1872 as a men's club for writers and artists of moderate means. Bynner participated in the club's one-week summer retreat with a thousand men in the Bohemian Grove on the Russian River. However, his selection as the author of the Bohemian Grove play for 1920 was aborted by a California Supreme Court justice and others who vehemently opposed Bynner's signing of a petition to release conscientious objectors from prison.[27]

Figure 6.2. Hotel Carlton, 1912, at the corner of Telegraph and Durant Avenues, Berkeley, California. Berkeley Public Library, Berkeley History Online. This was the residence of both Witter Bynner in 1918–1919 and Princess Der Ling in 1943–1944 when they were teaching at the University of California. Der Ling died while walking from the hotel to teach a Chinese language class and was hit by a grocery truck at the intersection of Telegraph and Bancroft.

It was in 1918 in Berkeley that Bynner met Jiang Kanghu (Kiang Kang-hu) (1883–1954), who was teaching Chinese there. Jiang was not only a scholar, but also a prominent and controversial leader of political reform in early twentieth-century China.

He was born into a scholar-official family in Jiangxi province. Both his grandfather and father were *jinshi* (holders of the highest degree in the traditional examination system) and had served as officials in both Beijing and the provinces.[28] Jiang was a precocious child who mastered the classical composition style at an early age. In 1900 he went to Japan to study Japanese and became a social and political radical who condemned capitalism, proposed the dissolution of the family, promoted women's education, advocated the romanization of the Chinese language, and became a leader of the Chinese Socialist Party. When Yuan Shikai banned the Socialist Party in 1913 because of its radicalism, Jiang fled to the United States where he lived from 1913 to 1920.

Jiang secured the goodwill of the University of California at Berkeley when he contributed thirteen thousand Chinese volumes from his father's library. While he was teaching Chinese at Berkeley, he and Bynner met and began their collaborative project in translating Tang dynasty poems. Jiang returned to China in 1920 (with Bynner), in the wake of the May Fourth Movement of 1919 when it seemed that socialism might receive a more receptive hearing by the reformers. In January 1922, he attended the Congress of Far Eastern Revolutionary Parties in Moscow where he had meetings with Lenin, Trotsky, and other leading Bolsheviks. However, what he saw in Russia convinced him that differences in China required another path, and he abandoned his belief in socialism and began to support democracy. However, his political instincts were less than acute and he was discredited. He eventually abandoned his radical views and gradually adopted the position that any reform of China must be built on a foundation of classical Confucian values.

By 1929, Jiang was back in the United States and then went to Montreal where he headed a new department of Chinese studies at McGill University. But in 1932 he wrote to Bynner that he was thinking of resigning in order to "return to China just to suffer with my people."[29] He once again demonstrated his political naïveté by becoming the minister of education in Wei Jingwei's Chinese puppet government controlled by the Japanese. When the war ended, the Nationalist government imprisoned him as a Japanese collaborator. Bynner's letters on his behalf may have saved him from being executed. When the Communists took control, they kept Wei in jail, where he died on December 6, 1954.

After meeting, Bynner and Jiang began an eleven-year collaboration that would culminate in the publication of *The Jade Mountain* in 1929. On June 22, 1920, they departed together for China. Bynner was accompanied by friends, including the controversial sculptor Beniamino Bufano.[30] In Shanghai, Jiang booked into a separate hotel. The heat was so intense that Bynner, along with Arthur Davison Ficke and his wife, fled for relief to a lake resort near Hangzhou.[31] While the Fickes moved on to the nearby mountain resort of Moganshan (Mokanshan) in search of cooler temperatures, Bynner stayed behind in Hangzhou. One wonders if he wanted to be alone to look for male sexual companions. In any case, he encountered two Chinese college students on the roof of a Hangzhou hotel who knew enough English to help him communicate. These twenty-year-old young men became Bynner's guides in Hangzhou. Bynner was particularly charmed by the elder of the two, named Nie Shizhang (Nieh Shih-chang), and he stayed in Hangzhou until Nie's school vacation ended. However, Nie seems to have joined him again later because elsewhere Bynner refers to Nie as "the young student and friend who piloted me on many trips."[32]

Nie was on the point of becoming a Christian, and Bynner discouraged him "from yielding one jot of his birthright in Confucius, in Buddha, in Laotzu." Bynner was a spiritual syncretist and was critical of how organized Christianity had distorted the original teachings of Jesus. He found something of value in each spiritual teaching, although he had a very superficial understanding of Buddhism and a romanticized understanding of both Confucianism and Daoism. His appreciation of Daoism was closely linked to his love of nature and was based largely on the Tang dynasty poems and the famous work attributed to Laozi, probably a composite figure of the fifth century BC.

Bynner moved on to join the Fickes at Moganshan, where "the holy wonders of this place, this Chinese mountaintop" moved him.[33] Moganshan (Carefree Mountain) was a favorite summer resort at an altitude of two thousand feet, located 30 miles north of Hangzhou and 150 miles west of Shanghai.[34] Elsewhere he described the experience as spending "three months on a Chinese mountaintop, with a poet and his family, in the kind of retirement the old fellows loved and wrote about, overlooking a landscape the like of which I had never seen from any dwelling on earth."[35] Bynner tried unsuccessfully to make contact with Jiang in Shanghai. The hotel where Jiang had planned to stay was already full, and the hotel staff did not forward the mail from Bynner. As a result, the two of them lost touch with one another, and it was not until four months later that they met by chance on a street in Shanghai. Bynner had in the meantime been working on the literal translation of the Tang poems that Jiang had made for him, and they were able to resume their collaboration and go over Bynner's renderings for accuracy.[36]

Bynner later moved on to Beijing where he stayed during the winter of 1920–1921. The second morning at his hotel, Hu Ji (Hu Chi), the "ricksha-boy" from his 1917 visit, was waiting for him at the hotel door.[37] Hu Ji spoke a little English, and when Bynner left Beijing in 1917, Hu had asked for his photograph. During World War I, Hu joined a group of Chinese laborers in France. Bynner was happy to see him, and when he moved into a Chinese house, he elevated Hu Ji from "ricksha-boy" to "house-boy." In Beijing, Bynner consulted various English-speaking Chinese about his translations of the Tang poems. These included eminent figures like Hu Shi, Princess Der Ling, and Gu Hongming (Ku Hung-ming). Bynner even consulted his guide Nie Shizhang, who had acquired enough English from Bynner to discuss such things.[38]

Using a Chinese guide, Bynner traveled widely throughout China, following an itinerary that was unusual for a tourist of that time. He bought scrolls and jade and learned enough to write widely on China in popular journals. The collaborative effort of translating Tang poems was conducted mainly by mail.[39] However, since Jiang was deeply involved in China's political reform from 1920 to 1925, his involvement in the project was probably irregular. Since Bynner did not read Chinese, he depended on Jiang to translate the Chinese poems into literal English. Bynner then transformed them into verse. Bynner's close collaboration with Jiang and his own status as an eminent poet worked well. Relying on Jiang's knowledge, Bynner was able to avoid the exaggeration of the ideographic aspects of Chinese characters which afflicted other translators of Chinese poetry.[40] The most influential expression of this exaggeration was voiced in *The Chinese Written Character as a Medium for Poetry*, composed by Ernest Fenollosa (1853–1908) and edited by Ezra Pound (1885–1972).[41] Bynner and Pound were longtime acquaintances, though not mutual admirers of one another's work, and both shared a minimal knowledge of Chinese, and yet Bynner never fell prey to the ideographic excesses that affected Pound.

The Jade Mountain is a translation of the famous collection *Tangshi sanbaishou* (Three-Hundred Poems of the Tang Dynasty). The Tang dynasty (618–907) was the golden age of Chinese poetry and included the leading poets Du Fu and Li Bo. Over the years the Chinese have produced 130 anthologies of Tang Poetry and of these, *Tangshi sanbaishou* is the most widely read.[42] It was compiled by the scholar-official Sun Zhu and published in 1763 or 1764. Although the different editions vary slightly, the original number of poems was 310.[43]

After receiving Jiang's initial renderings, Bynner repeatedly revised the translations throughout the 1920s, often working "eight to ten hours a day on nothing but these poems."[44] He published 238 of the poems in forty-eight different popular journals.[45] The wide variety of these journals—including *The Nation, The New Republic, The Dial, The North China Herald, The Virginia Quarterly Review*, and *The London Mercury*—indicated the breadth of popular attention that poetry received at that time. The book met with enthusiastic praise upon its publication in 1929, and by 1994 it had been republished in fifteen editions. Although scholars today find the work unsatisfactory, they concede that it may be the best English translation available.[46]

In a review of translations of Chinese literature, the scholar Paul W. Kroll recognized the importance of this work as a source of inspiration by writing, "For me, many years ago, it was Witter Bynner's *The Jade Mountain* whose sometimes impeachable but always moving translations from the *Tangshi sanbaishou* kindled a *Neigung* for Chinese literature that has kept me in pursuit for a lifetime."[47] The eminent translator Burton Watson praises the collaborative effort of Bynner and Jiang, noting that in the rendering of poetry, "splendid translations have been produced through collaboration, and countless dreadful ones by individuals who could read the original language to perfection."[48]

The significance of *The Jade Mountain* in American culture lies in its role as a harbinger of the reorientation from exclusively Eurocentric literary models to include Chinese works as sources of inspiration. Bynner clearly anticipated American multiculturalism when he wrote in his introduction, "I predict that future Western poets will go to school with the masters of the T'ang dynasty, as well as with the masters of the gold age of Greece, or with the Hebrew prophets, or with the English dramatists or romanticists."[49]

Bynner's second effort to translate a Chinese book was less successful than *The Jade Mountain*. Bynner was a poet, and in transforming Jiang's literal translations into verse, he was in his element. So long as his limited knowledge of Daoism formed the background to his translations, the translation was not appreciably diminished; however when Bynner turned to the translation of a philosophical work, the limits of his knowledge of Daoism became much more obvious. Although Bynner undertook both *The Jade Mountain* and *The Way of Life According to Laotzu* in wartime (World War I and World War II, respectively), his motives for undertaking them differed. The first he began in 1918 at the age of thirty-seven for artistic reasons, while the second was begun in 1943 out of a very different motivation. The United States was at war with Japan, which was inflicting enormous suffering on the Chinese. Gone was the pacifism that had so dominated Bynner's attitude toward the American entry into World War I. During 1942, Bynner had served as the New Mexico state chairman of the United China Relief effort. His frustration in this project led him to undertake a translation of Laozi's *Daode jing* in order to be of "more service to China."[50]

Bynner's choice of Laozi's work to translate was unfortunate. Whereas the poems in *The Jade Mountain* were not well known to the West, the *Daode jing*'s famously mystical lines have attracted more translators than any other Chinese classic. There have been over forty English translations, nine German translations, and renderings into numerous other languages.[51] The mystical ambiguity of its lines has become a magnet for Daoist enthusiasts, each trying to improve upon the other's translation. Bynner himself was reacting to the translation effort of the popular philosopher Lin Yutang, which he described as "feeble."[52] Whereas Bynner had worked for eleven years in collaboration with a Chinese scholar in producing *The Jade Mountain*, he produced his translation of Laozi in only one year while working alone.

Bynner's longtime publisher, Alfred A. Knopf, rejected *The Way of Life According to Laotzu*; however Bynner found a more receptive publisher in Richard Walsh Jr. at John Day Company. Walsh and his wife, Pearl S. Buck, who won the Novel Prize for Literature in 1938 for her depictions of Chinese peasants, were enthusiastic over Bynner's translation.[53] The book's appearance in 1944 was timely and met with initial success, selling out the first printing in three weeks and eventually selling over fifty thousand copies.[54] It surpassed *The Jade Mountain* in sales, but not in critical reception or staying power. While Bynner's translation was well received in the popular press, with complimentary reviews in the *New York Herald Tribune* and the *New York Times*, it was criticized by academics. One scathing review by the Sinologist Homer H. Dubs mocked Bynner's admission that he could not read Chinese and noted that, unlike with *The Jade Mountain*, he had no assistance from a Chinese scholar such as Jiang Kanghu.[55] One of the kinder academic assessments was provided by the China scholar Wm. Theodore de Bary, who called Bynner's work "more a stimulating poetic interpretation than a translation."[56]

In 1920 in China, Bynner wrote to a friend in the United States, saying that his intention was eventually to settle in Berkeley, but that never happened.[57] After returning from China, he wandered about the United States on a lecture tour; but ill health plagued him and he finally settled in Santa Fe, New Mexico, in 1922, with a vacation home in Chapala, Mexico, and that is where he spent most of the last forty-seven years of his life. When his mother died in 1937, she left him a considerable inheritance, but he continued to live modestly. A number of literary figures, including D. H. Lawrence and his wife Frieda, visited him in Santa Fe. He had a series of male secretaries who were also lovers. Although he lived discreetly, he was accused by one former friend of introducing homosexuality to New Mexico.[58] From 1930 until 1964, he lived together as partners with Robert Hunt, who was twenty-five years younger than he was. Bynner's health began to deteriorate after 1945, eventually causing almost total blindness. In 1965, one year after Hunt's death, he suffered a debilitating stroke and died three and a half years later.

MOVING THE MUSE OF POPULAR VERSE
AND DRAMA FROM EUROPE TO CHINA

The movement of the muse from Europe to China appeared not only in the work of the American poet Bynner, but also in the German aesthete-popularizer Vincenz Hundhausen (Hong Taosheng). Hundhausen's attraction to China was both homoerotic and explicitly homosexual. He lived in China for thirty-one years (1923–1954), composing and staging adaptations of classical Chinese dramas for Germans, who constituted one of the largest expatriate groups in China. Unlike most foreign residents in China, he remained after the Communist takeover until he was expelled, possibly because of the Communist government's homophobia.

Hundhausen was born in Grevenbroich (near Cologne) in 1878 into a successful middle-class Christian family. His maternal grandfather, Vincenz von Zuccalmaglio (1806–1876), was a jurist and author who used the pseudonym Montanus.[59] His father, Friedrich Hermann Hundhausen (1842–1883), was a factory owner. Hundhausen studied law at several German universities. During World War I he served as a captain in the reserves, and after the war he worked as an attorney and notary in Berlin. In 1923 he used the opportunity of being a court-appointed executor of a large estate to immigrate to China.

Hundhausen began studying Chinese literature and philosophy and became enthused over serving as a literary intermediary in an East-West cultural exchange. With the liquidation of his law practice in Berlin and the sale of his literary works, Hundhausen had the financial means to live independently in China. With his friend Wang Yo Deh, he acquired a small island in a lake opposite the Zhangyimen (Gate of Splendid Ceremonials) just outside the southwest side of the Beijing city wall (map 1). The site was probably Qingnian hu (Youth Lake) on contemporary maps of Beijing.[60] The area was said to have once been a pleasure garden of earlier emperors, but the buildings had fallen into disrepair. The Chinese called it the Lotus Pond, but Hundhausen renamed it "Nan He Pao Tse" (*Nanhai baize*) or "Pappelinsel" (Poplar Island) after the poplar trees that grew around it.[61] Over the one-floor Chinese-style building, Hundhausen built a second floor. After climbing a narrow, steep, and dark staircase, one entered two small rooms overflowing with what would eventually become a twelve-thousand-volume library.[62] A brewery occupied a neighboring plot of land.

Visitors to the Lotus Pond sometimes encountered this large, strongly built man wearing a loincloth and an old straw hat, standing on a flat dingy and clearing the overgrowth of water plants from the pond's surface. Hundhausen prided himself on his self-sufficiency that created ersatz coffee from the starchy kernels of burned lotus fruit growing on the pond. But he had a compassionate side as well. On his desk he kept a statue of Guanyin, the bodhisattva whose special concern was mercy and human suffering. The diplomat Walter Fuchs recalled how Hundhausen used to gaze upon it during conversations.[63] During the 1930s, Harold Acton was often invited to the outings at the Lotus Pond, where copious amounts of sausages and lager were served. He left this condescending portrait of Hundhausen:

> I think he pictured himself as a Chinese sage, but nobody could mistake his real nationality, for he was a robust and rubicund man of fifty with goggles, close-cropped hair, a white moustache and a big paunch, who welcomed you with loud *heils* of Heidelberg heartiness.[64]

In his memoirs, Acton drew on his contacts with numerous prominent people in the arts to describe their traits and idiosyncrasies in a light and humorous manner. If he liked someone, like the art historian Laurence Sickman, the anecdotes were serious and complimentary. If he disliked someone, like the art curator Alan Priest, the anecdotes had an edge. Acton's attitude toward Hundhausen seems to have been complicated by the fact that the two of them were competing cultural intermediaries between China and the West. Consequently, Acton tried to diminish Hundhausen by portraying him as a comical figure who guffawed in *gemütlich* fashion, drank lager in his shirtsleeves, and threw Lotus Lake gatherings at which Acton was "touched by the more jovial aspects of German *Kultur*." Acton mocks Hundhausen's Chinese poetry recitals by describing the reactions of prominent Chinese intellectuals:

> When he recited his translations of Li Po and Tu Fu it was like a Gothic tempest: he would bawl them against a crashing accompaniment of modernistic music. Nothing could have sounded more remote from the Chinese, and I noticed that V. K. Ting and Hu Shih, the most diplomatic of scholars, were struggling with all their might to check their laughter.[65]

Acton's mockery underscores the reality that while Hundhausen was actually engaged in artistic creativity, Acton played the much safer role of an elitist observer-critic.

In the division between elite and popular culture, Hundhausen clearly belonged to the popularizers. Richard Wilhelm (1873–1930), by contrast, belonged to the elite Sinological culture. Wilhelm first went to Qingdao in 1899, in the German sphere of interest in China, as a Protestant missionary. He took a serious interest in Chinese culture and developed into a Sinologist with a spiritualist bent. From 1921 until 1924, he was a professor of German literature at Beijing University (Beida) and a member of the scholarly advisory committee of the German embassy.[66] Wilhelm knew

Hundhausen and gently punned on his reputation as *"Der Trumpeter von Pekingen"* (the trumpeter from Peking).[67] This was an allusion to the famous novel *Der Trompeter von Säckingen* by Joseph Viktor von Scheffel.[68]

Now largely forgotten, *The Trompeter from Säckingen* was one of the most popular books of late nineteenth-century Germany. First published in 1854, by 1921 it had been reprinted 322 times.[69] This epic poem in unrhymed trochaic verse was set in the late seventeenth-century Black Forest region. It tells a simple story of a young man skilled in trumpet playing who discontinues his studies at the University of Heidelberg and falls in love with a woman whose noble status is an obstacle to marriage. Finally, when the pope ennobles him, the young man is able to consummate his love in matrimony. The poem's humor and sympathetic portrayal of the people of the Upper Rhine River region made it a favorite of the German middle classes. It was part of the *völkisch* (folk) ideology and *Heimatkunst* (domestic art) aesthetic of the conservative forces flourishing in Germany around 1900.[70] In referring to Hundhausen as "the Trumpeter of Peking," Wilhelm was implying that his work in China duplicated the spiritual tone of the middle-class, sentimental culture then thriving in Germany.

Acton and Hundhausen both were interested in the arts, although Acton's interests leaned toward classical drama and the visual arts while Hundhausen's focused more on poetry and popular drama. But Acton was like a literary meteor who burned brightest in his youth at Eton and Oxford, while Hundhausen's achievements grew as he aged. Hundhausen had far more energy and drive than Acton, and the results were more prolific. Acton's youthful gay indiscretions gave way to a tightly closeted maturity, while Hundhausen's same-sex activities were public knowledge in Beijing. Likewise in politics, while Acton was no lover of Mussolini's fascism, he avoided public criticism, unlike Hundhausen, whose criticism of Hitler's fascism was well known. Consequently, while Acton sailed through life largely unscathed by his politics or his sexuality, Hundhausen paid a price for his openness.

In 1924, Hundhausen was invited to teach German literature at Beijing University (Beida). He was well liked by his colleagues and students, one of whom became the well-known poet Feng Zhi (Feng Chih) (1906–1993). After graduating with a degree from the German Department at Beida in 1928, Feng traveled to Germany where he studied at the University of Berlin from 1930 to 1935, earning a doctorate.[71] He translated Rainer Maria Rilke's *Briefe an den jungen Dichter* (Letters to a Young Poet) into Chinese. After returning to China, he served as a member of the German Department at Beida from 1935 to 1938, when the Sino-Japanese War interrupted his career. After the war, Feng became a dedicated Communist and repudiated his earlier translations.

Unlike the large expatriate community in Beijing, Hundhausen moved increasingly in mixed European-Chinese circles. His translation work involved more than 120 Chinese texts (mostly poems) in the 1920s.[72] He was best known for his adaptations (*Nachdichtungen*) of Chinese poems and dramas. Although his knowledge of Chinese was quite limited, he collaborated with Chinese translators in transforming Chinese texts into German works of literary quality. His collaborators produced literal translations from Chinese into German, while Hundhausen transformed their translations into poetry.

Witter Bynner, whose knowledge of Chinese was also limited, had engaged in a similar type of collaboration with the Chinese translator Jiang Kanghu.[73] However, Bynner's translations inclined toward literate audiences, while Hundhausen's were more popular in appeal. In 1926, Hundhausen produced an adaptation of the musical drama *Xixiang ji* (The West Chamber Story), which he attributed to an unknown scholar of the Ming period (1368–1644). Recent scholarship attributes probable authorship to the thirteenth-century dramatist Wang Shihfu.[74] Hundhausen adapted this into *Das Westzimmer. Ein chinesisches Singspiel in deutscher Sprache* (The West Room: A Chinese Operetta in German). In 1930 he followed up with *Die Laute von Gau Ming* (The Flute by Gao Ming), an adaptation of the famous musical drama *Pipa ji* (The Lute) by Gao Ming (ca. 1305–1370).[75] Hundhausen's adaptation emphasized the strict adherence of Gao Ming to Confucian traditionalism.[76]

The appearance of *Das Westzimmer* provoked a famous legal battle. The reviewers' enthusiastic praise for Hundhausen's intuitive poetic adaptation of the *Das Westzimmer* aroused critical reactions from German Sinologists who noted Hundhausen's deficiencies as an amateur Sinologist. The most serious of these was written by the Bonn Sinologist Erich Schmitt (1893–1955), who accused Hundhausen of plagiarizing the French translation of *Xixiang ji* by the French Sinologist Stanislaus Julien.[77] Hundhausen responded as an attorney (which he was) rather than as a scholar by filing suit in court against Schmitt.

Critical reactions to *Das Westzimmer* divided largely on whether one's main interests were scholarly or literary and whether the emphasis was upon the translation's accuracy (a philological concern) or the artistic quality (an aesthetic concern). Those with literary concerns argued that Hundhausen's adaptation was different in nature from earlier translation efforts like those of Julien and should be appreciated as a work of art in German. One enthusiastic reviewer wrote, "This is the first time that poetry in the Chinese language has been rendered into poetry in some foreign language."[78] The reviewer argued that Hundhausen was not a Sinologue and should not be evaluated as one. Rather, he was a poet, whose talent was to adapt the poetry of Chinese culture into German.

The Sinological perspective on the dispute was presented by Erich Haenisch (1880–1966), a Berlin-born Sinologist who traveled in China and Tibet before assuming a chair at Leipzig and then moving to the chair in Berlin in 1932. His work was hindered by his intense dislike of the Nazis.[79] Haenisch recognized that Hundhausen's adaptation *Das Westzimmer* had popular appeal, but he differed from Schmitt in saying that the deficiencies in the adaptation were due less to Hundhausen plagiarizing Julien than to his inadequate knowledge of the Chinese language.[80] Nevertheless, Haenisch criticized Hundhausen for going to a civil court to defend himself against a scholarly criticism because of the intimidating effect such actions had on the freedom of scholars to criticize.

In addition to suing Schmitt for defamation, Hundhausen also published a brochure of rebuttal entitled *"Der Fall Erich Schmitt"* (The Case of Erich Schmitt) and distributed it widely to numerous Sinologists, including Paul Pelliot, who wrote in the journal *T'oung Pao* that he did not find Schmitt's accusation of plagiarism convincing.[81] Hundhausen's pamphlet is filled with polemical and intemperate language. On April 12, 1933, the court ruled in Hundhausen's favor by concluding that *Das Westzimmer* was an independent translation. However, the fine of one hundred Reichsmarks imposed on Schmitt for defamation was waived.[82]

Hundhausen's creativity extended beyond re-creations of Chinese poetry and drama in German. He played a leading role in introducing Chinese drama to Europe and functioned as an impresario who staged dramatic presentations. He began with lectures in which he read his own adaptations and later formed a theater group called the "Pekinger Bühnenspiele." While the words of the adaptations were German, the drama remained Chinese in character. Hundhausen attempted to reproduce the popular appeal of Chinese stage dramas and to broaden their audience beyond the limited, more educated audiences of German theater. Scenes from Hundhausen's adaptation of *Pipa ji* (The Lute) were staged for German audiences in Beijing and Tianjin in 1930.[83]

Other dramas followed. Hundhausen collaborated with a Chinese actor and dramatic arts teacher to found a theatrical school.[84] The company of actors consisted of both Germans and Chinese, and Hundhausen himself played roles, such as a Chinese magistrate. As a result of successful performances before German-speaking audiences in Beijing, Tianjin, Qingdao, and Shanghai, Hundhausen took the theater company to Europe in 1934. The company premiered in Vienna, followed by a four-month tour of theaters in most of the larger cities in Austria and Switzerland. However, Hundhausen was frustrated in his attempt to stage productions in Germany. The German authorities refused permission because of his outspoken opposition to National Socialism.

In 1937, Hundhausen lost his university lectureship at Beida because of political pressure exerted by the National Socialist government of Germany. The German ambassador informed him that instructors more supportive of the German government were desired. Barred from teaching, Hundhausen's enormous energy was diverted to other intellectual endeavors. When the Beijing University press was closed because of the Japanese incursion into north China, he revived it with his own funds and published over a hundred works. The publication included a German-language literary periodical called *Die Dschunke* (The Junk), which was published for five years. He produced several Festschrift collections that included contributions in both German and Chinese by leading Chinese poets and scholars of the time.

Hundhausen's creativity could not flourish in a society without basic freedoms. These included both freedom of speech and sexual freedom. Hundhausen was not a closeted homosexual. He was a charismatic figure who attracted young acolytes. The theatrical world tends to attract sexually ambiguous hangers-on. Hundhausen cultivated contacts with actors in his theater group as well as young Chinese students assisting in his translations and publications. His homosexuality was well known among the German expatriates in Beijing and was mocked by some of them.[85]

Hundhausen had contact with prominent leaders of the homosexual rights movement in Germany, including Magnus Hirschfeld. Although Hirschfeld was unsuccessful in his efforts to repeal Article 175, he established the Institut für Sexualwissenschaft in Berlin in 1919, dedicated to research on sexuality. The Nazis were particularly hostile to his efforts, and in May of 1933, National Socialist university students plundered and destroyed the institute.

In May of 1931, Hirschfeld spent an "unforgettable beautiful summer day" visiting Hundhausen at his Lotus Pond (Pappelinsel).[86] Hirschfeld described Hundhausen as "sharply satirical, but an extremely intelligent personality." Also present was Hundhausen's "highly talented" acolyte, the twenty-two-year-old Berliner Wolfgang von Januszkiewitz-Nathusius. Januskiewitz was the local news and arts editor of the *Deutsch-Chinesischen Nachrichten*. After July 1934, he moved to Shanghai where he worked for the automotive industry. He was active in the German theater society. However, he committed suicide, a form of death that ended the lives of many homosexual men who internalized the loathing of a society that viewed them as unnatural.

On that day in May, Hirschfeld was also accompanied by a young male companion known familiarly by his nickname Taoli (literally "peaches and plums," metaphorically "Fine Disciple"). Taoli was a richly metaphorical pun traceable to the ancient *Shijing* (Book of Poetry), but with additional reference to the "peach" as a metaphor for homosexuality, as in the *Han Feizi*'s "half-eaten peach" (*fentao*) that the male favorite Mizi Xia shared with his lover Duke Ling of Wei (534–493 BC). Taoli's real name was Li Shiu-tong (Li Zhaotang) (1907–1993). Li was the grandson of the famous Qing reformer and self-strengthener Li Hongzhang (1823–1901).[87] He was the son of the wealthy Hong Kong businessman Li Kam-tong. Li Shiu-tong was a medical student at St. John's University in Shanghai in 1931 when Hirschfield visited on his eighteen-month world tour. Li was an attractive and impressionable twenty-four-year-old who became so infatuated with Hirschfeld that he left Shanghai to follow him to Beijing, serving as Hirschfeld's traveling companion and Chinese interpreter (figure 6.3). It was during this trip to Beijing that Hirschfeld and Li visited Hundhausen at his home on Lotus Pond.

The gathering on that day at the Lotus Island appears to have consisted entirely of men of like-minded sexuality. The mellow same-sex tone of the day is captured in a bittersweet poem that Hundhausen inscribed in Hirschfeld's travel dairy. It might be read as a complaint against Western modernizing forces in China that were destroying traditional Chinese tolerance of homosexuality. It reads,

> The peaceful harmony to live
> With oneself, with others, with what is natural
> No longer to desire or gain
> China understands this. Merely by
> Its example, it would bring a healthy cure
> Yet there is resentment, there is blindness
> We want no practical lesson
> And do not rest, until the Chinese
> No longer are, what they were.

Li Shiu-tong later followed Hirschfeld when he left China, apparently with his father's support, who is quoted as saying, "It is my wish and my hope that my son will one day become the Dr. Hirschfeld of China."[88] However, Li was unable to undertake regular studies at Hirschfeld's institute in Berlin because Hirschfeld was forced out of Germany by the National Socialists who attacked and destroyed the institute. He tried to reestablish the institute in Nice, France, while Li attended medical school in Vienna and then Zurich. Li seems to have been a follower who needed Hirschfeld's paternal guidance. When Hirschfeld died of a stroke in 1935, Li began drifting, never finishing medical school. Hirschfeld left the institute's remaining assets to another young lover, Karl Giese, who served as his secretary, but he left his personal effects—including diaries, photographs, and books—to Li. Li carried these materials with him for the rest of his life, first when he moved to Zurich, then to Harvard's graduate school during the war, and then back in Zurich from 1945 to 1960, then

Figure 6.3. The German sexologist Dr. Magnus Hirschfeld visiting with faculty members of a Beijing university (probably Beida), 1931. Courtesy of Prof. Erwin J. Haeberle, founder and director of the Archive for Sexology, Humboldt University, Berlin. Hirschfeld's newfound disciple Li Shiutong (Zhaotong) (1907–1993) appears on the right side of the staircase in a dark jacket (without glasses). Li became one of Hirschfeld's lovers and returned to Europe with him. Forbidden by the Nazis from returning to his Institute in Berlin, Hirschfeld died in 1935 in France of a stroke, and Li was named one his two heirs.

Hong Kong, and then Vancouver from 1975 until his death in 1993 at the age of eighty-six.[89]

Hundhausen had emigrated from Germany to China to escape the oppression of a right-wing totalitarian regime. However, in 1949, China was taken over by a left-wing totalitarian regime. His status in China as a foreigner became precarious. Although he had opposed German imperialism and the "unequal treaties" and had a letter to the Reichstag in 1926 to prove it, he appears not to have been a Communist. The precariousness of his foreign status was compounded by his open homosexuality in a China that was now governed by a harshly homophobic regime. While a foreigner like Rewi Alley survived this homophobic atmosphere and was able to continue living in China, Hundhausen could not. Suddenly in the spring of 1954, after thirty years of residence in China, he was expelled. As a refugee he carried a single book from his large library—his German translations of Chinese poets *Chinesische Dichter in deutscher Sprache* (1926).[90] He was forced to return to his hometown of Grevenbroich where he fell ill and was hospitalized. He continued to dream of returning to China until the end (figure 6.4). He died on May 18, 1955, at the age of seventy-seven, with his dream unrealized.

Figure 6.4. Vincenz Hundhausen (1878–1955) after his expulsion from China in 1954 and shortly before his death. Courtesy of Dr. Hartmut Walravens and Dr. Gussone of Grevenbroich, Germany.

BRINGING CHINESE ART TO THE AMERICAN HEARTLAND

It is characteristically American that one of the finest collections of Chinese art in the world is to be found in the heartland of America, far from the coastal centers of culture. This collection in the Nelson-Atkins Museum in Kansas City, Missouri, is the result of capitalist philanthropy, regional loyalty, and the dedication of Laurence Chalfant Stevens Sickman, who was largely responsible for assembling the collection. Sickman was one of the greatest art historians and curators of Chinese art in the twentieth century. He was also a remarkable man who distinguished himself in military service to his country in World War II. Very few people are aware that he was homosexual.

Sickman was born in Denver, Colorado, in 1907. His interest in Asia was almost genetic and dated from when he was a little boy in Denver, collecting Japanese dolls and prints. There was one shop in Denver that he frequented. He recalled in later years that he had decided upon a career as a curator of Oriental art at the early age of seventeen.[91] He began his college career at the University of Denver, but he had never been to the East Coast, and its allure drew him there. John Ellerton Lodge was then the director of the Freer Gallery in Washington, D.C., a branch of the Smithsonian Museum that houses the East Asian art collection. When Sickman asked him for advice, Lodge suggested that he study at Harvard, which is where Sickman transferred. During his last two years of undergraduate education, Sickman studied Chinese and Japanese art under Langdon Warner. Harvard in the 1920s and 1930s was teeming with China scholars. Even the famous French Sinologist Paul Pelliot (1878–1945) was there, and Sickman studied Chinese archeology with him. There sometime between 1928 and 1930 he met Lincoln Kirstein, a bisexual who would become an impresario and leading figure in the New York City art world.[92]

In 1930, after graduating from Harvard, Sickman and William Acker were appointed the first two Harvard-Yenching fellows. This enabled Sickman to travel extensively in China. There in 1931 he again encountered Professor Warner who was a trustee of the newly established Nelson Gallery of Art in Kansas City.[93] William Rockhill Nelson, the founder of the *Kansas City Star*, had bequeathed $11 million to establish a museum, and Warner controlled part of this bequest, charged with the task of acquiring artworks for the new museum. Warner introduced Sickman to the antiquaries of Beijing, and when he left China, he recommended to the Nelson board that Sickman assume his responsibilities. Warner eventually gave Sickman broad responsibility to buy works of art for the museum, although he and Sickman often disagreed and Warner would overrule him.

The market for antiquities in China was highly fluid in the thirties, with bogus works along with genuine pieces flooding the market. Sickman learned a great deal about connoisseurship from Dr. Otto Burchard, the German art dealer with a doctorate from Heidelberg University who lived in Beijing. Burchard became Sickman's adviser, close friend, and informal tutor. Sickman learned how to negotiate the purchase of antiquities from the Beijing art dealers with shops in Liulichang and most notably from the legendary dealer Huang Jun (styled Bochuan). Sickman traveled widely in the north China countryside, searching for mural paintings in ancient temples and Buddhist cave sites. In 1932 and 1933, John and Wilma Fairbank, who were in China as students, accompanied him on trips to the Yungang Caves in northern Shanxi province and the Buddhist caves at Longmen, near the ancient capital of Luoyang in Henan province.[94]

It was during this time in Beijing that Harold Acton and Sickman met. They were fellow aesthetes, although Sickman was far more professional and scholarly. Also, Sickman made his living from this work, while Acton was wealthy enough not to be concerned about employment. Nevertheless their shared tastes and delight in Sickman's acquisitions are described by Acton in his memoirs: "Some of the most splendid moments of the day were when Laurence walked in with some treasure he had discovered, and he was constantly discovering treasures, from Chou bronzes to jade cicadas, for the fantastically fortunate Kansas City Museum."[95] Acton made many visits to Sickman at his house in Xiehe (Hsieh Ho) Hutung, which he shared with his mother, and viewed his wonderful finds.

Sickman and Acton often went together to visit the elegant prince and painter Puru, whose landscapes in the styles of past dynasties and outstanding calligraphy made him, in Sickman's view, "the best Chinese artist of the mid-twentieth century."[96] Sickman offered less generous praise for the self-styled rustic Qi Baishi, who used his forceful brush strokes to produce works which spanned the spectrum of quality. Qi's students produced a vast number of fakes, some of which Sickman "unwittingly acquired."

Sickman even had the use of an airplane in searching for acquisitions. Social and economic conditions in China made it a buyer's market for art collectors. Many Chinese were desperate to sell their art, either because of their financial circumstances or because they had acquired it by dubious means. The famous horizontal scroll of mountains by the Northern Song landscape painter Xu Daoning (Hsü Tao-ning) came to Sickman in the dead of night along with the need for urgent payment.[97] When the last emperor was evicted from the Forbidden City by the warlord general Feng Yuxiang in 1924, Puyi took many imperial art treasures with him in his flight to the Japanese compound in Tianjin. When Sickman visited him there, Puyi played with his new Japanese motorcycle, leaving Sickman alone to pick the works he wanted.

While Sickman was able to benefit from the desperation of these Chinese in acquiring their art, he was also able to preserve artworks that might otherwise have been lost or dispersed, such as the stone reliefs (ca. 522) from the Buddhist caves at Longmen, Henan province, that had already been broken up and separated among Beijing dealers.[98] Acton commented on Sickman's integrity which prevented him from keeping any of these artworks for himself, instead passing them all on to the Nelson-Atkins. His purchases elevated the Kansas City Museum to the level of one of the finest Asian collections in the United States.

In 1935, Sickman was appointed curator of Oriental art at the Nelson-Atkins. He was innovative in displaying major works together with minor art and furniture in order to convey the artworks' original settings. Harvard tried but failed to tempt him away from the Nelson-Atkins. In 1938–1940, Sickman was a lecturer in Far Eastern art at Harvard, and although he was offered a position at Harvard's Fogg Art Museum, his dedication to the Nelson-Atkins caused him to decline the offer and return to Kansas City.

When the United States entered World War II, Sickman enlisted and was assigned to intelligence (figure 6.5). He went to England, then on

Figure 6.5. Art historian Laurence Sickman (1906–1988) in uniform, ca. 1942. During World War II Sickman enlisted and served as a major in US intelligence (aerial surveillance), flying in a modified B-25 based in Kunming. Courtesy the Nelson-Atkins Museum of Art, Kansas City, Missouri.

to Lord Louis Mountbatten who was head of the British Southeast Asia Command in India and Burma. There he cheered up Acton who was unhappily stranded in service there. Finally he was sent on to General Chennault who placed him in charge of all aerial surveillance in China in order to call bombing strikes. He was assigned a pilot and a souped-up B-25 and operated out of the US airbase at Kunming. He played a central role in the bombing of the Japanese in China. Once he spotted a huge shipment of aviation fuel in transit across the large Lake Tai, west of Shanghai. The fuel had originally been flown over the Hump from India into southwest China by US planes to assist the Nationalists, and it was now being sold to the Japanese by corrupt Nationalist generals. When Sickman ordered an airstrike that destroyed the fuel, the generals were enraged. Sickman was also responsible for destroying the Japanese fuel dump in Kowloon, Hong Kong.

After the Hiroshima and Nagasaki bombings in August 1945, Major Sickman and a colonel flew the B-25 to Beijing. They were met by the Japanese general staff in Beijing who preferred to surrender to the Americans rather than to the Chinese. Sickman brought US$250,000 in cash to buy intelligence. He also used much of this cash to buy Chinese art, for which he later reimbursed the US government. After demobilization in 1945, he returned to the Nelson-Atkins and in 1953 was appointed director of the museum.

Sickman was very discreet and closeted about his sexuality, once complaining to a friend, "I have too many hormones." He appeared to have few sexual partners, although appearances among closeted homosexuals can be misleading, particularly if they complain of having too many hormones. His principal lover was Jim Wallace, who had a strong interest in Indian art and fostered Sickman's interest in it. They both lived in Kansas City, but in separate residences. The Nelson-Atkins Museum was located in a twenty-acre park, and Sickman lived nearby with his mother. Their relationship soured when Wallace crossed Sickman's strict wall of separation between his private sexual life and his professional museum life.

Kansas City lay in the center of the American heartland where in the 1950s and 1960s many people viewed homosexuality with a horror reserved for Communism and heroin addiction in their subversion of the American way of life. Art museum patrons are typically bastions of propriety and the patrons of the Nelson-Atkins were no exception. Rumor has it that at a museum event, Wallace—perhaps after too much to drink—replied to a question by saying, "Oh well, I'm the director's wife." Sickman felt personally betrayed by this indiscretion. He had devoted much of his life to the Nelson-Atkins, and his relationship to it was of paramount importance. Soon afterward, Wallace left Kansas City and relocated to the northeastern part of the country.

Although Sickman had an excellent knowledge of the Chinese language and published several scholarly works on art history, including the widely read *Art and Architecture of China* (1956) with Alexander Soper, his greatest strength lay in museum work. The unique and extraordinary nature of the Nelson-Atkins collection lies in its breadth, which covers every aspect of Chinese art, including bronzes, sculpture, painting, woodblock prints, furniture, and textiles. It was Sickman's stature and reputation that brought the 385-piece exhibition "Archeological Finds of the People's Republic of China" to Kansas City during the 1970s. This exhibition was one of the earliest signs of the thaw in Cold War relations between the United States and Communist China since its founding in 1949.

Sickman retired as director of the Nelson-Atkins in 1977. He was a long-time smoker and eventually contracted lung cancer. When he learned that the disease was incurable, he resigned himself to his fate and indulged in cigarettes and increasing amounts of Scotch whiskey. He had always been an aesthete who savored the pleasures of life. He died in 1988. His memorial is the Nelson-Atkins collection and the tremendous advance it made in cultivating an appreciation of Chinese art in the United States.

Epilogue

History allows us to re-create worlds and to revive attitudes that no longer exist. Today it is becoming increasingly difficult to conceive how gay men only fifty years ago were regarded with the most intense shame, subjected to the most blatant discrimination, terminated from their employment, arrested, and jailed on the basis of their sexuality. Words have their own way of revealing history. In 1969, *homophobia* was a new word that was not widely used because hostility toward homosexuality was not yet viewed as hatred.

Fifty years ago the conventional view in Western culture was that same-sex attraction was something unnatural and even evil. Of course, widespread loathing of homosexuality existed, but it was regarded as a natural and understandable reaction to a perverse phenomenon. Homosexuals sometimes encountered tolerance, but rarely understanding. Because the loathing of homosexuals had not yet been perceived as wrong or sinful, there had been no word in common usage, such as *homophobia*, that evoked guilt or at least put the user on the defensive for feeling this hatred. The twenty-three men treated in this book were not radicals. They were socially conventional figures, at most a bit eccentric, who just happened to feel same-sex desire. It was the widely accepted hatred of their same-sex attraction that drove them to flee their homelands and go to China, either physically or intellectually.

The image of flight evokes both escape and inspiration. These contrasting images certainly applied to the flight of queers to China. The remoteness of China has made it a place to which several oppressed groups have fled. In the nineteenth and twentieth centuries, homosexuals were joined by ambitious young Christian women fleeing the oppressive professional limitations of their culture to become missionaries in China, and in the 1930s by Jews who escaped Nazi oppression by fleeing to Shanghai. The nature of the oppression of men with same-sex desires varied by the individual. Clearly, Josef Schedel was fleeing from a blatant form of oppression which threatened him with arrest and imprisonment. Edmund Backhouse may have fled for the same reason. For others, such as W. Somerset Maugham and Rewi Alley, the flight to China was more of a precautionary move to avoid legal harassment and find a place more tolerant of their sexual activities with young men.

The flight of G. L. Dickenson, Vincenz Hundhausen, Victor Segalen, George Soulié de Morant, Witter Bynner, George N. Kates, Alan Priest, Christopher Isherwood, Harold Acton, Laurence Sickman, W. H. Auden, and David Kidd to China was far more sublimated sexually and was characterized as much by culture and homoeroticism as by homosexuality. For scholars like Ferdinand Karsch-Haack, J. J. M. De Groot, Arthur Waley, Glen William Baxter, Howard Wechsler, and Marston Anderson, the attraction was primarily intellectual and usually involved limited or no travel to China.

Although these twenty-three men with same-sex desires shared China as an object of attraction, their backgrounds, attitudes, interests, and motivations were neither unified nor cohesive. They shared a secret bond, but it functioned more in the nature of a defense against attack rather than as an activist agenda in the manner of a Homintern or gay mafia. For some of these men, Chinese boy-actors personified the object of their desires. Others cultivated friendships with Chinese men to realize the object of their desires. They tended to be disproportionately attracted to aesthetic fields, and in that sense they shared a sensibility. Most of them shared this aesthetic attraction to China—to its calligraphy, drama, painting, sculpture, and verse as well as to the bodies of its young men. This led them to play a significant role in opening the broader Western sensibility to the beauty and fascination of China. This reorientation involved a fundamental readjustment because our sense of beauty is often etched on our consciousness at an early age of development. The powerful force of same-sex attraction in these men seems to have played an important role in re-etching the sense of beauty in our consciousness and expanding the Western cultural sensibility to include elements from Chinese culture.

Apart from this shared aesthetic sensibility, there is little evidence that these men with same-sex desire were instinctually defined by their genes or inevitably shaped by their environment to focus exclusively on certain fields. As the subject matter becomes intellectually more complex, the link to same-sex attraction becomes more intangible. Consequently, the intellectual connections these twenty-three men made with China cannot be, in comparison with the aesthetic dimension, as clearly linked to their sexuality.

In spite of all the historical changes, China today continues to exert an appeal for gay men from the West. Philip Gambone is an accomplished American author of domestic gay fiction who presents gay characters as ordinary rather than deviant, and "out" rather than closeted. He has published a novel, *Beijing*, which is clearly semiautobiographical.[1] In the novel, the main character, David Masiello of Boston, accepts the job of an office manager in a medical clinic in Beijing for one year to go to China to escape his unhappiness following the AIDS death of his partner Johnny. In real life, Gambone went to China on a School Year Abroad program to teach for one semester in Beijing in the fall of 1996.

The novel *Beijing* reflects how a new chapter has begun in the history of men with same-sex desire being attracted to China, but it is a chapter filled with continuities with the past. Everything about the character in the novel is ordinary, except for his journey to China and falling in love with a Chinese man. The gay man went to China to escape an unhappy life, not to get away from a homophobic world where he was closeted. In fact, the atmosphere that the character finds in Beijing was far more homophobic than the atmosphere he left behind in Boston. In Boston the main character lived in a gay ghetto where his advancing age was making it more difficult for him to find a lover. He was attracted to China, but initially he did not find Asian men attractive.[2] In Beijing, his aging body became an exotic figure which attracted a deeply closeted younger Chinese gay man, and they fell in love.

Gambone's novel presents the lighter and happier side of the flight of Western gay men to China. For the deeper and darker side of this flight, we could go to a memoir by a Western gay man about his experiences in Japan. Because of the revolutionary upheaval in China in the aftermath of the Communist victory of 1949, Westerners were restricted in visiting China for three decades. A few Europeans were able to visit the mainland as a part of friendship association tours, but the lack of diplomatic relations with the PRC limited Americans to Hong Kong and Taiwan until 1979. Even during the 1980s, foreign visitors to China were rarely free to move about China without an official guide, which limited unsupervised contact with Chinese people. During this time, Japan became the destination for most Americans fascinated with East Asia.

Some of the most eminent translators of Japanese literature have been homosexuals who lived in Japan with Japanese lovers. In his candid memoir, the Japanologist John Whittier Treat reveals that the traditional pattern of Western dominance that existed in China over Chinese "boys" has continued in modified form in Japan. When Treat was thirty-four, he spent a year in Japan in 1986–1987 writing a study of literature in Hiroshima and Nagasaki. His stay coincided with a national panic over the AIDS epidemic. His fascination with having sex with Japanese men becomes a metaphor of miscegenation in which he continues a colonialist tradition—"the desire to miscegenate was apparently rife in the Empire."[3] Treat claimed that when Westerners were involved sexually with Japanese men, "it seemed a rule that we were supposed to be on top." He described his sexual encounter with a younger Japanese man called Oda (a pseudonym) in candidly racist terms. Although Treat was the one being sexually penetrated, he was, "when all was said and done and screwed, still on top."[4] The same thing might be said of several of the twenty-three men in this study and their relations with Chinese. However, if we stopped there, we would be leaving out a lot.

The racist candor of Treat's comments can be attributed, in part, to his personal egotism, which is sanctioned by the consciously cultivated subjectivity of queer theory. But it raises the question of why the fascination with Chinese "boys" persists. Is it a vestige of the recent racial and cultural dominance of the West over the East that lingers as an erotic image in the consciousness of gay men? Or does it represent something deeper and longer lasting? Are Chinese "boys" a unique metaphor for the aesthetics of China? Does the fascination with Chinese "boys," which was so deeply felt among the twenty-three men in this study, persist as a phenomenon based on a force outside of time? Is the beauty of young Chinese men, like a flower at the peak of its bloom, an object of timeless beauty?

Notes

1. My comments on Edmund White's study of Chinese are based on e-mail correspondence with the author in November and December of 2010. However, I note that in his *The Beautiful Room Is Empty* (New York: Knopf, 1988), the second volume of a trilogy of semiautobiographical novels, White gives a different reason for not entering the graduate program in Chinese at Harvard. He wrote, "My father was unwilling to keep me on his payroll, and his income was too high for me to qualify for a fellowship" (p. 160). This explanation is at odds with the way graduate fellowships were usually awarded in the 1960s. Whereas undergraduate scholarships were partially need based, graduate fellowships were based primarily on merit. Moreover, as a self-supporting adult, as he claims that he was, he would not have been obliged to include his father's income in his financial aid statement. The more likely explanation for the discrepancy between what he wrote to me in 2010 and what he wrote in *The Beautiful Room Is Empty* lay in White's use of his life as an impressionistic sketch that he freely modified for artistic purposes. One of the dominant themes of his trilogy is his portrayal of his father as a homophobic and very unsympathetic man, and this seems to be the key to understanding the novel's slightly different explanation of why White did not go to Harvard to do graduate work in Chinese. For another perspective on White's artistic prevarications, see the chapter "White Lies" in Reed Woodhouse's *Unlimited Embrace: A Canon of Gay Fiction, 1945–1995* (Amherst: University of Massachusetts Press, 1998), 263–295.

2. Charles Kaiser, *The Gay Metropolis, 1940–1996* (San Diego: Harcourt, Brace, 1997), 287.

3. Eve Kosofsky Sedgwick, *Epistemology of the Closet* (Berkeley: University of California Press, 1990), 16–17.

4. Alan Helms, *Young Man from the Provinces: A Gay Life before Stonewall* (New York: Avon, 1997), 208.

5. "BTW," *Gay and Lesbian Review*, 17, no. 1 (2010): 10.

6. Francis Mark Mondimore, *A Natural History of Homosexuality* (Baltimore, MD: Johns Hopkins University Press, 1996), 86; Douglass Shand-Tucci, *The Crimson Letter: Harvard, Homosexuality, and the Shaping of American Culture* (New York: St. Martin's, 2003), 263, 287.

7. Sedgwick, *Epistemology of the Closet*, 40–44.

8. See Larry Kramer, "Queer Theory's Heist of Our History," *Gay and Lesbian Review* 16, no. 5 (2009): 11–13.

9. Rudyard Kipling, "The Ballad of East and West," 1889.

10. Bao Ruo-wang (Jean Pasqualini) and Rudolph Chelminski, *Prisoner of Mao* (1973; reprinted, New York: Penguin, 1976), 189–190. Also see Fang-fu Juan, *Sex in China: Studies in Sexology in Chinese Culture* (New York: Plenum, 1991), 120–134.

11. Jens Damm, "Same Sex Desire and Society in Taiwan, 1970–1987," *China Quarterly* 181 (2005): 75.

12. Pai Hsien-yung, *Crystal Boys*, trans. by Howard Goldblatt (San Francisco: Gay Sunshine Press, 1990).

13. Alfred C. Kinsey et al., *Sexual Behavior in the Human Male* (Philadelphia: W. B. Saunders, 1948), 636–659.

14. George Chauncey, *Gay New York: Gender, Urban Culture, and the Making of the Gay Male World, 1890–1940* (New York: Basic Books, 1994), 6–7.

1. FLIGHT TO THE LAND OF OZ

1. Josef Schedel, "China-Tagebuch, 1909–1919," in *Josef Schedel (1856–1943) Ein deutscher Apotheker in Ostasien*, ed. Hartmut Walravens (Berlin: Staatsbibliothek zu Berlin, 2008), 55–58.

2. Schedel, "China-Tagebuch, 1909–1919," 63.

3. Jens Damm, "Ferdinand Karsch-Haack," In *Who's Who in Gay and Lesbian History: From Antiquity to World War II*, ed. Robert Aldrich and Garry Wotherspoon (London: Routledge, 2001), 238–239.

4. Matt Houlbrook, *Queer London: Perils and Pleasures in the Sexual Metropolis, 1918–1957* (Chicago: University of Chicago Press, 2005), 19.

5. Frank Harris, *Oscar Wilde* (1916; reprinted, New York: Carroll & Graf, 1992), 146–147.

6. Hugh Trevor-Roper, *Hermit of Peking: The Hidden Life of Sir Edmund Backhouse*, rev. ed. (Harmondsworth, England: Penguin, 1978), 255.

7. Trevor-Roper, *Hermit of Peking*, 32–33. For the origins of the term *Uranianism*, see Neil McKenna, *The Secret Life of Oscar Wilde* (New York: Basic Books, 2005), 80.

8. McKenna, *The Secret Life of Oscar Wilde*, 90–91; Douglas Murray, *Bosie: A Biography of Lord Alfred Douglas* (New York: Hyperion, 2000), 36.

9. Lord Alfred Douglas, "Two Loves," in *The Penguin Book of Homosexual Verse*, ed. Stephen Coote (London: Penguin, 1986), 262–264.

10. Trevor-Roper, *Hermit of Peking*, 33–35.

11. Trevor-Roper, *Hermit of Peking*, 33–34.

12. The tendency to explain Backhouse's behavior in terms of eccentricity and "aberrant behavior" without regard to his closeted homosexuality continues today. In a retrospective review of Trevor-Roper's *Hermit of Peking* that appeared in the *Wall Street Journal* (January 22, 2011, C13), Joseph Epstein fails to discuss the homosexuality not only of Backhouse, but also of Frederick Rolfe (Baron Corvo), explaining them instead as fellow charlatans.

13. Gaius Suetonius Tranquillus, *The Twelve Caesars*, trans. Michael Grant (Harmondsworth, England: Penguin, 1957), 135–136. See also Graham Robb, *Strangers: Homosexual Love in the Nineteenth Century* (New York: Norton, 2003), 168.

14. Robert Aldrich, *The Seduction of the Mediterranean: Writing, Art and Homosexual Fantasy* (London: Routledge, 1993), 58–65.

15. McKenna, *The Secret Life of Oscar Wilde*, 440–449.

16. Thekla Clark, *Wystan and Chester* (New York: Columbia University Press, 1995), 3–37.

17. Michael Davidson, *Some Boys* (London: Gay Men's Press, 1988), 61–68; Frank Browning, *A Queer Geography* (New York: Crown, 1996), 51–98.

18. Aldrich, *The Seduction of the Mediterranean*, 143–146.

19. Aldrich, *The Seduction of the Mediterranean*, illustration 11, "Neapel, c. 1890–1900."

20. Aldrich, *The Seduction of the Mediterranean*, 127–128.

21. Roger Peyrefitte, *L'Exilé de Capri* (Paris: Ernest Flammarion, 1959). See the English translation by Edward Hyams, *The Exile of Capri* (New York: Fleet Publishing, 1965).

22. Sir Richard Francis Burton, "Terminal Essay," in *A Plain and Literal Translation of the Arabian Nights Entertainment*, 10 vols. (Benares: Kamashastra Society, 1885–1895).

23. Vivien W. Ng, "Homosexuality and the State in Late Imperial China," in *Reclaiming the Gay and Lesbian Past*, ed. Martin Duberman et al. (New York: New American Library, 1989), 76–77.

24. Matthew H. Sommer, "The Penetrated Male in Late Imperial China: Judicial Constructions and Social Stigma," *Modern China* 23 (1997): 141; M. J. Meijer, "Homosexual Offences in Ch'ing Law," *T'oung Pao* 71 (1985): 109–110.

25. Meijer, "Homosexual Offenses in Ch'ing Law," 129–131.

26. Vivien W. Ng, "Ideology and Sexuality: Rape Laws in Qing China," *Journal of Asian Studies* 46 (1987): 68.

27. Meijer, "Homosexual Offenses in Ch'ing Law," 114.

28. "Editor's Note," in *Dictionary of Ming Biography*, 2 vols., ed. L. Carrington Goodrich and Chaoying Fang (New York: Columbia University Press, 1976), 314; Bret Hinsch, *Passions of the Cut Sleeve: The Male Homosexual Tradition in China* (Berkeley: University of California Press, 1990), 142–143.

29. Craig A. Williams, *Roman Homosexuality: Ideologies of Masculinity in Classical Antiquity* (New York: Oxford, 1999), 18–19.

30. Aldrich, *The Seduction of the Mediterranean*, 174–178.

31. Sommer, "The Penetrated Male in Late Imperial China," 161–163, 170–171.

32. Witter Bynner, *Selected Letters*, ed. James Kraft (New York: Farrar, Straus & Giroux, 1981), xi.

33. James Kraft, *Who Is Witter Bynner? A Biography* (Albuquerque: University of New Mexico Press, 1995), 15–16.

34. James Kraft, "Biographical Introduction," in *Selected Poems*, by Witter Bynner (New York: Farrar, Straus & Giroux, 1978), xxxiii.

35. Kraft, "Biographical Introduction," xlv–xv.

36. Kraft, "Biographical Introduction," lxv.

37. Kraft, *Who Is Witter Bynner?*, 41–42.

38. Martin Green, *Children of the Sun: A Narrative of "Decadence" in England after 1918* (New York: Basic Books, 1976), 118–119.

39. Paula Byrne, *Mad World: Evelyn Waugh and the Secrets of Brideshead* (New York: HarperCollins, 2009), 297.

40. Green, *Children of the Sun*, 160–161.

41. Harold Acton, *Memoirs of an Aesthete* (London: Methuen, 1948), 231–233.

42. James Lord, *Some Remarkable Men: Further Memoirs* (New York: Farrar, Straus & Giroux, 1996), 79.

43. Acton, *Memoirs of an Aesthete*, 255.

44. Acton, *Memoirs of an Aesthete*, 275–276.

45. Kraft, *Who Is Witter Bynner?*, 84–85.

46. Witter Bynner, *Selected Poems*, ed. Richard Wilbur (New York: Farrar, Straus & Giroux 1977), 145.

47. "Professor Vincenz Hundhausen: Mein Lebenslauf," in Hartmut Walravens, *Vincenz Hundhausen: Leben und Werk* (Wiesbaden: Harrossowitz, 1999), 59.

48. Pamela Atwell, "Obituary: George N. Kates (1895–1990)," *Journal of Asian Studies* 49 (1990): 1014–1015.

49. George N. Kates, *The Years that Were Fat: The Last of Old China* (New York: Harper, 1952), 82.

50. George N. Kates, *Chinese Household Furniture* (London: Constable, 1948), ix.

2. THE EXOTIC APPEAL OF CHINESE BOY-ACTORS

1. George Soulié de Morant, *Bijou-de-Ceinture, ou le Jeune home qui porte robe, se poudre et se farde, roman* (Paris: Flammarion, 1925).

2. Soulié de Morant, *Bijou-de-Ceinture*, 25.

3. George Solié de Morant, *Pei Yu: Boy Actress*, trans. by Gerald Fabian and Guy Wernham. (San Francisco: Alamo Square Press, 1991).

4. Colin P. MacKerras, *The Rise of Peking Opera, 1770–1870: Social Aspects of the Theatre in Manchu China* (Oxford: Clarendon, 1972), 42–43.

5. Wu Cuncun, *Homoerotic Sensibilities in Late Imperial China* (London: Routledge, 2004), 123–132; Ichisada Miyazaki, *China's Examination Hell: The Civil Service Examinations of Imperial China*, trans. by Conrad Schirokauer (New Haven, CT: Yale University Press, 1981), 19.

6. L. C. Arlington and William Lewisohn, *In Search of Old Peking* (Beijing: Henri Vetch, 1935), 28, 211–213, 363.

7. Robert L. Thorp, *Visiting Historic Beijing: A Guide to Sites and Resources* (Warren, CT: Floating World Editions, 2008), 82.

8. Susan Naquin, *Peking Temples and City Life, 1400–1900* (Berkeley: University of California Press, 2000), 410–411.

9. Arlington and Lewisohn, *In Search of Old Peking*, 215–216.

10. Arlington and Lewisohn, *In Search of Old Peking*, 269–270.

11. MacKerras, *The Rise of Peking Opera*, 206–207.

12. Zhuangzi, *Jiaozheng Zhuangzi jishi*, 2 vols. (Taipei: Shihjie Shuju, 1971), 1:1.

13. The names of these seven theaters are given in Arlington and Lewisohn, *In Search of Old Peking*, 274.

14. Cuncun Wu and Mark Stevenson, "Male Love Lost: The Fate of Male Same-Sex Prostitution in Beijing in the Late Nineteenth and Early Twentieth Centuries," in *Embodied Modernities: Corporeality, Representation and Chinese Culture*, ed. Larissa Heinrich (Honolulu: University of Hawai'i Press, 2006), 45.

15. Wu and Stevenson, "Male Love Lost," 48–49.

16. Wu, *Homoerotic Sensibilities*, 140–144.

17. Wu, *Homoerotic Sensibilities*, 143; Soulié de Morant, *Bijou-de-Ceinture*, 94; Solié de Morant, *Pei Yu*, 54.

18. Wu, *Homoerotic Sensibilities*, 149–154.

19. Joseph Schedel, "China-Tagebuch," in *Josef Schedel (1856–1943), Ein deutscher Apotheker in Ostasien*, ed. Hartmut Walravens (Berlin: Staatsbibliothek zu Berlin, 2008), 65–66.

20. Schedel, "China-Tagebuch," 97.

21. John Minford and Robert E. Hegel, "Hong-lou meng," in *Indiana Companion to Traditional Chinese Literature*, ed. William H. Nienhauser Jr. (Bloomington: Indiana University Press, 1986), 452.

22. Cao Xueqin, *Gengchen chaoben shitouji*, 80 hui, 4 vols. (Taipei: Guangwen Bookstore Company, 1977), 2: 604. See Cao Xueqin, *The Story of the Stone*, trans. by David Hawkes, 4 vols. (London: Penguin, 1977), 2:53–62, 2:145–146.

23. Chen Sen, *Pinhua baojian*, 4 *juan* (1849; reprint, Taipei: Tianyi Publishing Society, 1974). See David Der-wei Wang, *Fin-de-siècle Splendour: Repressed Modernities of Late Qing Fiction, 1849–1911* (Stanford, CA: Stanford University Press, 1997), 61–65.

24. Wu, *Homoerotic Sensibilities*, 30–33.

25. Wu, *Homoerotic Sensibilities*, 119–123 and MacKerras, *The Rise of Peking Opera*, 44–45.

26. Soulié de Morant, *Bijou-de-Ceinture*, 235 and Solié de Morant, *Pei Yu*, 141.

27. Wu and Stevenson, "Male Love Lost," 53.

28. Wu and Stevenson, "Male Love Lost," 54–55.

29. Lao She (Shu Qingchun)'s "Tu" was first published in *Wenyi yuekan* 11, no. 1 (July 1937). For an English translation, see Lao She, "Rabbit." In *Blades of Grass: The Stories of Lao She*, translated by William A. Lyell and Sarah Wei-ming Chen (Honolulu: University of Hawai'i Press, 1999), 183–210.

30. William A. Lyell and Sarah Wei-ming Chen, "Translator's Postscript: The Man and the Stories." In Lao She, *Blades of Grass*, 275–276.

31. David Der-wei Wang, "Impersonating China," *Chinese Literature: Essays, Articles, Reviews (CLEAR)* 25 (2003): 134.

32. Pa Chin, *The Family*, trans. Sidney Shapiro (Peking: Foreign Language Press, 1958), 205.

33. Solié de Morant, *Pei Yu*, 150–151; Paul Zmiewski, "Introduction," in *Chinese Acupuncture*, by George Solié de Morant, trans. Lawrence Grinnell, Claudy Jeanmougin, and Maurice Leveque, ed. Paul Zmiewski (Brookline, MA: Paradigm, 1994), v.

34. Soulié de Morant, *Pei Yu*, 20.

35. Cf. Gerald Fabian's "Glossary" in Soulié de Morant, *Pei Yu*, 155; Arthur Hummel, ed. *Eminent Chinese of the Ch'ing Period* (Washington, DC: United States Government Printing Office, 1943), 80.

36. Soulié de Morant, *Pei Yu*, 6.

37. Hummel, 945–948.

38. Hummel, 312–313.

39. Soulié de Morant, *Pei Yu*, 45; Soulié de Morant, *Bijou-de-Ceinture*, 76–77.

40. Soulié de Morant, *Pei Yu*, 57, 65.

41. Soulié de Morant, *Pei Yu*, 8.

42. Jean Cocteau, *The White Book/Le Livre Blanc*, trans. Margaret Crosland (San Francisco: City Lights Books, 1989); see also Francis Steegmuller, *Cocteau: A Biography* (Boston: Little, Brown, 1970), 13.

43. Harold Acton, *Memoirs of an Aesthete, 1939–1969* [original title: *More Memoirs of an Aesthete*] (New York: Viking, 1971), 2–3.

44. Cyril Birch, "Harold Acton as a Translator from the Chinese," in *Oxford China and Italy: Writings in Honour of Sir Harold Acton on His Eightieth Birthday*, ed. Edward Cheney and Neil Ritchie (London: Thames and Hudson, 1984), 42.

45. "Mei Lan-fang," in *Biographical Dictionary of Republican China*, ed. Howard L. Boorman (New York: Columbia University Press, 1970) 3:26–29; A. C. Scott, *The Classical Theatre of China* (New York: Macmillan, 1957), 38.

46. Wang, "Impersonating China," 136.

47. Harold Acton, *Peonies and Ponies* (London: Chatto & Windus, 1941), 99.

48. Acton, *Peonies*, 138.

49. Acton, *Peonies*, 84.

50. Acton, *Peonies*, 272.

51. Giovanni Vitiello, "The Dragon's Whim: Ming and Qing Homoerotic Tales from *The Cut Sleeve*," *T'oung Pao* 78 (1992): 361–362.

52. Timothy Brook, *The Confusions of Pleasure: Commerce and Culture in Ming China* (Berkeley: University of California Press, 1998), 231–233.

53. Keith McMahon, "Eroticism in Late Ming, Early Qing Fiction: The Beauteous Realm and the Sexual Battlefield," *T'oung Pao* 73 (1987): 229–235; Giovanni Vitiello, "The Fantastic Journey of an Ugly Boy: Homosexuality and Salvation in Late Ming Pornography," *Positions: East Asian Culture Critique* 4 (1996): 295, 299.

54. This contrary interpretation is voiced by Sophie Volpp in "Classifying Lust: The Seventeenth-Century Vogue for Male Love," *Harvard Journal of Asiatic Studies* 61 (2001): 80–84; "The Literary Circulation of

Actors in Seventeenth-Century China," *Journal of Asian Studies* 61 (2002): 952–953. This emotive excess in late Qing fiction is also discussed in David Der-wei Wang, *Fin-de-siècle Splendour*, 36–52.

55. Jonathan D. Spence, *Emperor of China: Self-Portrait of K'ang-hsi* (New York: Random House, 1975), xxi, 125–126, 129.

56. Matthew H. Sommer, "The Penetrated Male in Late Imperial China: Judicial Constructions and Social Stigma," *Modern China* 23 (1997): 146.

57. Francis Mark Mondimore, *A Natural History of Homosexuality* (Baltimore, MD: Johns Hopkins University Press, 1996), 3.

58. Vitiello, "The Dragon's Whim," 347–350. See also Bret Hinsch, *Passions of the Cut Sleeve: The Male Homosexual Tradition in China* (Berkeley: University of California Press, 1990), 7.

59. Han Fei Tzu, *Basic Writings*, trans. Burton Watson (New York: Columbia University Press, 1964), 78–79.

60. Jens Damm, "Kuer vs. tongzhi—Diskurse der Homosexualität oder das Entstehen sexualler Identitäten in glokalieierten Taiwan und im postkolonialen Hongkong," in *Berliner Chinahefte*, no. 18 (May 2000): 60–63.

61. For examples of short stories in *Tongzhi* and *Kuer* literature from Taiwan, see Fran Martin, trans., *Angelwings: Contemporary Queer Fiction from Taiwan* (Honolulu: University Hawai'i Press, 2003).

62. Damm, "Kuer vs. tongzhi," 69. For one of the better-known examples of *kuer* literature, see Chu T'ien-wen (Zhu Tianwen)'s novel *Huangren shouji*, translated by Howard Goldblatt and Sylvia Li-chun Lin as *Notes of a Desolate Man* (New York: Columbia University Press, 1999).

63. F. E. Peters, *Ours, the Making and Unmaking of a Jesuit* (New York: Richard Marek, 1981), 24.

64. "El Padre B. de Angelis a los Padres Provinciales, de Roma a 12 de Octubre 1601," in *Monumenta Missionum Societatis Iesu Vol. XLII. Missiones Occidentales. Monumenta Mexicana VII (1599–1602)*, ed. Felix Zubillaga, SI (Rome: Institutum Historicum Societtais Iesu, 1981), 766–771.

65. D. E. Mungello, *The Great Encounter of China and the West, 1500–1800*, 3rd ed. (Lanham, MD: Rowman & Littlefield, 2009), 114–116.

66. D. E. Mungello, *The Spirit and the Flesh in Shandong, 1650–1785* (Lanham, MD: Rowman & Littlefield, 2001), 125, 129.

67. Irwin T. Hyatt Jr., *Our Ordered Lives Confess: Three Nineteenth-Century American Missionaries in East Shantung* (Cambridge, MA: Harvard University Press, 1976), 68.

3. ESTABLISHING FRIENDSHIPS IN IMPERIAL CHINA

1. Donald F. Lach, *Asia in the Making of Europe*, vol. 1, *The Century of Discovery*, 2 bks. (Chicago: University of Chicago Press, 1965), 211, 748.

2. C. R. Boxer, ed., *South China in the Sixteenth Century* (London: Hakluyt Society, 1953), 223.

3. Matteo Ricci, SI, *Fonti Ricciane*, ed. Pasquale M. D'Elia, SI, 3 vols. (Rome: La Libreria dello Stato, 1942), 1:98.

4. Irene Pih, *Le Pere Gabriel de Magalhães, un Jésuite portugais en Chine au XVIIe siècle* (Paris: Centro Cultural Português, 1979), 79–80.

5. Alfons Väth, SJ, *Johann Adam Schall von Bell S.J., Missionar in China, kaiserlicher Astronom und Ratgeber am Hofe von Peking 1592–1666*, unter Mitwirkung von Louis Van Hee, SJ, rev. ed. (Nettetal: Steyler, 1991), 249.

6. *Sinica Franciscana*, vol. 6, *Relationes et epistolas primorum Fratrum Minorum Italorum in Sinis (Saeculis 17 et 18)*, ed. Georgius Mensaert, OFM, in collaboration with Fortunato Margiotti, OFM, and [Antonius] Sisto Rosso, OFM, 2 pts. (Rome: Segreteria delle Missioni, 1961), 359. Also see Claudia von Collani, "Charles Maigrot's Role in the Chinese Rites Controversy," in *The Chinese Rites Controversy: Its History and Meaning*, ed. D. E. Mungello (Nettetal: Steyler, 1994), 164.

7. Joseph Brucker, SJ, "Schall von Bell," in *The Catholic Encyclopedia* (New York, 1912), 13:522–523.

8. Joseph Brucker, SJ, "Les missionaries catholiques aujourd'hui et autrefois," *Études*, July 5, 1901, 62–68.

9. George H. Dunne, *Generation of Giants: The Story of the Jesuits in China in the Last Decades of the Ming Dynasty* (Notre Dame, IN: University of Notre Dame Press, 1962), 329–331.

10. Louis Pfister, SJ, *Notices biographiques et bibliographiqes sur les Jésuites de l'ancienne mission de Chine 1552–1773* (Shanghai: Imprimerie de la Mission Catholique T'ou-sè-wè, 1932–1934), 172.

11. Väth, *Johann Adam Schall von Bell S.J.*, 250.

12. Lo-shu Fu, *A Documentary Chronicle of Sino-Western Relations (1644–1820)*, 2 vols. (Tucson: University of Arizona Press, 1966), 447.

13. Fang Chao-ying, "Yang Kuang-hsien," in *Eminent Chinese of the Ch'ing Period*, ed. Arthur Hummel (Washington, DC: United States Government Printing Office, 1943), 889–892.

14. Fu, *A Documentary Chronicle*, 37–38, 447.

15. Ferdinand Verbiest, ed., *Xichao ding'an* (collection of documents from the Kangxi reign), in *Tianzhujiao dongchuan wenxian* (collection of documents from the eastern mission of the Catholic Church) (Taipei: Taiwan Student Bookshop, 1965), 175.

16. Brucker, "Schall von Bell," 523.

17. John Boswell, *Christianity, Social Tolerance, and Homosexuality* (Chicago: University of Chicago Press, 1980), 315, 318–332. See also Michael Goodrich, *The Unmentionable Vice: Homosexuality in the Later Medieval Period* (Santa Barbara, CA: Ross-Erikson, 1979).

18. Jeffrey Richards, *Sex, Dissidence and Damnation: Minority Groups in the Middle Ages* (New York: Barnes & Noble, 1996).

19. Matteo Ripa, *Storia della fondazione della Congregazione e del Collegio de' Chinese sotto it titolo della Sagra Famiglia di Gesù Cristo, scritta dallo stesso fondatore Matteo Ripa e de' viaggi da lui fatti*, 3 vols. (Napoli: Manfredi, 1832), 1:8–9. There is an abridged English translation by Fortunato Prandi entitled *Memoirs of Father Ripa during Thirteen Years' Residence at the court of Peking in the Service of the Emperor of China* (London: John Murray, 1844). However, many details have been omitted, and at times the translation is very loose, almost a paraphrase.

20. Giacomo di Fiore, "Un cinese a Castel Sant'Angelo: La vicenda di un alumno del Collegio di Matteo Ripa fra transgressione e reclusione," *La Conoscenza dell'Asia e dell'Africa in Italia nei Secoli XVIII e XIX* (1985), 281–282.

21. Ripa, *Memoirs*, 33.

22. Ripa, *Memoirs*, 93–95. See Joseph Dehergne, SJ, "La Mission de Pékin vers 1700," *Archivum historicum Societatis Iesu* 22 (1953): 333.

23. Ripa, *Memoirs*, 98.

24. Ripa, *Storia*, 2:133.

25. Ripa, *Memoirs*, 133; Ripa, *S.F.*, 2:142, cited in Di Fiore, "Un cinese," 220–221.

26. Ripa, *Storia*, 2:145.

27. Ripa, *Storia*, 2:146.

28. Ripa, *Storia*, 2:153–154.

29. Ripa, *Storia*, 2:168–169.

30. Ripa, *Storia*, 2:193–194.

31. Ripa, *Storia*, 2:260.

32. Di Fiori, "Un cinese," 222, citing Ripa, *Storia*, 2:451.

33. Ripa, *Storia*, 3:195.

34. Ripa, *Storia*, 3:201. See Di Fiore, "Un cinese," 281–282.

35. Di Fiori, "Un cinese," 224, citing Ripa, *Storia*, 3:300, 308.

36. Di Fiori, "Un cinese," 227, citing Ripa *Storia*, 3:330, 345.

37. Di Fiori, "Un cinese, 227.

38. Di Fiori, "Un cinese," 228, citing Ripa, *Storia*, 3:411.

39. Di Fiori, "Carità e reclusione nell'Europa del Settecento. La disavventure carcerairie di due cinesi al seguito di Jean-François Foucquet e di Matteo Ripa," in *Scritture di Storia*, 49–89 (Napoli: Edizioni Scientifiche Italiane, 2005), 78.

40. Di Fiori, "Un cinese," 230.

41. Di Fiore, "Un cinese," 252.

42. Di Fiore, "Carità," 85–86.

43. Dr Fiori, "Un cinese," 235.

44. Di Fiore, "Carità," 79.

45. Di Fiore, "Un cinese," 253.

46. Di Fiore, "Un cinese," 233–235.
47. Di Fiore, "Un cinese," 237.
48. Di Fiore, "Un cinese," 239; "Carità," 80.
49. Di Fiore, "Carita," 83.
50. Di Fiore, "Un cinese," 242.
51. Di Fiore, "Un cinese," 250–251.
52. Di Fiore, "Carità," 81.
53. Di Fiore, "Un cinese," 244–245.
54. Di Fiore, "Un cinese," 261; "Carità," 75.
55. There has been considerable confusion about Ripa's date of death, which was 1746. Most sources have given his date of death as November 22, 1745. These sources have included Samuel Couling, *Encyclopedia Sinica* (Shanghai, 1917), 485, and Fang Hao, *Zhongguo Tianzhujiao shi renwu chuan*, 3 vols. (Hong Kong: Gongjiao Renlixue Hui, 1970–1973), 2:347. Fang Chao-ying's article on "Yin-jeng" in *Eminent Chinese of the Ch'ing Period 1644–1911* (Washington, DC, 1943), 925, gives the year as 1745. By contrast, Nigel Cameron, *Barbarians and Mandarins* (Chicago: University of Chicago Press, 1976), 287, gives Ripa's year of death as 1756.
56. Di Fiore, "Un cinese," 264.
57. Di Fiore, "Un cinese," 269.
58. Di Fiore, "Un cinese," 270.
59. Francesco D'Arelli, "The Chinese College in Eighteenth-Century Naples," *East and West* 58 (2008): 306.

4. ESTABLISHING FRIENDSHIPS IN POST-1911 CHINA

1. Matteo Ricci, *On Friendship: One Hundred Maxims for a Chinese Prince*, trans. Timothy Billings (New York: Columbia University Press, 2009), 10–13.
2. James Kraft, *Who Is Witter Bynner? A Biography* (Albuquerque: University of New Mexico Press, 1995), 50, 63–64.
3. Harold Acton, *Memoirs of an Aesthete* (London: Methuen, 1948), 365.
4. Cyril Birch, "Harold Acton as a Translator from the Chinese," in *Oxford, China, and Italy: Writings in Honour of Sir Harold Acton on His Eightieth Birthday*, ed. Edward Chaney and Neil Ritchie (London: Thames and Hudson, 1984), 43.
5. In his preface to *The Peach Blossom Fan*, Acton states that he and Chen had made a draft translation of "all but the last seven scenes," which would represent thirty-three, but in a later article, Cyril Birch stated that Chen and Acton had completed thirty-four of the forty scenes. See K'ung Shang-jen, *The Peach Blossom Fan* [T'an-hua-shan], trans. Chen Shih-hsiang and Harold Acton, with the collaboration of Cyril Birch (Berkeley: University of California Press, 1976), vii; Birch, "Harold Acton as a Translator from the Chinese," 43.

6. Private correspondence with Professor Cyril Birch, July 16, 2010.

7. Selina Hastings, *The Secret Lives of Somerset Maugham: A Biography* (New York: Random House, 2010), 3–4.

8. Hastings, *The Secret Lives of Somerset Maugham*, 187.

9. Hastings, *The Secret Lives of Somerset Maugham*, 178–181.

10. Hastings, *The Secret Lives of Somerset Maugham*, 291–293.

11. Hastings, *The Secret Lives of Somerset Maugham*, 241–248; H. J. Lethbridge, introduction to *On a Chinese Screen*, by W. Somerset Maugham (1922; reprinted, New York: Paragon House, 1990), xi.

12. Maugham, *On a Chinese Screen*, 193–203.

13. "Ku Hung-ming," in *Biographical Dictionary of Republican China*, ed. Howard L. Boorman, 5 vols. (New York: Columbia University Press, 1968), 2:250–252.

14. Maugham, *On a Chinese Screen*, 152.

15. Maugham, *On a Chinese Screen*, 78–79.

16. Hastings, *The Secret Lives of Somerset Maugham*, 180, 244, 263.

17. Hastings, *The Secret Lives of Somerset Maugham*, 263.

18. Hastings, *The Secret Lives of Somerset Maugham*, 293.

19. Green, *Children of the Sun: A Narrative of "Decadence" in England after 1918* (New York: Basic Books, 1976), 287.

20. Stephen Spender, *World within World: The Autobiography of Stephen Spender* (1951; reprinted, New York: St. Martin's, 1994), 121–129.

21. W. H. Auden and Christopher Isherwood, *Journey to a War* (New York: Random House, 1939), 13.

22. Auden and Isherwood, *Journey to a War*, 56.

23. Auden and Isherwood, *Journey to a War*, 65.

24. Auden and Isherwood, *Journey to a War*, 60–61.

25. Auden and Isherwood, *Journey to a War*, 51.

26. Auden and Isherwood, *Journey to a War*, 178–179.

27. Patricia Laurence, *Lilly Briscoe's Chinese Eyes: Bloomsbury, Modernism, and China.* (Columbia: University of South Carolina Press, 2003), 50, 186, 415.

28. Auden and Isherwood, *Journey to a War*, 237.

29. Soulié de Morant, *Pei Yu: Boy Actress*, trans. Gerald Fabian and Guy Wernham (San Francisco: Alamo Square Press, 1991), 109–111.

30. Wang Dingjiu, *Shanghai menjing* (Shanghai: Zhongyang shudian, 1932). This guide to Shanghai is discussed in Wenqing Kang, *Obsession: Male Same-Sex Relations in China, 1900–1950* (Hong Kong: Hong Kong University Press, 2009), 104–105.

31. Frederick Wakeman Jr., *Policing Shanghai, 1927–1937* (Berkeley: University of California Press, 1995), 12–13, 105–106.

32. Anne-Marie Brady, *Friend of China: The Myth of Rewi Alley* (London: Routledge, 2002), 31, 122–123.

33. Anne-Marie Brady, "'Treat Insiders and Outsiders Differently': The Use and Control of Foreigners in the PRC," *China Quarterly* 164 (2000): 952.

34. Brady, *Friend of China*, 8–12.

35. Rewi Alley, *At 90: Memoirs of My China Years* (Beijing: New World Press, 1987), 41.

36. Brady, *Friend of China*, 14–15.

37. Brady, *Friend of China*, 16.

38. Brady, *Friend of China*, 18–19.

39. Giovanni Vitiello, "The Dragon's Whim: Ming and Qing Homoerotic Tales from *The Cut Sleeve*," *T'oung Pao* 78 (1992): 349; Albert Chan, "Chinese-Philippine Relations in the Late Sixteenth Century and to 1603," *Philippine Studies* 26 (1978): 71.

40. Ihara Saikaku, *The Great Mirror of Male Love*, trans. Paul Gordon Schalow (Stanford, CA: Stanford University Press, 1990), 28.

41. Brady, *Friend of China*, 21.

42. Brady, *Friend of China*, 28–29.

43. Auden and Isherwood, *Journey to a War*, 245–246.

44. Brady, *Friend of China*, 30–31.

45. Brady, *Friend of China*, 37.

46. Brady, *Friend of China*, 39–47.

47. Brady, *Friend of China*, 48–49.

48. On Mao's sexual activity and use of Daoist sexual techniques, see the book written by his personal physician Li Zhisui, with editorial assistance of Anne F. Thurston, *The Private Life of Chairman Mao*, trans. Tai Hung-chao (New York: Random House, 1994), 356–364.

49. Brady, *Friend of China*, 50–56.

50. Brady, *Friend of China*, 63.

51. Brady, *Friend of China*, 101.

52. Brady, *Friend of China*, 119.

53. Brady, *Friend of China*, 122–124.

54. Andrea Weiss, *In the Shadow of the Magic Mountain: The Erika and Klaus Mann Story* (Chicago: University of Chicago Press, 2008), 113–116.

55. John Blofeld, *City of Lingering Splendour* (Boston: Shambala, 1989), 25–26.

56. David Kidd, *Peking Story: The Last Days of Old China* (New York: New York Review of Books, 2003), 3–5.

57. Nien Cheng, "The Bride Wore Platform Shoes," *New York Times Book Review*, April 17, 1988, 30.

58. Kidd, *Peking Story*, 30.

59. Kidd, *Peking Story*, 6.

60. Kidd, *Peking Story*, 15.

61. Kidd, *Peking Story*, 168–169.

62. Kidd, *Peking Story*, 169–170.

63. Private correspondence of the author with Professor Gaye Chan, chair of the Department of Art and Art History, University of Hawai'i at Manoa, July 6, 2010.

64. Michael Davidson, *The World, the Flesh and Myself* (Washington, DC: Guild Press, 1962), 261–262.

5. ESTABLISHING INTELLECTUAL CONNECTIONS WITH CHINA

1. R. J. Zwi Werblowsky, *The Beaten Track of Science: The Life and Work of J. J. M. De Groot*, ed. Hartmut Walravens (Wiesbaden: Harrossowitz, 2002), 12f.

2. Werblowsky, *The Beaten Track of Science*, 19–20.

3. Maurice Freedman, *The Study of Chinese Society: Essays by Maurice Freedman*, ed. G. W. Skinner (Stanford, CA: Stanford University Press, 1979), 356–357.

4. Kristopher Schipper, "The History of Taoist Studies in Europe/the West," in *Europe Studies China: Papers from an International Symposium on the History of European Sinology*, ed. Ming Wilson and John Cayley (Warren, CT: Floating World Editions, 2007), 472.

5. Werblowsky, *The Beaten Track of Science*, 25–26.

6. Werblowsky, *The Beaten Track of Science*, 33.

7. Werblowsky, *The Beaten Track of Science*, 16.

8. Marcel Granet, *La pensée chinoise* (Paris: La Renaissance du Livre, 1934; reprinted, Éditions Albin Michel, 1968), 491n214.

9. Werblowsky, *The Beaten Track of Science*, 18.

10. Werblowsky, *The Beaten Track of Science*, 29–30.

11. David B. Honey, *Incense at the Altar: Pioneering Sinologists and the Development of Classical Chinese Philology* (New Haven, CT: American Oriental Society, 2001), 129–130.

12. Werblowsky, *The Beaten Track of Science*, 18, 32.

13. Werblowsky, *The Beaten Track of Science*, 18.

14. W. Otterspeer, *De opvoedende kracht van den groentijd: Het Leidse ontgroenschandaal van 1911*(Leiden: Burgersdijk & Niermans, 1995), 21.

15. Werblowsky, *The Beaten Track of Science*, 31.

16. W. Otterspeer, *De opvoedende kracht van den groentijd*, 8–17.

17. Ottospeer, *De opvoedende kracht van den groentijd*, 22–23.

18. [J. J. M. De Groot], *Groenloopen. Een ernstig woord aan ouders en voogden van aanstaande studenten, door een hoogleeraar* (Amsterdam: Höveker & Wormser, 1904).

19. Otterspeer, *De opvoedende kracht van den groentijd* 18–19.

20. Otterspeer, *De opvoedende kracht van den groentijd*, 18.

21. Otterspeer, *De opvoedende kracht van den groentijd*, 18–19.

22. Otterspeer, *De opvoedende kracht van den groentijd*, 24. In 1910, forty-four professors responded to a survey on the question of reforming the degreening process. Eleven were opposed to the degreening process, nine supported it, twenty-two were for reform, and two were for radical reform.

23. J. J. M. De Groot, "Gesloten Brief aan de Leden der Staten-Generaal in zake het Groenlopen," Leiden, November 1911. De Groot's letter, along with the "green revue" libretto, is reproduced in Otterspeer, *De opvoedende kracht van den groentijd*, 42–51.

24. Otterspeer, *De opvoedende kracht van den groentijd*, 29.

25. Otterspeer, *De opvoedende kracht van den groentijd*, 49.

26. Otterspeer, *De opvoedende kracht van den groentijd*, 41.

27. Honey, *Incense at the Altar*, 224–225.

28. David Hawkes, "Obituary of Dr. Arthur Waley," *Asia Major* 12 (1966): 143f.

29. E. Bruce Brooks, "Arthur Waley," http:www.umass.edu/wsp/sinology/persons/waley.html (accessed November 15, 2009).

30. Patricia Laurence, *Lily Briscoe's Chinese Eyes: Bloomsbury, Modernism, and China* (Columbia: University of South Carolina Press, 2003), 306.

31. Gerald Brenan, *Personal Record, 1920–1972* (Cambridge, England: Cambridge University Press, 1974), 94.

32. Brooks, "Arthur Waley," 4.

33. Laurence, *Lily Briscoe's Chinese Eyes*, 309.

34. Hawkes, "Obituary of Dr. Arthur Waley," 147.

35. Laurence, *Lily Briscoe's Chinese Eyes*, 120, 400.

36. Virginia Woolf, *Letters*, 3:183, cited in Laurence, *Lily Briscoe's Chinese Eyes*, 308.

37. Harold Acton, *Memoirs of an Aesthete, 1939–1969* (New York: Viking, 1971), 26–27.

38. Speculation suggesting that Waley might have been homosexual has been voiced by several authors. Wyndham Lewis portrayed Waley (in the character Arthur Wildsmith) as an eccentric and repellant homosexual in his satirical novel of English society of the 1920s. See Wyndham Lewis, *The Apes of God* (1930; reprinted Santa Barbara, CA: Black Sparrow Press, 1981), 201–207. More recently, John Whittier Treat has written: "Both [Sir Richard Francis] Burton and Waley married, but neither fathered any children. Both led what biographers called 'separate domestic lives' from their wives. Their work, we are told was their true love. . . . Is there something about being a translator that especially appeals to us homosexuals?" John Whittier Treat, *Great Mirrors Shattered: Homosexuality, Orientalism, and Japan* (New York: Oxford University Press, 1999), 158–159. Additional speculation on Waley's homosexuality is found in John Walter de Gruchy, *Orienting*

Arthur Waley: Japonism, Orientalism, and the Creation of Japanese Literature in English (Honolulu: University of Hawai'i Press, 2003), 44–49 and 172–173.

39. Alison Waley, *A Half of Two Lives* (New York: McGraw-Hill, 1982), xvi–xvii.

40. Laurence, *Lily Briscoe's Chinese Eyes*, 309.

41. Brenan, *Personal Record*, 94–100.

42. Michael Holroyd, *Lytton Strachey: The New Biography* (New York: Farrar, Straus & Giroux, 1995), 462.

43. Brenan, *Personal Record*, 95.

44. Acton, *Memoirs of an Aesthete 1939–1969*, 28.

45. Acton, *Memoirs of an Aesthete 1939–1969*, 27.

46. Alison Waley, *A Half of Two Lives*, 10–12.

47. Alison Waley, *A Half of Two Lives*, 178–179.

48. Hilary Spurling, introduction to *A Half of Two Lives*, by Alison Waley, xxv.

49. Alison Waley, *A Half of Two Lives*, 98.

50. Hilary Spurling, introduction to *A Half of Two Lives*, by Alison Waley, xxii–xxiii.

51. Carmen Blacker, "Intent of Courtesy," in *Madly Singing in the Mountains*, ed. Ivan Morris (New York: Walker, 1970), 24–25.

52. Blacker, "Intent of Courtesy," 26–27.

53. Richard Deacon, *The Cambridge Apostles* (New York: Farrar, Straus & Giroux, 1986), 17.

54. G. Lowes Dickinson, *Letters from John Chinaman* (London: R. Brimley Johnson, 1901).

55. G. Lowes Dickinson, *The Autobiography of G. Lowes Dickinson*, ed. Dennis Proctor (London: Duckworth, 1973), 68.

56. Deacon, *Cambridge Apostles*, 59.

57. Deacon, *Cambridge Apostles* 62–65.

58. Brooks, "Arthur Waley," 11.

59. The claim that Wittgenstein was a closeted homosexual was first made by W. W. Bartley III in his book *Wittgenstein* (1973; rev. ed., Lasalle, IL: Open Court, 1985). As is often the case with closeted men, Bartley's claim about Wittgenstein's homosexuality has been disputed. For a summary of this dispute, see Ray Monk, *Ludwig Wittgenstein: The Duty of Genius* (New York: Penguin, 1990), 581–586.

60. Deacon, *Cambridge Apostles*, 68.

61. Michael S. Sherry, *Gay Artists in Modern American Culture: An Imagined Conspiracy* (Chapel Hill: University of North Carolina Press, 2007), 1–2, 42–44.

62. Deacon, *Cambridge Apostles*, 65.

63. George Piggford, "Rupert Brooke," in *Who's Who in Gay and Lesbian History: From Antiquity to World War II* (London: Routledge, 2001), 70.

64. Alison Waley, *A Half of Two Lives*, 289–290.

65. Acton, *Memoirs of an Aesthete 1939–1969*, 140.

66. The leading scholar and translator of the entire *Xiyu ji*, Professor Anthony Yu, has no knowledge of this additional chapter and did not find it in *Monkey*. Private correspondence of Professor Yu with the author, August 6, 2010.

67. Steve Hogan and Lee Hudson, eds., *Completely Queer: Gay and Lesbian Encyclopedia* (New York: Henry Holt, 1998), 91–92.

68. Laurence, *Lily Briscoe's Chinese Eyes*, 266–279, 284–288.

69. Alison Waley, *A Half of Two Lives*, 67–68.

70. Hugh Trevor-Roper, *Hermit of Peking: The Hidden Life of Sir Edmund Backhouse*, rev. ed. (Harmondsworth, England: Penguin, 1978), 24.

71. Harold Acton, *Memoirs of an Aesthete 1939–1969*, 25–27.

72. It seems that this work was never published by Kelley and Walsh. The closest work to Acton's description seems to be *Famous Chinese Plays*, trans. and ed. by L. C. Arlington and H. Acton, illustrated (with musical notes) (Peiping: Henri Vetch, 1937).

73. Man-kuei Li, "Yüan Mei," in *Eminent Chinese of the Ch'ing Period*, ed. Arthur Hummel, 955 (Washington, DC: United States Government Printing Office, 1943).

74. Arthur Waley, *Yuan Mei, Eighteenth Century Chinese Poet* (London: George Allen and Unwin, 1956), 34.

75. Waley, *Yuan Mei*, 27.

76. Waley, *Yuan Mei*, 109.

77. Waley, *Yuan Mei*, 101, 210.

78. Jonathan Spence, "Yuan Mei," in *The Indiana Companion to Traditional Chinese Literature*, ed. William H. Nienhauser Jr. (Bloomington: Indiana University Press, 1986), 957.

79. Laurence Sickman, "Harold Acton in Peking," in *Oxford China and Italy: Writings in Honour of Sir Harold Acton on His Eightieth Birthday*, ed. Edward Chaney and Neil Ritchie (London: Thames & Hudson, 1984), 69.

80. Acton, *Memoirs of an Aesthete*, 323.

81. Grant Hayter-Menzies, *Imperial Masquerade: The Legend of Princess Der Ling* (Hong Kong: Hong Kong University Press, 2008); Shuo Wang, "Der Ling: Manchu Princess, Cultural Advisor, and Author," in *The Human Tradition in Modern China*, ed. Kenneth J. Hammond and Kristin Stapleton (Lanham, MD: Rowman & Littlefield, 2008), 73–91.

82. Princess Der Ling, *Two Years in the Forbidden City* (New York: Moffat, Yard, 1911).

83. Acton, *Memoirs of an Aesthete*, 278–279.

84. Acton, *Memoirs of an Aesthete*, 276 facing.

85. Acton, *Memoirs of an Aesthete*, 370.

86. Acton, *Memoirs of an Aesthete*, 328.

87. Cyril Birch, "Harold Acton as a Translator from the Chinese," in *Oxford China and Italy: Writings in Honour of Sir Harold Acton on his Eightieth Birthday*, ed. Edward Chaney and Neil Ritchie (London: Thames & Hudson, 1984), 40–41.

88. "Alan Priest Dies," *New York Times*, January 23, 1969, 27.

89. Acton, *Memoirs of an Aesthete*, 252.

90. A. C. Scott, *The Classical Theatre of China* (New York: Macmillan, 1957), 32–37.

91. Acton, *Memoirs of an Aesthete 1939–1969*, 251.

92. Frances Wood, *The Lure of China: Writers from Marco Polo to J. G. Ballard* (South San Francisco: Long River Press, 2009), 179.

93. Acton, *Memoirs of an Aesthete*, 353.

94. Acton, *Memoirs of an Aesthete*, 393–394.

95. Acton, *Memoirs of an Aesthete*, 353–354.

96. Acton, *Memoirs of an Aesthete*, 368.

97. A. M. Wentink, "Harold Acton," in *Who's Who in Gay and Lesbian History*, ed. Robert Aldrich and Garry Wotherspoon (London: Routledge, 2001), 3–4.

98. Acton, *Memoirs of an Aesthete*, 393–394.

99. Letter of Julian Bell to E. P., March 20, 1936, cited in Laurence, *Lily Briscoe's Chinese Eyes*, 68–69.

100. Quentin Bell, ed., *Julian Bell: Essays, Poems and Letters* (London: Hogarth Press, 1938), 79.

101. Letter of Julian Bell to E. P., October 21, 1936, cited in Laurence, *Lily Briscoe's Chinese Eyes*, 68.

102. James Lord, *Some Remarkable Men: Further Memoirs* (New York: Farrar, Straus & Giroux, 1996), 13.

103. Acton, *Memoirs of an Aesthete 1939–1969*, 2–3.

104. Acton, *Memoirs of an Aesthete*, 323–324.

105. For the sake of simplicity, I have converted Acton's Wade-Giles romanization to pinyin. Hence his reference to Prince P'u Ju (P'u Hsin-yü) is rendered in this book as Pu Ru (Pu Xinyu). *Memoirs of an Aesthete*, 372–375.

106. "Ch'i Pai-shih," in *Biographical Dictionary of Republican China*, ed. Howard L. Boorman, 1:302–304 (New York: Columbia University Press, 1967).

107. Bell, *Julian Bell*, 80.

108. Acton refers to Ling Shuhua by her married name of "Mrs. Ch'en Yin-k'o." Acton, *Memoirs of an Aesthete*, 376–378.

109. Wen Fong, *The Lohans and a Bridge to Heaven*, Freer Gallery of Art Occasional Papers, vol. 3, no. 1 (Washington, DC: Smithsonian, 1958), 24–27.

110. Qu Yuan (340?–278 BC) is one of the most famous poets in Chinese culture.

111. Lord, *Some Remarkable Men*, 54. There is a ceramic Tang dynasty horse that seems to fit this description in the catalog *Handbook of the Collections in the William Rockhill Nelson Gallery of Art and Mary Atkins Museum of Fine Arts*, vol. 2, *Art of the Orient*, 5th ed. (Kansas City, MO: University Trustees W. R. Nelson Trust, 1973), 83. The caption on the illustration is "Saddle Horse, Tang Dynasty (618–906), 8th century. Glazed pottery, 23" high. The body is cream-white, the mane yellow and the saddle-cloth is a brilliant blue."

112. Acton, *Memoirs of an Aesthete 1939–1969*, 90.

113. Acton, *Memoirs of an Aesthete 1939–1969*, 116–117.

114. Lord, *Some Remarkable Men*, 20, 63–64.

115. Acton, *Memoirs of an Aesthete 1939–1969*, xiv.

116. Harold Acton, *The Bourbons of Naples (1734–1825)* (London: Methuen, 1956); *The Last Bourbons of Naples (1825–1861)* (London: Methuen, 1961).

117. Because Chiang Kai-shek's Nationalist government moved the capital from Beijing to Nanjing during the years 1928 to 1949, the name of Beijing during those years was changed to Beiping.

118. J. D. Schmidt, *"Ching-chü"* and *"K'un-ch'u,"* in *The Indian Companion to Traditional Chinese Literature*, ed. William H. Nienhauser Jr. (Bloomington: Indiana University Press, 1986), 316–318, 514–516.

119. A. C. Scott, *The Classical Theatre of China* (New York: Macmillan, 1957), 33–37.

120. Beatrice Kit Fun Leung, "The Missionaries," in *Handbook of Christianity in China*, vol. 2, *1800–Present*, ed. R. G. Tiedemann (Leiden: Brill, 2010), 794.

121. William Wright, *Harvard's Secret Court: The Savage 1920 Purge of Campus Homosexuals* (New York: St. Martin's, 2005).

122. Private communication of the author with Douglass Shand Tucci of January 23, 2010. See Douglass Shand-Tucci, *The Crimson Letter: Harvard, Homosexuality, and the Shaping of American Culture* (New York: St. Martin's, 2003).

123. Glen W. Baxter, "Hua-chien chi; Songs of the Tenth Century China: A Study of the First Tz'u Anthology," PhD diss., Harvard University, 1952.

124. Sima Guang, Achilles Fang, Bernard S. Solomon, and Glen W. Baxter, *The Chronicle of the Three Kingdoms (220–265): Chapters 69–78 from the Tzu Chih t'ung chien of Ssu-ma Kuang.* (Cambridge, MA: Harvard University Press, 1952).

125. Private communication with Professor Patrick Hanan, December 21, 2009.

126. Patricia Ebrey and Robert Crawford, "Obituary of Howard Wechsler (1942–1980)," *Journal of Asian Studies* 46, no.1 (1987): 227.

127. "Prof. Arthur Wright of Yale, 62, Scholar of Chinese History, Dies," *New York Times*, August 14, 1976, 19.

128. Personal correspondence of July 20, 2011; name of letter writer withheld by this author.

129. Marston Anderson, "The Fiction of Wu Zu-xiang," MA thesis, University of California Press, Berkeley, 1978.

130. Marston Anderson, "Narrative and Critique: The Construction of Social Reality in Modern Chinese Literature," PhD thesis, University of California Press, Berkeley, 1985.

131. Marston Anderson, *The Limits of Realism: Chinese Fiction in the Revolutionary Period* (Berkeley: University of California Press, 1990), vii.

132. Kang-I Sun, "Zuihou yige judian" [Final Words], first published in the Taiwanese journal *Zhongwai wenxue* [Chung-wai Literary Review], February 1993, 160–162; reprinted in *Yesu qianxue ji* (Xi'an: Shaanxi Shifandaxue chubanshe, 1998), 38–39.

133. Private correspondence of Kang-I Sun Chang to the author, June 22, 2010.

6. THE REORIENTATION OF WESTERN AESTHETICS

1. Paul Demiéville, "Aperçu historique des etudes sinologiques en France," *Acta Asiatica* 11 (1966): 79–107.

2. Jonathan Spence, *The Chan's Great Continent: China in Western Minds* (New York: Norton, 1998), 146.

3. The differences in interpretation are apparent in two recent editions of Segalen's novel *René Leys*. The edition edited by Marie Dollé and Christian Doumet gives more emphasis to Segalen's homosexuality than does the edition edited by Sophie Labatut. Cf. Victor Segalen, *René Leys*, ed. Marie Dollé and Christian Doumet (Paris: Librairie Générale Française, 1999); Victor Segalen, *René Leys*, ed. Sophie Labatut (Paris: Gallimard, 2000).

4. Segalen, *René Leys*, ed. Dollé and Doumet, 278f.

5. Segalen, *René Leys*, ed. Dollé and Doumet, 271.

6. Victor Segalen, *Stèles*, trans. Timothy Billings and Christopher Bush (Wesleyan University Press, 2007).

7. Spence, *Emperor of China: Self-Portrait of K'ang-hsi* (New York: Random House, 1975), 119–122.

8. Arthur Hummel, ed., *Eminent Chinese of the Ch'ing Period* (Washington, DC: United States Government Printing Office, 1943), 729–731.

9. Jerome Ch'en, "The Last Emperor of China," *Bulletin of the School of Oriental and African Studies* 28 (1965): 340–341.

10. Fang Chao-ying, "Tsai-t'ien," in *Eminent Chinese of the Ch'ing Period*, ed. Hummel, 732.

11. Segalen, *René Leys*, ed. Dollé and Doumet, 181.

12. Segalen, *René Leys*, ed. Dollé and Doumet, 184.

13. Segalen, *René Leys*, ed. Dollé and Doumet, 253.

14. Hummel, *Eminent Chinese of the Ch'ing Period*, 385.

15. Segalen, *René Leys*, ed. Dollé and Doumet, 115. Cf. Victor Segalen, *René Leys*, trans. J. A. Underwood (New York: New York Review of Books, 2003), 66.

16. Segalen, *René Leys*, ed. Dollé and Doumet, 260–261; cf. Segalen, *René Leys*, trans. Underwood, 201–202.

17. Ian Buruma, preface to Segalen, *René Leys*, trans. Underwood, x.

18. Trevor-Roper, *Hermit of Peking: The Hidden Life of Sir Edmund Backhouse*, rev. ed. (Harmondsworth, England: Penguin, 1978), 361.

19. The muses and their respective arts were as follows: Calliope (epic poetry), Clio (history), Euterpe (flute playing), Melpomene (tragedy), Terpsichore (dancing), Erato (the lyre), Polyhymnia (sacred song), Urania (astronomy), and Thalia (comedy). See Paul Harvey, *The Oxford Companion to Classical Literature* (Oxford: Oxford University Press, 1937), 280–281.

20. James Kraft, *Who Is Witter Bynner? A Biography* (Albuquerque: University of New Mexico Press, 1995), 41–42.

21. Witter Bynner, *Selected Letters*, ed. James Kraft (New York: Farrar, Straus & Giroux, 1981), 55.

22. Bynner letter to Barry Faulkner, Shanghai, May 22, 1917, in Bynner, *Selected Letters*, 59.

23. Bynner to Faulkner, *Selected Letters*, 59–61.

24. Bynner, *Selected Letters*, 66.

25. Kraft, *Who Is Witter Bynner?*, 49.

26. Bynner, *Selected Letters*, 65; Kraft, "Biographical Introduction," in *Selected Poems*, by Witter Bynner, xlix; Kraft, *Who Is Witter Bynner?*, 42, 47–48.

27. Bynner, *Selected Letters*, 70.

28. "Chiang K'ang-hu," in *Biographical Dictionary of Republican China*, ed. Howard L. Boorman (New York: Columbia University Press, 1967), 338–344.

29. Bynner, *Selected Letters*, 68–69.

30. Kraft, "Biographical Information," in *Selected Poems*, by Bynner, l.

31. Witter Bynner, *The Chinese Translations* (New York: Farrar, Straus & Giroux, 1978), 6–7; Bynner, *Selected Letters*, 74–75.

32. Witter Bynner, *Prose Pieces*, ed. James Kraft (New York: Farrar, Straus & Giroux, 1979), 80.

33. Bynner letter to Edna St. Vincent Millay, September 10, 1920, in *Selected Letters*, 77.

34. Samuel Couling, *The Encyclopedia Sinica* (Shanghai: Kelly & Walsh, 1917), 379.

35. Bynner, *Prose Pieces*, 71.

36. Bynner, *Chinese Translations*, 6–7.

37. Bynner, *Prose Pieces*, 86.

38. Bynner, *Prose Pieces*, 80.

39. Kraft, *Who Is Witter Bynner?*, 44–45.

40. Bynner, "Tempest in a China Teapot," in *Prose Pieces*, 241–246.

41. Ernest Fenollosa, *The Chinese Written Character as a Medium for Poetry*, ed. Ezra Pound (London: Stanley Nott, 1936).

42. Shuen-fu Lin, "Tangshi sanbaishou," in *Indiana Companion to Traditional Chinese Literature*, ed. Wm. H. Nienhauser Jr., 755 (Bloomington: Indiana University Press, 1986).

43. Burton Watson, "Introduction to *The Jade Mountain*," in *The Chinese Translations*, by Bynner, 15–16.

44. Bynner, *Prose Pieces*, 69.

45. *The Jade Mountain*, trans. Witter Bynner, from the texts of Kiang Kang-hu (1929; Garden City, New York: Anchor, 1964), vii.

46. Nienhauser, *Indiana Companion to Traditional Chinese Literature*, 756.

47. Paul W. Kroll, "Reflections on Recent Anthologies of Chinese Literature in Translation," *Journal of Asian Studies* 61 (2002): 988.

48. Watson, "Introduction to *The Jade Mountain*," 23.

49. Bynner, *The Jade Mountain*, xvii.

50. David Lattimore, "Introduction to *The Way of Life According to Laotzu*," in *Chinese Translations*, by Bynner, 313.

51. Lattimore, "Introduction to *The Way of Life According to Laotzu*," in *Chinese Translations*, by Bynner, 309–310.

52. Lattimore, "Introduction to *The Way of Life According to Laotzu*," in *Chinese Translations*, by Bynner, 314.

53. Lattimore, "Introduction to *The Way of Life According to Laotzu*," in *Chinese Translations*, by Bynner, 324–325.

54. Kraft, "Biographical Introduction," in *Selected Poems*, by Bynner, lxxiii–lxxiv.

55. Homer H. Dubs, review of *The Way of Life According to Laotzu*, *Journal of the American Oriental Society* 65 (1945): 212.

56. Wm. Theodore de Bary and Ainslie T. Embree, *A Guide to Oriental Classics* (New York: Columbia University Press, 1964), 132.

57. Bynner letter to Haniel Long, August 1, 1920, in *Selected Letters*, 75.

58. Kraft, "Biographical Introduction," in *Selected Poems*, by Bynner, lviii.

59. Hartmut Walravens, *Vincenz Hundhausen (1878–1955): Leben und Werk des Dichters, Druckers, Verlegers, Professors, Regisseurs und Anwalts in Peking* (Wiesbaden: Harrossowitz, 1999), 19.

60. Lutz Bieg, "Literary Translations of the Classical Lyric and Drama of China in the First Half of the 20th Century: The 'Case' of Vincenz Hundhausen (1878–1955)," in *De l'un au multiple: traductions du chinois vers les langues europeennes*, ed. Viviane Alleton and Michael Lackner (Paris: Maison des sciences de l'homme, 1999), 69–70.

61. Sunglin [d.i. Herbert Mueller], "Auf der Pappelinsel, Vincenz Hundhausen in Peking zum Fünfundsiebzigsten," in *Vincenz Hundhause Leben und Werk*, by Walravens, 40.

62. Herbert Mueller, "Vincenz Hundhausen, 1878–1955," in *Vincenz Hundhausen: Leben und Werk*, by Walravens, 13–14.

63. Walter Fuchs, "Vincenz Hundhausen, 1878–1955," *Journal of Oriental Studies* 3, no. 2 (1956): 322–323.

64. Harold Acton, *Memoirs of an Aesthete* (London: Methuen, 1948), 326–327.

65. Acton, *Memoirs of an Aesthete*, 327.

66. Hartmut Walravens, ed., *Richard Wilhelm (1873–1930). Missionar in China und Vermittler chinesischen Geistesguts* (Nettetal: Steyler, 2008), 7.

67. Irmgard Grimm, *Erinnerungen aus meinem bunten Leben* (Hannover: Author, 1992), 67.

68. Joseph Viktor von Scheffel, *Der Trompeter von Säckingen* (Stuttgart: Metzler, 1854).

69. Ulrich Scheck, "Joseph Viktor von Scheffel," in *Nineteenth-Century German Writers, 1841–1900* (Detroit, MI: Gale Research, 1993), 129:336.

70. Sherwin Simmons, "Advertising Seizes Control of Life: Berlin Dada and the Power of Advertising," *Oxford Art Journal* 22, no. 1 (1999): 119.

71. *Biographical Dictionary of Republican China*, ed. Howard L. Boorman (New York: Columbia University Press, 1967), 2:21–24.

72. Bieg, "Literary Translations," 69.

73. John C. Ferguson's review of *Die Rückkehr der Seele* by Professor Hundhausen, 3 vols. (Zürich and Leipzig: Rascher Verlag, 1937), in *Vincenz Hundhausen (1878–1955) Nachdichtungen, Pekinger Bühnenspiele und zeitgenössische Kritik*, by Walravens (Wiesbaden: Harrassowitz, 2000), 99.

74. James M. Hargett, "Hsi-hsiang chi," in *Indiana Companion to Traditional Chinese Literature*, ed. Nienhauser, 407–409.

75. K. C. Leung, "Kao Ming," in *Indiana Companion to Traditional Chinese Literature*, ed. Nienhauser, 473–474.

76. Herman Hiltbrunner, review of Hundhausen's adaptation of Gau Ming, "Laute," in *Deutsch-Chinesische Nachrichten*, April 22, 1934, 4.

77. Erich Schmitt, review of Vincenz Hundhausen's *Das Westzimmer, Orientalische Literaturzeitung* 4 (1929): col. 300–304. The translation by Julien was "*Si-siang-ki ou l'Histoire du Pavillon d'Occident. Comédie en seize actes,*" Atsume Gusa, 1872–1880.

78. Dr. M. E. R. F. Meerkerk, "A German Translation of the His Hsiang Chi (A Review)," in *Vincenz Hundhausen Nachdichtungen*, by Walravens, 77.

79. David B. Honey, *Incense at the Alter: Pioneering Sinologists and the Development of Classical Chinese Philology* (New Haven, CT: American Oriental Society, 2001), 130–131.

80. E. Haenisch, review of Hundhausen's *Das Westzimmer, Asia Major* 8 (1933): 278–282, reprinted in Walravens, *Vincenz Hundhausen Nachdichtungen*, 79–83.

81. Paul Pelliot, *T'oung Pao* 27 (1930): 220.

82. Bieg, "Literary Translations," 76–77.

83. Walravens, *Vincenz Hundhausen Nachdichtungen*, 110–111.

84. Vincenz Hundhausen, "Mein Lebenslauf," in *Vincenz Hundhausen: Leben und Werk*, by Walravens, 59–60.

85. Bieg, "Literary Translations," 72.

86. Magnus Hirschfeld, "Die Lotusinsel," in *Vincenz Hundhausen: Leben und Werk*, by Walravens, 29–30.

87. Jason Gagliardi, "Mystery Man Could Unlock Sexology Files," *South China Morning Post* (Hong Kong), August 22, 1999.

88. Ron Dutton, "The Mystery of Li Shiu Tong," *Xtra West*, October 16, 2003, http://archives.extra.ca/Story.aspx?s=2265328 7/11/2011.

89. In 2006, the Tretter Collection of the University of Minnesota Libraries purchased the Hirschfeld materials from the Li family. *Tretter Letter (Newsletter for the Friends of the Tretter Collection)* 2, no. 1 rev. (January 2007): 1, 3.

90. Walravens, *Vincenz Hundhausen: Leben und Werk*, 93–97.

91. Wilma Fairbank, "Laurence Chalfant Stevens Sickman, 1906–1988," *Archives of Asian Art* 42 (1989): 82.

92. David Leddick, *Intimate Companions: A Triography of George Platt Lynes, Paul Cadmus, Lincoln Kirstein, and Their Circle* (New York: St. Martin's, 2000), 55–58; Martin Duberman, *The World of Lincoln Kirstein* (New York: Knopf, 2007), 29–92.

93. *Dictionary of Art Historians*, at www.dictionaryofarthistorians.org.

94. Fairbank, "Laurence Chalfant Stevens Sickman," 82.

95. Acton, *Memoirs of an Aesthete*, 324.

96. Laurence Sickman, "Harold Acton in Peking," in *Oxford China and Italy: Writings in Honour of Sir Harold Acton on His Eightieth Birthday*, ed. Edward Chaney and Neil Ritchie (London: Thames & Hudson, 1984), 70.

97. See *Fishermen* (handscroll detail), by Hsü Tao-ning (died about 1066–1067), ink on silk, 82" long, 19" wide, in *Handbook of the Collections in the William Rockhill Nelson Gallery of Art and Mary Atkins Museum of Fine Arts*, vol. 2, *Art of the Orient*, ed. Ross E. Taggart, George L. McKenna, and Marc F. Wilson, 5th ed. (Kansas City, MO: Nelson-Atkins Museum, 1973), 51.

98. See "The Empress as Donor with Attendants" (about 522), from the Pin-yang cave at the Buddhist cave chapels of Lung-men, Honan, in *Handbook of the Collections in the William Rockhill Nelson Gallery of Art*, 31.

EPILOGUE

1. Philip Gambone, *Beijing* (Madison: University of Wisconsin Press, 2003).

2. Gambone, *Beijing*, 27.

3. John Whittier Treat, *Great Mirrors Shattered: Homosexuality, Orientalism, and Japan* (New York: Oxford University Press, 1999), 154.

4. Treat, *Great Mirrors Shattered*, 174–175.

Chinese Character Glossary

Aikedun	艾克敦
An Mincheng	安敏成
Ba Jin	巴金
Bai Xianyong	白先勇
baobei	寶貝
Beidaihe	北戴河
beiyu	貝玉
bi	嬖
Bian er chai	辯而釵
Cao Xueqin	曹雪芹
changpao	長袍
Changsheng dian	長生殿
Chen Sen	陳森
Chen Shixiang	陳世驤
Cheng Yanqiu	程硯秋
Chun Qinwang, Zaifeng	醇親王, 載灃
ci	詞
dan	旦
Dapeng	大鵬
Daqing luli	大清律例
Dashijie	大世界
Dazhalan	大柵欄
Der Ling	德齡
duanxiu	斷袖
Fang Hao	方豪

Feng Zhi	馮至
fentao	分桃
Ganyu Hutung	甘雨胡同
Gao Ming	高明
Gengchen chaoben shitouji	庚辰鈔本石頭記
Gong Wang Fu	恭王府
Gu Hongming	辜鴻銘
Gubeikou	古北口
Guling	牯嶺
guoji zhuyizhe	國際主義者
Hadamendajie	哈大門大街
hei guanyin	黑觀音
Hong Sheng	洪昇
Hong Taosheng	洪濤生
Honglou meng	紅樓夢
Houdefu	厚德福
hua	花
Huang Batong	黃巴桐
Huang Jun	黃濬, zi 字, Bochuan 百川, 伯川
Huangren shouji	荒人手記
hutong	胡同
jia	家
Jiang Kanghu	江亢虎
Jiang Yuhan	蔣玉函
Jiaozhou	膠州
jijian	雞姦
jing pibei	敬皮杯
Jinghua yuan	鏡花緣
jingju	京劇
Jingshan	景善
Jinshan	金山
jingxi	京戲
jinshi	進士
Jiujiang	九江
Kang-I Sun	孫康宜
Kong Shangren	孔尚任
kuer	酷兒
kuer wenxue	酷兒文學
Kunqu	崑曲
Lao She	老舍
Li Hongzhang	李鴻章
Li Ruzhen	李汝珍
Li Shiu-tong (Li Zhaotang), Tao Li	李兆堂, 桃李

Li xinwang	禮親王
Li Yaotang	李堯棠
liangren	良人
Ling Shuhua	凌叔華
Liulichang	琉璃廠
liumang	流氓
longyang	龍陽
Longyu Huangtaihou	隆裕皇太后
Lu Xun	魯迅
luohan	羅漢
Luyi Aili	路易。艾黎
Ma Guoxian	馬國賢
Mei Li	美麗
Mei Lanfang	梅蘭芳
Moganshan	莫干山
nanfeng	南風
nanfeng	男風
Nanhai baize	南海柏子
nanse	男色
Neicheng	內城
Nie Shizhang	聶世璋
Niezi	孽子
Ning Dacheng	寧大成
Pan Jinxiao	潘盡孝
Pan Shihong	潘士弘
Pinhua baojian	品花寶鑒
Pipa ji	琵琶記
Puru	溥儒
Puyi	溥儀
qi	奇
Qi Baishi	齊白石
Qianmen	前門
qidi	契弟
Qiguan	琪官
qing	情
Qingnian hu	青年湖
qixiong	契兄
qiyang	戚養
Qu Yuan	屈原
San Malu	三馬路
Shanghai menjing	上海門徑
Shen Ruilin	沈瑞麟
shezhengwang	攝政王

Shitouji	石頭記
Shiduo	世鐸
Shoushan quan tu	首善全圖
Shu Qingchun	舒慶春
siyu	私寓
Suiyuan	隨園
Sun Zhu	孫洙
Tang Ruowang	湯若望
Tangshi sanbaishou	唐時三百首
Taohuashan	桃花扇
Tianqiao	天橋
Tianzhujiao dongchuan wenxian	天主教東傳文獻
tongxingai	同姓愛
tongxinglian	同姓戀
tongzhi	同志
tongzhi wenxue	同志文學
Tsai-feng	載灃
tu'er	兔兒
tuzi	兔子
Waicheng	外城
Wang Dingjiu	王定九
Wang Shihfu	王實甫
wangba	王八
Wei Zheng	魏徵
Wu Chengan	吳承恩
Wu Cuncun	吳存存
Wu Duomo	吳多默
Wu Lujue	吳露爵
Xia Gui	夏珪
xianggong	相公
xiaochang	小唱
Xichao ding'an	熙朝定案
Xin Gongyuan	新公園
xing	性
xingbie	性別
Xixiang ji	西廂記
Xiyou ji	西游記
Xu Jingcheng	許景澄
Yang Guangxian	楊光先
Yao shan shu yan	遙山書鴈
Yesu qianxue ji	耶穌潛学集
Yu Geng	裕庚
Yuan Chang	袁昶

Yuan Mei	袁枚
zan	贊
Zhangyi men	彰儀門
Zhaolian	昭槤
Zhengyangmen	正陽門
Zhongguo Tianzhujiao shi renwu chuan	中國天主教史人物傳
Zhongwai wenxue	中外文學
Zhongyang shudian	中央書店
Zhu Tianwen	朱天文
Zizhi tongjian	資治通鑒
Zongli Yamen	總理衙門
Zuihou yige judian	最后一个句点

Bibliography

Acton, Harold. *The Bourbons of Naples (1734–1825)*. London: Methuen, 1956.

———. *The Last Bourbons of Naples (1825–1861)*. London: Methuen, 1961.

———. *Memoirs of an Aesthete*. London: Methuen, 1948.

———. *Memoirs of an Aesthete 1939–1969* (originally entitled *More Memoirs of an Aesthete*). New York: Viking, 1971.

———. *Peonies and Ponies*. London: Chatto and Windus, 1941.

Aldrich, Robert. *The Seduction of the Mediterranean: Writing, Art and Homosexual Fantasy*. London: Routledge, 1993.

Aldrich, Robert, and Garry Wotherspoon, eds. *Who's Who in Gay and Lesbian History: From Antiquity to World War II*. London: Routledge, 2001.

Alley, Rewi. *At 90: Memoirs of My China Years*. Beijing: New World Press, 1987.

Anderson, Marston. "The Fiction of Wu Zu-xiang." MA thesis, University of California, Berkeley, 1978.

———. *The Limits of Realism: Chinese Fiction in the Revolutionary Period*. Berkeley: University of California Press, 1990.

———. "Narrative and Critique: The Construction of Social Reality in Modern Chinese Literature." PhD thesis, University of California, Berkeley, 1985.

Arlington, L. C., and H. Acton, trans. and eds. *Famous Chinese Plays*. Illustrated (with musical notes). Peiping: Henri Vetch, 1937.

Arlington, L. C., and William Lewisohn. *In Search of Old Peking*. Beijing: Henri Vetch, 1935.

Atwell, Pamela. "Obituary: George N. Kates (1895–1990)." *Journal of Asian Studies* 49 (1990): 1014–1015.

Auden, W. H., and Christopher Isherwood. *Journey to a War*. New York: Random House, 1939.

Bao Ruo-wang (Jean Pasqualini), and Rudolph Chelminski. *Prisoner of Mao*. Harmondsworth, England: Penguin, 1976.

Bartley, W. W., III. *Wittgenstein*. 1973. Revised edition, Lasalle, IL: Open Court, 1985.

Baxter, Glen W. "Hua-chien chi; Songs of the Tenth Century China: A Study of the First Tz'u Anthology." PhD dissertation, Harvard University, 1952.

Bell, Quentin. *Julian Bell: Essays, Poems and Letters*. London: Hogarth Press, 1938.

Biblioteca Nazionale Vittorio Emanuele III—Napoli (BNN).

Bieg, Lutz. "Literary Translations of the Classical Lyric and Drama of China in the First Half of the 20th Century: The 'Case' of Vincenz Hundhausen (1878–1955)." In *De l'un au multiple: Traductions du chinois vers les langues europeennes*, edited by Viviane Alleton and Michael Lackner, 63–83. Paris: Maison des sciences de l'homme, 1999.

Birch, Cyril. "Harold Acton as a Translator from the Chinese." In *Oxford China and Italy: Writings in Honour of Sir Harold Acton on His Eightieth Birthday*, edited by Edward Cheney and Neil Ritchie. London: Thames and Hudson, 1984, 37–44.

Bland, J. O. P., and Sir Edmund Backhouse. *China under the Empress Dowager: Being the History of the Life and Times of Tzu Hsi, Compiled from the State Papers and the Private Diary of the Comptroller of Her Household*. London: W. Heinemann, 1910.

Blofeld, John. *City of Lingering Splendour*. Boston: Shambala, 1989.

Boorman, Howard L., ed. *Biographical Dictionary of Republican China*. 5 vols. New York: Columbia University Press, 1967–1979.

Boswell, John. *Christianity, Social Tolerance, and Homosexuality*. Chicago: University of Chicago Press, 1980.

Boxer, C. R., ed. *South China in the Sixteenth Century*. London: Hakluyt Society, 1953.

Brady, Anne-Marie. *Friend of China: The Myth of Rewi Alley*. London: Routledge, 2002.

———. "'Treat Insiders and Outsiders Differently': The Use and Control of Foreigners in the PRC." *China Quarterly* 164 (2000): 943–964.

Brenan, Gerald. *Personal Record, 1920–1972*. Cambridge, England: Cambridge University Press, 1974.

Brook, Timothy. *The Confusions of Pleasure: Commerce and Culture in Ming China*. Berkeley: University of California Press, 1998.

Brooks, Bruce. "Arthur Waley." http:www.umass.edu/wsp/sinology/persons/waley.html (accessed November 15, 2009).

Browning, Frank. *A Queer Geography*. New York: Crown, 1996.

Brucker, Joseph, SJ. "Les missionaries catholiques aujourd'hui et autrefois." *Études*, July 5, 1901, 44–71.

———. "Schall von Bell." In *Catholic Encyclopedia*, vol. 13. New York, 1912.

Burton, Sir Richard Francis. "Terminal Essay." In *A Plain and Literal Translation of the Arabian Nights Entertainment*, 10 vols. Benares: Kamashastra Society, 1885–1895.

Bynner, Witter. *The Chinese Translations*. New York: Farrar, Straus & Giroux, 1978.

———, trans. *The Jade Mountain*, translated from the texts of Kiang Kanghu. 1929; Garden City, NY: Anchor, 1964.

———. *Prose Pieces*. Edited by James Kraft. New York: Farrar, Straus & Giroux, 1979.

———. *Selected Poems*. Edited by Richard Wilbur. New York: Farrar, Straus & Giroux, 1977.

———. *Selected Letters*. Edited by James Kraft. New York: Farrar, Straus & Giroux, 1981.

Byrne, Paula. *Mad World: Evelyn Waugh and the Secrets of Brideshead*. New York: HarperCollins, 2009.

Cameron, Nigel. *Barbarians and Mandarins*. Chicago: University of Chicago Press, 1976.

Cao Xueqin. *Gengchen chaoben shitouji*. 80 hui. 4 vols. Taipei: Guangwen Bookstore Company, 1977.

———. *The Story of the Stone*. Translated by David Hawkes and John Minford. 4 vols. London: Penguin, 1973–1982.

Catholic Encyclopedia. 16 vols. New York: Robert Appleton Co./Encyclopedia Press, 1907–1914.

Chan, Albert. "Chinese-Philippine Relations in the Late Sixteenth Century and to 1603." *Philippine Studies* 26 (1978): 51–82.

Chauncey, George. *Gay New York: Gender, Urban Culture, and the Making of the Gay Male World, 1890–1940*. New York: Basic Books, 1994.

Ch'en, Jerome. "The Last Emperor of China." *Bulletin of the School of Oriental and African Studies* 28 (1965): 336–355.

Chen Sen. *Pinhua baojian*. 4 *juan*. 1849; reprinted, Taipei: Tianyi Publishing Society, 1974.

Cheney, Edward, and Neil Ritchie, eds. *Oxford China and Italy: Writings in Honour of Sir Harold Acton on His Eightieth Birthday*. London: Thames and Hudson, 1984.

Choi, Won-shik. "West Goes East: Pearl Buck's *The Good Earth*." *Korea Journal* (Fall 2001).

Chu T'ien-wen. *Notes of a Desolate Man* [Huangren shouji]. Translated by Howard Goldblatt and Sylvia Li-chun Lin. New York: Columbia University Press, 1999.

Clark, Thekla. *Wystan and Chester*. New York: Columbia University Press, 1995.

Cocteau, Jean. *The White Book/Le Livre Blanc*. Translated by Margaret Crosland. San Francisco: City Lights Books, 1989.

Collani, Claudia von. "Charles Maigrot's Role in the Chinese Rites Controversy." In *The Chinese Rites Controversy: Its History and Meaning*, edited by D. E. Mungello, 149–183. Nettetal: Steyler, 1994.

Coote, Stephen, ed. *The Penguin Book of Homosexual Verse*. London: Penguin, 1986.

Couling, Samuel. *Encyclopedia Sinica*. Shanghai: Kelly & Walsh, 1917.

Damm, Jens. "Kuer vs. tongzhi—Diskurse der Homosexualität oder das Entstehen sexueller Identitäten in glokalieierten Taiwan und im postkolonialen Hongkong." *Berliner Chinahefte*, no. 18 (May 2000): 60–75.

———. "Same Sex Desire and Society in Taiwan, 1970–1987." *China Quarterly* 181 (2005): 67–81.

D'Arelli, Francesco. "The Chinese College in Eighteenth-Century Naples." *East and West* 58 (2008): 283–312.

Davidson, Michael. *Some Boys*. London: Gay Men's Press, 1988.

———. *The World, The Flesh and Myself*. Washington, DC: Guild Press, 1962.

De Bary, Wm. Theodore, and Ainslie T. Embree. *A Guide to Oriental Classics*. New York: Columbia University Press, 1964.

De Groot, J. J. M. "Gesloten Brief aan de Leden der Staten-Generaal in zake het Groenlopen." Leiden, November 1911.

[De Groot, J. J. M.]. *Groenloopen. Een ernstig woord aan ouders en voogden van aanstaande studenten, door een hoogleeraar*. Amsterdam: Höveker & Wormser, 1904.

———. *The Religious System of China: Its Ancient Forms, Evolution, History and Present Aspect, Manners, Customs and Social Institutions Connected Therewith*. 6 vols. Leiden: E. J. Brill, 1892–1910.

Deacon, Richard. *The Cambridge Apostles*. New York: Farrar, Straus & Giroux, 1986.

Dehergne, Joseph, SJ. "La Mission de Pékin vers 1700." *Archivum historicum Societatis Iesu* 22 (1953): 314–338.

———. *Répertoire des Jésuites de Chine de 1552 à 1800*. Rome: Institutum Historicum S.I., 1973.

Demiéville, Paul. "Aperçu historique des etudes sinologiques en France." *Acta Asiatica* 11 (1966): 56–110.

Der Ling, Princess. *Two Years in the Forbidden City*. New York: Moffat, Yard and Company, 1911.

Di Fiore, Giacomo. "Carità e reclusione nell'Europa del Settecento. La disavventure carcerairie di due cinesi al seguito di Jean-François Fouquet e di Matteo Ripa." In *Scritture di Storia*, 49–89. Napoli: Edizioni Scientifiche Italiane, 2005.

———. "Un cinese a Castel Sant'Angelo: La vicenda di un alumno del Collegio di Matteo Ripa fra transgressione e reclusione." In *La Conoscenza dell'Asia e dell'Africa in Italia nei Secoli XVIII e XIX*, 219–286 (1985).

Dickinson, G. Lowes. *The Autobiography of G. Lowes Dickinson*. Edited by Dennis Proctor. London: Duckworth, 1973.

———. *Letters from John Chinaman*. London: R. Brimley Johnson, 1901.

Dictionary of Art Historians. At www.dictionaryofarthistorians.org.

Duberman, Martin. *The World of Lincoln Kirstein*. New York: Knopf, 2007.

Dubs, Homer H. Review of *The Way of Life According to Laotzu*. *Journal of the American Oriental Society* 65 (1945): 212.

Dunne, George H., SJ. *Generation of Giants: The Story of the Jesuits in China in the Last Decades of the Ming Dynasty*. Notre Dame, IN: University of Notre Dame Press, 1962.

Ebrey, Patricia, and Robert Crawford. "Obituary of Howard Wechsler (1942–1980)." *Journal of Asian Studies* 46, no. 1 (February 1987): 227.

Fairbank, John King. "The Confidence Man." *New York Review of Books*, April 14, 1977. Reprinted in John King Fairbank, "Sinology Gone Astray: A Peking Confidence Man." In *China Watch*, 35–42. Cambridge, MA: Harvard University Press, 1987.

Fairbank, Wilma. "Laurence Chalfant Stevens Sickman, 1906–1988." *Archives of Asian Art* 42 (1989): 82–84.

Fang Hao. *Zhongguo Tianzhujiao shi renwu chuan*. 3 vols. Hong Kong: Gongjiao Renlixue Hui, 1970–1973.

Fenollosa, Ernest. *The Chinese Written Character as a Medium for Poetry*, edited by Ezra Pound. London: Stanley Nott, 1936.

Fong, Wen. *The Lohans and a Bridge to Heaven*. Freer Gallery of Art Occasional Papers, vol. 3, number 1. Washington, DC: Smithsonian, 1958.

Freedman, Maurice. *The Study of Chinese Society: Essays by Maurice Freedman*. Edited by G. W. Skinner. Stanford, CA: Stanford University Press, 1979.

Fu, Lo-shu. *A Documentary Chronicle of Sino-Western Relations (1644–1820)*. 2 vols. Tucson: University of Arizona Press, 1966.

Fuchs, Walter. "Vincenz Hundhausen, 1878–1955." *Journal of Oriental Studies* 3, no. 2 (1956): 322–323.

Gambone, Philip. *Beijing*. Madison: University of Wisconsin Press, 2003.

Goodrich, L. Carrington, and Chaoying Fang, eds. *Dictionary of Ming Biography*. 2 vols. New York: Columbia University Press, 1976.

Goodrich, Michael. *The Unmentionable Vice: Homosexuality in the Later Medieval Period*. Santa Barbara, CA: Ross-Erikson, 1979.

Granet, Marcel. *La pensée chinoise*. Paris: La Renaissance du Livre, 1934; reprinted Éditions Albin Michel, 1968.

Green, Martin. *Children of the Sun: A Narrative of "Decadence" in England after 1918*. New York: Basic Books, 1976.

Grimm, Irmgard. *Erinnerungen aus meinem bunten Leben*. Hannover: Author, 1992.

Han Fei Tzu. *Basic Writings*. Translated by Burton Watson. New York: Columbia University Press, 1964.

Handbook of the Collections in the William Rockhill Nelson Gallery of Art and Mary Atkins Museum of Fine Arts. Vol. 2, *Art of the Orient*. Edited by Ross E. Taggart, George L. McKenna, and Marc F. Wilson. 5th ed. Kansas City: Nelson-Atkins Museum, 1973.

Handforth, Thomas. *Mei Li*. New York: Doubleday, 1938.

Harris, Frank. *Oscar Wilde*. 1916; reprinted, New York: Carroll & Graf, 1992.

Hastings, Selina. *The Secret Lives of Somerset Maugham: A Biography*. New York: Random House, 2010.

Hawkes, David. "Obituary of Dr. Arthur Waley." *Asia Major* 12 (1966): 143–147.

Hayter-Menzies, Grant. *Imperial Masquerade: The Legend of Princess Der Ling*. Hong Kong: Hong Kong University Press, 2008.

Helms, Alan. *Young Man from the Provinces: A Gay Life Before Stonewall*. New York: Avon, 1997.

Hinsch, Bret. *Passions of the Cut Sleeve: The Male Homosexual Tradition in China*. Berkeley: University of California Press, 1990.

Hogan, Steve, and Lee Hudson, eds. *Completely Queer: Gay and Lesbian Encyclopedia*. New York: Henry Holt, 1998.

Holroyd, Michael. *Lytton Strachey: The New Biography*. New York: Farrar, Straus & Giroux, 1995.

Honey, David B. *Incense at the Altar: Pioneering Sinologists and the Development of Classical Chinese Philology*. New Haven, CT: American Oriental Society, 2001.

Houlbrook, Matt. *Queer London: Perils and Pleasures in the Sexual Metropolis, 1918–1957*. Chicago: University of Chicago Press, 2005.

Hummel, Arthur, ed. *Eminent Chinese of the Ch'ing Period*. Washington, DC: United States Government Printing Office, 1943.

Hyatt, Irwin T., Jr. *Our Ordered Lives Confess: Three Nineteenth-Century American Missionaries in East Shantung*. Cambridge, MA: Harvard University Press, 1976.

Juan, Fang-fu. *Sex in China: Studies in Sexology in Chinese Culture*. New York: Plenum, 1991.

Kaiser, Charles. *The Gay Metropolis, 1940–1996*. San Diego: Harcourt, Brace 1997.

Kang, Wenqing. *Obsession: Male Same-Sex Relations in China, 1900–1950*. Hong Kong: Hong Kong University Press, 2009.

Kates, George N. *Chinese Household Furniture*. London: Constable, 1948.

————. *The Years that Were Fat: The Last of Old China*. New York: Harper, 1952.

Kidd, David. *Peking Story: The Last Days of Old China*. 1988; New York: New York Review of Books, 2003.

Kinsey, Alfred C., et al. *Sexual Behavior in the Human Male*. Philadelphia: W. B. Saunders, 1948.

Kipling, Rudyard. "The Ballad of East and West." 1889.

Kraft, James. *Who Is Witter Bynner? A Biography*. Albuquerque: University of New Mexico Press, 1995.

Kramer, Larry. "Queer Theory's Heist of Our History." *Gay and Lesbian Review* 16, no. 5 (2009): 11–13.

Kroll, Paul W. "Reflections on Recent Anthologies of Chinese Literature in Translation." *Journal of Asian Studies* 61 (2002): 985–999.

K'ung Shang-jen. *The Peach Blossom Fan* [T'an-hua-shan]. Translated by Chen Shih-hsiang and Harold Acton with the collaboration of Cyril Birch. Berkeley: University of California Press, 1976.

Lach, Donald F. *Asia in the Making of Europe*. Vol. 1, *The Century of Discovery*. 2 bks. Chicago: University of Chicago Press, 1965.

Lao She [Shu Qingchun]. "Rabbit" [Tu], translated by William A. Lyell. In *Blades of Grass: The Stories of Lao She*, translated by William A. Lyell and Sarah Wei-ming Chen, 183–210. Honolulu: University of Hawai'i Press, 1999.

Laurence, Patricia. *Lilly Briscoe's Chinese Eyes: Bloomsbury, Modernism, and China*. Columbia: University of South Carolina Press, 2003.

Leddick, David. *Intimate Companions: A Triography of George Platt Lynes, Paul Cadmus, Lincoln Kirstein, and Their Circle*. New York: St. Martin's, 2000.

Li Zhisui, with editorial assistance of Anne F. Thurston. *The Private Life of Chairman Mao*. Translated by Tai Hung-chao. New York: Random House, 1994.

Lord, James. *Some Remarkable Men: Further Memoirs*. New York: Farrar, Straus & Giroux, 1996.

MacKerras, Colin P. *The Rise of the Peking Opera, 1770–1870*. Oxford: Clarendon, 1972.

Martin, Fran, trans. *Angelwings: Contemporary Queer Fiction from Taiwan*. Honolulu: University of Hawai'i Press, 2003.

Maugham, W. Somerset. *On a Chinese Screen*. 1922; reprinted, New York: Paragon House, 1990.

McKenna, Neil. *The Secret Life of Oscar Wilde*. New York: Basic Books, 2005.

McMahon, Keith. "Eroticism in Late Ming, Early Qing Fiction: The Beauteous Realm and the Sexual Battlefield." *T'oung Pao* 73 (1987): 217–264.

Meijer, M. J. "Homosexual Offences in Ch'ing Law." *T'oung Pao* 71 (1985): 140–180.

Miyazaki, Ichisada. *China's Examination Hell: The Civil Service Examinations of Imperial China*. Translated by Conrad Schirokauer. New Haven, CT: Yale University Press, 1981.

Mondimore, Francis Mark. *A Natural History of Homosexuality*. Baltimore, MD: Johns Hopkins University Press, 1996.

Monk, Ray. *Ludwig Wittgenstein: The Duty of Genius*. New York: Penguin, 1990.

Monumenta Missionum Societatis Iesu Vol. XLII. Missiones Occidentales. Monumenta Mexicana VII (1599–1602). Edited by Felix Zubillaga, SI. Rome: Institutum Historicum Societtais Iesu, 1981.

Morris, Ivan, ed. *Madly Singing in the Mountains: An Appreciation and Anthology of Arthur Waley*. New York: Walker, 1970.

Mungello, D. E. *The Great Encounter of China and the West, 1500–1800*. 3rd ed. Lanham, MD: Rowman & Littlefield, 2009.

———. "The Sad Tale of Lucio Wu (1713–1763)." *Sino-Western Cultural Relations Journal* 29 (2007): 19–33.

———. *The Spirit and the Flesh in Shandong, 1650–1785*. Lanham, MD: Rowman and Littlefield, 2001.

Murray, Douglas. *Bosie: A Biography of Lord Alfred Douglas*. New York: Hyperion, 2000.

Naquin, Susan. *Peking Temples and City Life, 1400–1900*. Berkeley: University of California Press, 2000.

Ng, Vivien W. "Homosexuality and the State in Late Imperial China." In *Reclaiming the Gay and Lesbian Past*, ed. Martin Duberman et al., 76–89. New York: New American Library, 1989.

———. "Ideology and Sexuality: Rape Laws in Qing China." *Journal of Asian Studies* 46 (1987): 57–70.

Nienhauser, William H., Jr., ed. *Indiana Companion to Traditional Chinese Literature*. Bloomington: Indiana University Press, 1986.

Otterspeer, W. *De opvoedende kracht van den groentijd: Het Leidse ontgroenschandaal van 1911*. Leiden: Burgersdijk & Niermans, 1995.

Oxford Dictionary of National Biography. www.oxforddnb.com.

Pa Chin. *The Family*. Translated by Sidney Shapiro. Peking: Foreign Language Press, 1958.

Pai Hsien-yung. *Crystal Boys*. Translated by Howard Goldblatt. San Francisco: Gay Sunshine Press, 1990.

Pelliot, Paul. *T'oung Pao* 27 (1930): 220.

Peters, F. E. *Ours: The Making and Unmaking of a Jesuit*. New York: Richard Marek, 1981.

Peyrefitte, Roger. *L'Exilé de Capri*. Paris: Ernest Flammarion, 1959.

———. *The Exile of Capri*. Translated by Edward Hyams. New York: Fleet Publishing, 1965.

Pfister, Louis, SJ. *Notices biographiques et bibliographiqes sur les Jésuites de l'ancienne mission de Chine, 1552–1773*. Shanghai: Imprimerie de la Mission Catholique T'ou-sè-wè, 1932–1934.

Pih, Irene. *Le Pere Gabriel de Magalhães, un Jésuite portugais en Chine au XVIIe siècle*. Paris: Centro Cultural Português, 1979.

Plant, Richard. *The Pink Triangle: The Nazi War against Homosexuals*. New York: Henry Holt, 1986.

Ricci, Matteo, SI. *Fonti Ricciane*. Edited by Pasquale M. D'Elia, SI. 3 vols. Rome: La Libreria dello Stato, 1942–1949.

Richards, Jeffrey. *Sex, Dissidence and Damnation: Minority Groups in the Middle Ages*. New York: Barnes & Noble, 1996.

Ripa, Matteo. *Memoirs of Father Ripa during Thirteen Years' Residence at the Court of Peking in the Service of the Emperor of China*. Translated by Fortunato Prandi. London: John Murray, 1844.

―――. *Storia della fondazione della Congregazione e del Collegio de' Chinese sotto it titolo della Sagra Famiglia di Gesù Cristo, scritta dallo stesso fondatore Matteo Ripa e de' viaggi da lui fatti*. 3 vols. Napoli: Manfredi, 1832.

Robb, Graham. *Strangers: Homosexual Love in the Nineteenth Century*. New York: Norton, 2003.

Saikaku, Ihara. *The Great Mirror of Male Love*. Translated by Paul Gordon Schalow. Stanford, CA: Stanford University Press, 1990.

Scheck, Ulrich. "Joseph Viktor von Scheffel." In *Nineteenth-Century German Writers, 1841–1900*, vol. 129. Detroit: Gale Research, 1993.

Schedel, Joseph, "China-Tagebuch." In *Josef Schedel (1856–1943), Ein deutscher Apotheker in Ostasien*, edited by Hartmut Walravens. Berlin: Staatsbibliothek zu Berlin, 2008, 55–102.

Scheffel, Joseph Viktor von. *Der Trompeter von Säckingen*. Stuttgart: Metzler, 1854.

Schipper, Kristopher. "The History of Taoist Studies in Europe/the West." In *Europe Studies China: Papers from an International Symposium on the History of European Sinology*, edited by Ming Wilson and John Cayley. Warren, CT: Floating World Editions, 2007.

Schmidt, J. D. "*Ching-chü*" and "*K'un-ch'u*." In *Indian Companion to Traditional Chinese Literature*, edited by William H. Nienhauser Jr. Bloomington: Indiana University Press, 1986, 316–318, 514–516.

Schmitt, Erich. Review of Vincenz Hundhausen's *Das Westzimmer*. *Orientalische Literaturzeitung* 4 (1929): col. 300–304.

Scott, A. C. *The Classical Theatre of China*. New York: Macmillan, 1957.

Sedgwick, Eve Kosofsky. *Epistemology of the Closet*. Berkeley: University of California Press, 1990.

Segalen, Victor. *René Leys*. Edited by Marie Dollé and Christian Doumet. Paris: Librairie Générale Française, 1999.

―――. *René Leys*. Edited by Sophie Labatut. Paris: Gallimard, 2000.

————. *René Leys*. Translated by J. A. Underwood. New York: New York Review of Books, 2003.

————. *Stèles*. Translated by Timothy Billings and Christopher Bush. Middletown, CT: Wesleyan University Press, 2007.

Shand-Tucci, Douglass. *The Crimson Letter: Harvard, Homosexuality, and the Shaping of American Culture*. New York: St. Martin's, 2003.

Sherry, Michael S. *Gay Artists in Modern American Culture: An Imagined Conspiracy*. Chapel Hill: University of North Carolina Press, 2007.

Sima Guang, Achilles Fang, Bernard S. Solomon, and Glen W. Baxter. *The Chronicle of the Three Kingdoms (220–265): Chapters 69–78 from the Tzu Chih t'ung chien of Ssu-ma Kuang*. Cambridge, MA: Harvard University Press, 1952.

Simmons, Sherwin. "Advertising Seizes Control of Life: Berlin Dada and the Power of Advertising." *Oxford Art Journal* 22, no. 1 (1999): 119–146.

Sinica Franciscana. Vol. 6, *Relationes et epistolas primorum Fratrum Minorum Italorum in Sinis (Saeculis 17 et 18)*. Edited by Georgius Mensaert, OFM, in collaboration with Fortunato Margiotti, OFM, and [Antonius] Sisto Rosso, OFM. 2 pts. Rome: Segreteria delle Missioni, 1961.

Sommer, Matthew H. "The Penetrated Male in Late Imperial China: Judicial Constructions and Social Stigma." *Modern China* 23 (1997): 140–180.

Soulié de Morant, George. *Bijou-de-ceinture, ou le Jeune home qui porte robe, se poudre et se farde, roman (Précédé d'une letter de M. Claude Farrére)*. Paris: Flammarion, 1925.

————. *Chinese Acupuncture*. Translated by Lawrence Grinnell, Claudy Jeanmougin, and Maurice Leveque. Edited by Paul Zmiewski. Brookline, MA: Paradigm, 1994.

————. *Pei Yu: Boy Actress*. Translated by Gerald Fabian and Guy Wernham. San Francisco: Alamo Square Press, 1991.

Spence, Jonathan D. *The Chan's Great Continent: China in Western Minds*. New York: Norton, 1998.

————. *Emperor of China: Self-Portrait of K'ang-hsi*. New York: Random House, 1975.

Spender, Stephen. *World within World: The Autobiography of Stephen Spender*. 1951; reprinted, New York: St. Martin's, 1994.

Standaert, Nicolas, ed. *Handbook of Christianity in China*. Vol. 1, *635–1800*. Leiden: Brill, 2001.

Steegmuller, Francis. *Cocteau: A Biography*. Boston: Little, Brown, 1970.

Suetonius Tranquillus, Gaius. *The Twelve Caesars*. Translated by Michael Grant. Harmondsworth, England: Penguin, 1957.

Sun, Kang-I, "Zuihou yige judian" (Final Words), *Zhongwai wenxue* (Chung-wai Literary Review), February 1993, 160–162; reprinted in *Yesu qianxue ji*, 38–39. Xi'an: Shaanxi Shifandaxue chubanshe, 1998.

Sutton, Stephanne B. *In China's Border Provinces: The Turbulent Career of Joseph Rock, Botanist-Explorer.* New York: Hastings House, 1974.

Thorp, Robert L. *Visiting Historic Beijing: A Guide to Sites and Resources.* Warren, CT: Floating World Editions, 2008.

Treat, John Whittier. *Great Mirrors Shattered: Homosexuality, Orientalism, and Japan.* New York: Oxford University Press, 1999.

Trevor-Roper, Hugh. *Hermit of Peking: The Hidden Life of Sir Edmund Backhouse.* Revised ed. Harmondsworth, England: Penguin, 1978.

Väth, Alfons, SJ. *Johann Adam Schall von Bell S.J., Missionar in China, kaiserlicher Astronom und Ratgeber am Hofe von Peking, 1592–1666.* Unter Mitwirkung von Lous Van Hee, SJ, revised ed. Nettetal: Steyler, 1991.

Verbiest, Ferdinand, ed. *Xichao ding'an.* In *Tianzhujiao dongchuan wenxian,* 71–224. Taipei: Taiwan Student Bookshop, 1965.

Vitiello, Giovanni. "The Dragon's Whim: Ming and Qing Homoerotic Tales from *The Cut Sleeve.*" *T'oung Pao* 78 (1992): 341–372.

———. "The Fantastic Journey of an Ugly Boy: Homosexuality and Salvation in Late Ming Pornography." *Positions: East Asian Culture Critique* 4 (1996): 291–320.

Volpp, Sophie. "Classifying Lust: The Seventeenth-Century Vogue for Male Love." *Harvard Journal of Asiatic Studies* 61 (2001): 77–117.

———. "The Literary Circulation of Actors in Seventeenth-Century China." *Journal of Asian Studies* 61 (2002): 949–984.

Wakeman, Frederic, Jr. *Policing Shanghai, 1927–1937.* Berkeley: University of California Press, 1995.

Waley, Alison. *A Half of Two Lives.* New York: McGraw-Hill, 1982.

Waley, Arthur. *Yuan Mei, Eighteenth Century Chinese Poet.* London: Allen and Unwin, 1956.

Walravens, Hartmut, ed. *Josef Schedel (1856–1943), Ein deutscher Apotheker in Ostasien.* Berlin: Staatsbibliothek zu Berlin, 2008.

———. *Vincenz Hundhausen (1878–1955): Leben und Werk des Dichters, Druckers, Verlegers, Professors, Regisseurs und Anwalts in Peking.* Wiesbaden: Harrossowitz, 1999.

Wang, David Der-wei. *Fin-de-siècle Splendor: Repressed Modernities of Late Qing Fiction, 1849–1911.* Stanford, CA: Stanford University Press, 1997.

———. "Impersonating China." *Chinese Literature: Essays, Articles, Reviews (CLEAR)* 25 (2003): 133–161.

Wang Dingju. *Shanghai menjing.* Shanghai: Zhongyang shudian, 1932.

Wang, Shuo. "Der Ling: Manchu Princess, Cultural Advisor, and Author." In *The Human Tradition in Modern China,* edited by Kenneth J. Hammond and Kristin Stapleton, 73–91. Lanham, MD: Rowman and Littlefield, 2008.

Waugh, Evelyn. *Brideshead Revisited.* Boston: Little, Brown, 1945.

Weiss, Andrea. *In the Shadow of the Magic Mountain: The Erika and Klaus Mann Story*. Chicago: University of Chicago Press, 2008.

Werblowsky, R. J. Zwi. *The Beaten Track of Science: The Life and Work of J. J. M. de Groot*. Edited by Hartmut Walravens. Wiesbaden: Harrossowitz, 2002.

White, Edmund. *The Beautiful Room Is Empty*. New York: Knopf, 1988.

Williams, Craig A. *Roman Homosexuality: Ideologies of Masculinity in Classical Antiquity*. New York: Oxford, 1999.

Wood, Frances. *The Lure of China: Writers from Marco Polo to J. G. Ballard*. South San Francisco: Long River Press, 2009.

Woodhouse, Reed. *Unlimited Embrace: A Canon of Gay Fiction, 1945–1995*. Amherst: University of Massachusetts Press, 1998.

Wright, William. *Harvard's Secret Court: The Savage 1920 Purge of Campus Homosexuals*. New York: St. Martin's, 2005.

Wu, Ch'eng-en. *Monkey, Folk Novel of China*. Translated by Arthur Waley. London: John Day, 1943.

Wu, Cuncun, and Mark Stevenson. "Male Love Lost: The Fate of Male Same-Sex Prostitution in Beijing in the Late Nineteenth and Early Twentieth Centuries." In *Embodied Modernities: Corporeality, Representation and Chinese Culture*. Edited by Larissa Heinrich. Honolulu: University of Hawai'i Press, 2006.

Wu, Cuncun. *Homoerotic Sensibilities in Late Imperial China*. London: Routledge, 2004.

Index

Note: Page numbers in italics refer to illustrations and maps.

185

About the Author

D. E. Mungello, the grandson of Italian immigrants, was raised in a small town in southwestern Pennsylvania. After obtaining his doctorate in history from the University of California at Berkeley, he chose to focus on Sino-Western history. He pursued research in Europe and China and published several books on the early intellectual contacts between Europe and China while specializing in the history of Christianity in China. In 1979 in Germany he founded the *Sino-Western Cultural Relations Journal*. In his previous book, *Drowning Girls in China: Female Infanticide since 1650*, he examined the neglected and politically sensitive historical plight of infant girls in China. He has published articles in a wide range of publications, including *VIA* (*Voices in Italian Americana*) and the *Gay and Lesbian Review*. His first teaching position was at Lingnan College in Hong Kong, and he is currently professor of history at Baylor University in Waco, Texas.